*For Lucy & Dennis —*

## PERFORMING THE PILGRIMS

*To thank you both
for Thanksgiving 2004.*

*Papa & Ma —*
*♥*

*Alastair & Patricia*

PERFORMANCE STUDIES
*Expressive Behavior in Culture*

Sally Harrison-Pepper, General Editor

# Performing the Pilgrims

## A STUDY OF ETHNOHISTORICAL
## ROLE-PLAYING AT PLIMOTH PLANTATION

by

Stephen Eddy Snow

*Foreword by Barbara Kirshenblatt-Gimblett*

UNIVERSITY PRESS OF MISSISSIPPI
*Jackson*

Copyright © 1993 by the University Press of Mississippi
All rights reserved
Manufactured in the United States of America
96  95  94  93    4  3  2  1
The paper in this book meets the guidelines for permanence and durability of
the Committee on Production Guidelines for Book Longevity of the Council on
Library Resources.

Snow, Stephen Eddy.
     Performing the pilgrims : a study of ethnohistorical role playing
at Plimoth Plantation / by Stephen Eddy Snow ; foreword by Barbara
Kirshenblatt-Gimblett.
          p.  cm. -- (Performance studies)
     Includes bibliographical references and index.
     ISBN 0-87805-570-3
          1. Historic sites--Massachusetts--Plymouth--Interpretive programs.
     2. Pilgrims (New Plymouth Colony)   3. Theater--Massachusetts--
     Plymouth.   4. Massachusetts--History--New Plymouth, 1620–1691.
     I. Title   II. Series.
     F74.P8S68   1993                                             92-45587
     974.4'82--dc20                                                   CIP


British Library Cataloging-in-Publication data available

*This work is dedicated to my mother and father,*
*Bernice Frances Eddy Snow and Ernest Augustus Snow, Jr.,*
*both descendants of those hardy English souls*
*who first settled New Plimoth,*
*in what is now called Plymouth, Massachusetts.*

# Contents

# Illustrations

FIGURES

# Foreword

Plimoth Plantation is a beautifully faceted jewel (or perhaps a Chinese puzzle). Its meaning cannot be exhausted, nor its paradoxes resolved. Turning and examining the site from every angle, *Performing the Pilgrims* demonstrates brilliantly just how good Plimoth Plantation is to think with. Stephen Eddy Snow, a pilgrim thrice over, is our expert guide. Descended from Pilgrims, he played Pilgrim roles for two seasons at the Pilgrim village. His vivid analysis of this experience is itself the result of an intellectual pilgrimage.

An unscripted ensemble performance that is environmental and improvisational, the Pilgrim village aligns itself more with experimental performance modes than with conventional theatre, understood as European drama constructed on Aristotelian principles for a proscenium stage. To capture the distinctive quality of this tangible yet elusive site, Snow works with an expanded notion of the performative. He draws not only on the history of avant-garde performance, postwar experimental theatre, and postmodern performance art, but also on his experience with Asian performance forms. The result is an important contribution not only to the emergent discipline of performance studies, but also to the history of museums and theatre, which stand in a complex relation to one another, and to new forms of performances at the electronic frontier. Living history, as explored here, goes beyond recreation and simulation. It is an extraordinary experiment in virtuality.

As Snow so vividly demonstrates, the legacy of the Pilgrims' antipathy to theatre is encoded in the history of how the site has been commemorated, represented, and animated. Ceremonies, banquets, orations, processions, festivals, tableaux, pageants, and exhibitions have celebrated the Pilgrims for almost two centuries, blurring the boundaries of ritual, theatre, and museum. During the early nineteenth century performances that would have been objectionable to conservative Protestants if staged in a theatre were acceptable when presented in a museum (or as civic ceremony), even if there was little else to distinguish them. Reframing performances in terms of nature, science, history, education, and commemoration made them respectable. In what might be characterized as a reciprocity of means and complementarity of function, museums used the theatrical craft of scene painting for exhibits and staged performances in their lecture rooms, while theatres used the subjects presented in museums. Museums served as surrogate theatres during periods when theatres came under attack for religious reasons, while theatres brought a note of seriousness to their offerings by presenting edifying entertainment.[1]

Today's Plimoth Plantation is both museum and theatre, literally. Plimoth Village, the living historical museum, has not displaced the exhibit gallery, where archeological actualities are labelled and displayed in vitrines. Rather "experience theatre" stands in a strategic relationship to the "theatre of objects."[2] There is a drama in objects—in the processes by which they are made and used. Consider the visual narratives of Diderot's plates in the Encyclopedie, which show the object, its parts, how it is made, and how it is used.[3] Or the work displays so central to agricultural fairs. Otis T. Mason, an anthropologist at the Smithsonian Institution, addressed the theatricality of objects in 1891 when he defined "the important elements of the specimen" as "the dramatis personae and incidents."[4] Archaeologists understand this when they try out tools, whether replicas or present-day versions, as a way to better understand them and the processes of which they are part. Most recently, Elaine Scarry reimagined the object as "a projection of the human body" that "deprives the external world of the privilege of being inanimate."[5] That privilege is fully forfeited in the Pilgrim village.

The Pilgrim village is a homunculous of history, fashioned not from clay but from the living tissue of twentieth-century actors. More than an embodiment of history, the village is an imaginary space into which the visitor enters. Gone is the fourth wall. Immersed in a total environment, the visitor negotiates a path through the site, both physically and conceptually. The brochure invites the visitor to interact with the Pilgrims, to "talk with them, ask them about their lives, and listen as they tell you, in the seventeen regional dialects heard throughout the Village, what it was like to come to this foreign place and build their future." In contrast with the exhibit gallery, which is silent as a tomb, Plimoth Village is full of "the sounds of life, laughter, songs, and voices. Although the days of the Pilgrims and native people are filled with chores, there's always time to include you in the lively discussions, storytelling and games that balance their lives." The visitor inhabits the icon.

Two trajectories—the history of archaeology and the history of theatrical commemoration—converge at Plimoth Plantation. Digging painstakingly in the dirt, meticulously sifting and recording every scrap of evidence from the garbage heap of history, the archaeologist infers a totality that is utterly virtual. Living history takes the archaeological imagination—reconstituting wholes from parts—the extra mile. If the archaeologist cannot excavate the whole pot in tact, or all of the fragments, then he can fill in the gaps, inferring from a few shards what the whole might have been. Having reconstituted the pot, why not the potter? Why not his studio, home, and marketplace? And why limit the reconstruction, let alone the exhibition, to drawings and words? The curator is a dramaturg of the metonyms of history, fashioning a mimetic recreation of the totality of Pilgrim daily life from archaeological fragments, some of them on display in the exhibit gallery. The Pilgrim village is a consummate performance of connoisseurship.

Several display traditions are at work here. First, living historical museums are an extreme example of the passion to imagine the past in the most literal detail, a passion perhaps most familiar in meticulous reconstructions of what is described in the Bible. Architectural drawings and scale models of the Tabernacle, the Temple, Noah's Ark, and the entire city of Jerusalem have a long history, stimulated in part by the Protestant Reformation and the fascination with the literal truth of the Biblical text. In this respect, it is perhaps less ironic that the Pilgrims, who so detested theatre, should be represented so literally at Plimoth Plantation. Second, the habitat group became popular during the nineteenth century as a way to display natural and cultural specimens. Rather than arranging them in a decorative pattern or according to some purely formal taxonomy, curators staged objects within their "habitat." The legacy of this approach may be seen today in the dioramas at the American Museum of Natural History, the recreated environments of animals in zoos, period rooms, wax museums, and the foreign villages at world's fairs. Such exhibitions are surrogates for the sites, near and far, that they represent. Third, even when tourists travel to distant destinations, what they encounter is often an exhibition of where they are or of somewhere else. Travel panoramas so popular in the nineteenth century offered a "you are there" experience, including the very cities in which they were staged. Indonesia in miniature is installed just outside Jakarta.[6]

Even as historic recreations in our own day model themselves on the tourist experience, tourism itself recodes space as time. Travellers are routinely promised idyllic escapes from their harried lives to destinations where time "stands still" or the past lives on, untouched by modernity—typically tropical islands, rural areas, exotic locales, and historic recreations. Time does indeed stand still at the Pilgrim village—it is always 1627 in the virtual world that emanates from the deep hole of archaeology. Traces once fixed in layered sediments of time can be seen in the exhibit gallery.

There is at work here, in both the archaeological and the curatorial imagination, a performance epistemology that places a premium on experience—visceral, kinesthetic, haptic, intimate—and a performative pedagogy more akin to the nascent medium of virtual reality than to older models of learning. Immersed in an experiential situation, the visitor uses all her senses to plot her own path, at her own pace, through an imagined world. She is never told what questions to ask or given definitive answers. Learning here is all process and discovery. It is partial, negotiable, polyvocal. More like hypermedia than a play, the site is truly interactive. Visitors do not "passively" watch a performance on a stage, look at displays in a museum, or take "rides" through installations in a theme park. They actively engage the site and those in it. The virtual world they are exploring "pushes back."

We can see in the display history of the site a shift from ceremonial to virtual, from commemorative to exploratory, from discrete moments, objects, and scenes, to the waking dream of a virtual Pilgrim world. But Plimoth Plantation keeps alive the tension between actualities and virtualities. Denigrated by some as Disneyworld his-

tory, as ersatz, the Pilgrim village should be seen in relation to the history of exhibiting copies. In many ways, American museums of the
nineteenth century were virtual museums, consisting in large measure
of copies of the great works of western civilization. Copies did not
have the degraded sense they do today, when they were commissioned
or collected and exhibited by museums with pride. Whether wax, plaster, marble, autotypes, or created in some other reproductive medium,
copies were subject to their own distinctive aesthetic values. Copies
might even be preferred to originals because their very presence indicated that education was the primary objective of the exhibition.

Modelling is the way of knowing, whether projecting back to a past
that must be imagined into completeness, or forward to what has not
yet been experienced. Even the older notion of copy, while submissive
to its source, is more than a surrogate for a missing original. Why else
keep alive the relationship between archaeological artifacts displayed
in the exhibit gallery and the "full-sense fantasy" of the Pilgrim village. The brochure invites the visitor to compare them: "Many of the
originals upon which the copies have been based may be viewed in the
museum's exhibit gallery." The pleasure of the Pilgrim village derives
in part from the tour de force of its staging, which is all the more
amazing given the fragmentary nature of the archaeological remains.
But realness, or the fidelity of the virtual world of the Village, is not
enough. The "actual" must be exhibited alongside the "virtual" in a
show of truth.

The result is a shifting locus of authenticity, a trade-off between the
aura of actuality, of the archaeological remain, and the (tele)presence of
virtuality, the recreated Pilgrim world. The mediating term is process.
Visitors are urged to "Browse through the museum's renowned gift
shop, where many items created using authentic seventeenth-century
methods are available for your own private collection." Authenticity is
located not in the artifacts per se or in the models on which they are
based, but in the *methods* by which they were made—in a way of
doing, which is a way of knowing, in a performance. The Village as
a whole is based on this principle, which is taken to an extreme in
the technique of first-person interpretation. It is as if the tool not only
animated a hand, but also a total sensibility—and so fully, that using
an adze to understand how it works extends from the hand to the
body to the mind to the inner state and way of being in the world that

constitutes the person who might have used the tool in 1627. The mementos in the giftshop acquire their authenticity from this chain of effects.

What are the implications of Plimoth Plantation for the historical consciousness of actors and visitors alike? Forfeiting third person omniscience for the partiality of the first person seems a small price to pay, for what is lost in historical comprehensiveness is gained in immediacy and detail, in the completeness and penetrability of a small virtual world. The Pilgrims live in a narrow strip of time defined by particular moments in 1627 and repeated annually, even though they work hard to create deeper and richer "memory" of the years preceding. A major task of the pilgrims is to deny that which came after 1627, to deny the time that intervenes between 1627 and 1993. This puts the visitor in the fascinating position of seer into the future. It is not so much that the visitor enters the world of the Pilgrim to experience 1627 (there are no doubt flashes when that happens, when the time machine as an instrument recedes from consciousness). Nor is it so much that 1993 confronts 1627. Rather, the visitor has the uncanny sense of seeing into the future, converting what he understands to be our past into the Pilgrim's future. In a curious sense, actors and visitors collaborate in an historical imaginary that denies and jumbles time by sustaining one small slice of it indefinitely, even while abutting it with the present moment.

It is in the nature of tourist productions to produce just such an effect. However persuasive the representation, finally what you experience is the site itself. The juxtaposition of simulation and tourist amenities, the intercalation of quotidians (theirs and ours), the breaking of frames, is deliberately engineered and a source of pleasure in its own right. The brochure instructs the visitor: "Upon your return from the village and homesite, take a break from the arduousness of Pilgrim living conditions before travelling to *Mayflower II*. Have a bite to eat in the courtyard, Gainsborough Room or Picnic Pavilion." This is always a *double* experience, an experience of then and now, which enhances its role as historiographic corrective: "At the waterfront a double treat awaits you. After your visit to the ship, enjoy authentic seventeenth-century baked goods—not at all the bland taste so often imagined—at the J. Barnes Bake Shop." History at Plimoth is so real you can taste it.

Freeze frame, by making time stand still, also interrupts the inexorable narrative of origins in its tracks and displaces the unbroken line of its exclusive genealogy. Pilgrim displays past and present are in conflict, not only in relation to each other, but also internally. The refusal of the Wampanoag to pretend to be themselves, their refusal to give up actuality for virtuality, is but one indication. Snow's account of difficulties that arose when an African-American became part of the virtual village is another. Such tensions give the Pilgrim quotidian and its virtuality their ideologically charge. As Snow notes, the Pilgrim village, billed as one of the "Living Museums of Everyman's History," is supposed to be more democratic because "Total history gives rhyme and reason to everyone in a historical community, the nobodies no less than the somebodies." Everyone is offered a chance to (re)live Pilgrim daily life in all its detail and elusiveness—or at least to walk among the living dead.

But can the "democratizing effect" of Plimoth Plantation really remedy the exclusions and inequities of history? The recent Ellis Island restoration faces the same problem. As does the Columbus Quincentenary. We are witnessing the era of historical identification by consent (and dissent), rather than descent. Sites long associated with a discrete historical experience and exclusive set of participants, whether Pilgrims landing at Plymouth Rock or immigrants coming through Ellis Island, compete for the status of definitive master narrative. How shall the founding of the nation be told? Which site can be more inclusive, which is to say, more "democratic"? At Ellis Island, virtually anyone, no matter when he arrived in the United States or through which port, can pay $100 to have his name or the name of an ancestor inscribed on the American Immigrant Wall of Honor that rings the island—and that includes the Pilgrims and their descendents! Ellis Island, in a slick taxonomic move, has absorbed Plimoth. The rock is just another port of entry for just another group of immigrants.

Just how all of this works is the subject of *Performing the Pilgrims*, which may well speak to the Nintendo generation in ways never anticipated.

Barbara Kirshenblatt-Gimblett

1. For an extended discussion of these and related topics, see Barbara Kirshenblatt-Gimblett, "Objects of Ethnography," *Exhibiting Cultures: The Poetics and Politics of Museum Display,* eds. Ivan Karp, and Steven D. Lavine (Washington, D.C.: Smithsonian Institution Press, 1991), pp. 386–443.

2. The discussion here of virtual reality is indebted to Brenda Laurel, *Computers as Theatre* (Reading, Mass.: Addison-Wesley, 1991).

3. See Roland Barthes, "The Plates of the Encyclopedia," *New Critical Essays,* trans. Richard Howard (New York: Hill and Wang, 1980). pp. 23–40.

4. Otis T. Mason, "The Natural History of Folklore," *Journal of American Folklore* 4 (13) 1891: 99.

5. Elaine Scarry, *The Body in Pain: The Making and Unmaking of the World* (New York: Oxford University Press, 1985), pp. 281, 285.

6. The Polynesian Village in Hawaii offers all of Polynesia—there is no need to travel the length and breadth of the Pacific to see the Cook Islands, Samoa, Tahiti, Fiji, etc.

# Preface

This is a book about a performance that tells the story of the first English settlers in Plymouth, Massachusetts.[1] At the center stage of this performance are those strange yet familiar figures, the Pilgrims. Since for many Americans the Pilgrim image is indelibly associated with a major national holiday, we have seen in the last half of the twentieth century, this image mechanically and electronically reproduced by every conceivable method. This overexposure in popular culture has resulted in a sometimes denigrative attitude toward the Pilgrims. However, regardless of the many spurious, superficial, and downright silly representations of these early settlers, their story remains an important part of American history, folklore, and culture.

The performance of the Pilgrim story at Plimoth Plantation, an outdoor "living history" museum in Plymouth, Massachusetts, can be described as a cultural performance because it serves to "dramatize our collective myths and history" (MacAloon 1984, 1). This performance has been shaped by significant forces of cultural creativity in American society. The study of its evolution and organization can help us gain insight about changing perspectives in American culture. Beverly J. Stoeltje writes that "the most productive way to study a complex society, then, is through observation of such units of performance" (1981, 124).

The focus of the present study is the transformation of this cultural performance. In 1969, a momentous change occurred at Plimoth Plantation: the antiques were removed from the restored village. This event signaled the end of an attitude of protective reverence for the "sainted ancestors." No longer worshipped as such, the Pilgrims became the objects of rigorous ethnohistorical scrutiny. Under the direction of Harvard-educated anthropologist James Deetz, Plimoth was put on course to become a "living museum," in which the material culture of the period would be reproduced and the mental and behavioral culture of the people (the *ethnoi*) would be re-created. This occasion marked the initial phase of what Dell Hymes calls a complex "metaphrasis," "a technical term for interpretive transformation of genre" (Ben-Amos 1975, 20). In his own study, Hymes analyzed the transition from one style of presentation of a Chinookan narrative cycle—myth—to another—tale. He observed the performers of a traditional coyote tale as they switched from the formal narrative style associated with myth to a more colloquial storytelling format. A similar kind of "interpretive transformation of genre" began to occur at Plimoth in 1969. The third-person narrative presentation of the "Pilgrim Fathers" (mythic figures) by museum guides who were frequently dressed in inauthentic period attire was replaced by a format in which the cultural life of the Pilgrims was re-created by "interpreters" dressed in well-researched historical costumes and giving, as Deetz said, "the appearance of seventeenth-century Pilgrims." This was the beginning of the concept for "Performing the Pilgrims."

The next phase of this metaphrasis came in the early 1970s, when interpreters began to experiment with speaking in period dialect and in the first person. As Deetz told me in a 1987 telephone interview, these attempts to speak in the first person evolved naturally from the new practice of *doing* Pilgrim tasks rather than merely talking about them: an interpreter could easily say, "*I* used to do such and such this way, because . . ." Thus, first-person interpretation took hold at Plimoth Plantation. By 1978, this living history method was the modus operandi in the re-creation of Pilgrim life at Plimoth. Interpreters were trained to embody fully the ethnohistorical roles, to act as if they truly were seventeenth-century Pilgrims. This study concentrates especially on the years 1984 to 1986, when the first-person approach had matured and stabilized. By this time, history at Plimoth was history *performed,* and the performance had begun to take on some very theatrical characteristics.

Throughout this text, I will refer to the contemporary living history performance at Plimoth as the Theatre of the Pilgrims. This term is meant to be both realistic and metaphorical. The re-creation of Pilgrim personages who would appear on the "set" of the restored village has required many of the procedures and paraphernalia of theatre to produce the illusory representation of early seventeenth-century New England life: costumes, props, speeches, dialogues, singing, dancing, characterization, and the acting out of stories. A central question of this study is: is this really theatre?

I will cite many scholars, writers, journalists, visitors, and interpreters themselves who concur that the present-day Living Museum of 17th Century Plymouth has, indeed, become a kind of theatre. In arguing this case, I am especially indebted to my teacher, Richard Schechner, who developed the concept of environmental theater (1973) and who has also written eloquently about the theatrical effectiveness of Plimoth (1981). Based on his experience in experimental theatre and his research on performances in Asia and elsewhere, Schechner has enlarged the conceptual framework of theatre. He writes: "The first scenic principle of environmental theater is to create and use whole spaces. Literally spheres of spaces, spaces within spaces, spaces which contain, or envelop, or relate, or touch all the areas where the audience is and/or the performers perform" (1973, 2). This notion of theatrical space in which performers and spectators interact and in which the total playing area is used for many different kinds of performative possibilities is crucial to an understanding of Plimoth as a kind of theatre. It is my belief that Plimoth has become an environmental theater, one which attempts to reactualize the full cultural life of the Pilgrims in 1627, the year that is represented.

My analysis is undertaken from the perspective of performance studies, a new scholarly discipline that widens the definition of performance, focuses on the complexities of cultural performances, and aims to provide some answers. The emergence of this field and the developing theatricality at Plimoth are both manifestations of what anthropologist Clifford Geertz, at the beginning of the 1980s, identified as the "blurring of genres" in the social sciences and humanities. In his seminal essay, "Blurred Genres: The Refiguration of Social Thought," Geertz described an important "cultural shift" in which interpretive explanations in the social sciences derived more and more from the "contrivances of cultural performance" (1980, 168). Geertz's explication of the "drama analogy" has been of invaluable help to me in my examination of the aspects of dramatic ritual in the performance at Plimoth and in my analysis of the power of the drama to persuade through the creation of illusion.

This new "dramatistic perspective," with its incisive use of theatrical metaphor and paradigm, has resulted in the collaboration of anthropologists and theatre specialists in performance studies and in the commingling of anthropology, history, museum studies, and theatre at Plimoth Plantation. Geertz put his finger on a significant cultural transition which, for some time, had been restructuring the vision of social scientists and scholars in the humanities.

The performance at Plimoth is based upon what is sometimes called "simulation." Jay Anderson, who has written widely on the phenomena of living museums and living history, describes this approach as "using simulation as a mode of interpreting the realities of life in the past more effectively" (1984, 12). This kind of imitative reenactment of a historical scene was also utilized by Alex Haley in preparation for writing his book *Roots*. Wanting to know what it was like to cross the ocean in the belly of a slaveship, he took a ship from Africa to America and attempted to simulate the experience:

> After each late evening's dinner, I climbed down successive metal ladders into her deep, dark, cold cargo hold. Stripping to my underwear, I lay on my back on a wide rough bare dunnage plank and forced myself to stay there through all ten nights of the crossing, trying to imagine what did he see, hear, feel, smell, taste—and above all, in knowing Kunta, what things did he think? (1976, 726)

Here, Haley is much like a Method actor preparing for a role.[2] He recreates his character's physical environment and sensory experience so that he can evoke what the character might have thought and felt in that particular historical moment. This is precisely the method of recreation that was developed at Plimoth Plantation.

As James Deetz tells us in his 1969 *Natural History* article, in the late 1960s interpreters began to experiment with living as the Pilgrims had so as to get some sense of what that daily life was like. They practiced actually using the restored houses; they chopped wood, carried water to the hearth, plucked chickens, and ate with their fingers. This simulation of behavior continued through the 1970s and into the 1980s; a 1985 report in the *Boston Globe Magazine* exclaimed: "Around

Plimoth Plantation you've got to walk like a Pilgrim, talk like a Pilgrim" (Engstrom 1985, 12). The interpreters were now speaking and acting as if they really were the historical characters whom they represented. An anthropological Pandora's box had been opened: these first-person portrayals of the Pilgrim dramatis personae necessitated the full expression of all the complex workings of symbolic culture as they were experienced by individuals in a specific ethnohistorical setting. Since then, the greatest challenge for the ethnohistorical role-player at Plimoth has been how to achieve a full and honest characterization that presents the mental, psychological, and spiritual perspective of his or her Pilgrim character.

In recent years, Plimoth's type of performative simulation of ethnohistorical data has become a significant pedagogical tool in anthropology and has catalyzed an important interface between the disciplines of anthropology and theatre. In fact, Deetz's early explorations with simulation were a harbinger of what anthropologist Victor Turner came to call "performing ethnography." In 1982, Turner and his co-author and wife, Edith, wrote:

> For several years, as teachers of anthropology, we have been experimenting with the performance of ethnography to aid students' understanding of how people in other cultures experience the richness of their social existence, what moral pressures they expect to receive as a reward for following certain patterns of action, and how they express joy, grief, deference, and affection, in accordance with cultural expectations. (1982, 33)

The point of this approach is to get beyond the merely cognitive aspect of ethnography, thus allowing participants, actors and audience alike, to get a sense of how a particular cultural group experienced themselves, "to put experiential flesh on these cognitive bones," as the Turners wrote (1982, 41).

The Turners and their colleagues at such institutions as the University of Chicago, the University of Virginia, and New York University were re-creating frames of social process from the ethnographic records of cultural Others: Ndembu name-inheritance rituals, sacred winter ceremonials of the Kwakiutl, and Barok initiation rites. Their aim was to come to a greater understanding of these groups. The Living Museum of 17th Century Plymouth puts on performances for the same reason. Based on ethnographic data from period texts such as *Mourt's Relation* (Heath 1963), the inner and outer lives of the people known as the Pilgrims are reconstructed and presented *via* living history performance. By the 1980s, what the Turners considered the primary function of performing ethnography was being realized at Plimoth Plantation: it had become a kind of "instructional theater" (1982, 41). This unique village was now the Theatre of the Pilgrims.

This living history re-creation provides a particularly valuable subject of research in the field of performance studies for several reasons. First, it is the performative representation of a cultural history. Second, it represents this culture in both authentic and inauthentic ways. Third, the actual cultural context in which the performers live—the style of their own period—impresses itself upon the historical representation: the "Pilgrims" have changed in each decade since the 1950s. Finally, this performative re-creation of Pilgrim history serves as a paradigm for an emerging genre of cultural performance that has important implications for the future representations of other famous historical scenes.

In researching my subject, I used the participant observation approach in order to build up what Geertz calls a "thick description" (1973). I examined this cultural performance from many angles and within different frames. As Geertz points out in his brilliant essay on this subject, the ethnographer, or "inscriber," must find his or her way through myriad complex conceptual structures that are frequently superimposed on one another—for instance, Pilgrim impersonators performing for a Japanese television crew that is creating a program to teach Japanese businessmen how to speak better English! What can it all mean? Geertz outlines the double task that is required to produce a thick description of such complicated cultural performance as "setting down the meaning particular social actions have for the actors whose actions they are, and stating, as explicitly as we can manage, what the knowledge thus attained demonstrates about the society in which it is found and, beyond that, about social life as such" (1973, 27). In this book, I will attempt to delineate the many levels of the living history performance at Plimoth and to explain the meaning of it all to American society in the last two decades of the twentieth century.

It was both ironic and unexpected that I ended up choosing the restored village at Plimoth as the subject of my study. I had been planning to do fieldwork and hoping to focus on a cultural performance in Asia, probably Indonesia. I was drawn to the faraway, to the cultural Other. However, a serious illness in my family brought me back to Plimoth. My mother was stricken with cancer and, after her death in January 1984, I decided to stay on with my father, in Plymouth, and to take a position as an interpreter at Plimoth Plantation. This provided me with a unique opportunity to study a cultural performance not of an Other, but of my own people. I discovered that the culture of the original inhabitants of Plimoth was so different from ours in contemporary America that the experience was similar to exploring a foreign land.

I had known vaguely that I was a descendant of the early English settlers of Plimoth but had not paid much attention to the fact. What I did know before I began my study was that Nicholas Snow, the progenitor of my father's line in America, had actually lived in the original Pilgrim village in 1627. My mother's family also descended from early Seventeenth-century residents of New Plimoth. Thus the process of exploring the cultural life of the Pilgrims also gave me the opportunity to examine and perform my own history.

For fifteen months, I portrayed two Pilgrim characters in the re-created Pilgrim Village: first, Richard Warren; then, Edward Winslow. I returned in 1986 to play the role of Governor William Bradford in the three-day reenactment of the "Harvest Feast." I tried to balance this subjective perspective by taking regular field notes (between 1984 and 1986, I frequently entered the village as a visitor); doing many interviews with performers, spectators, and Plimoth Plantation staff; making sound recordings of the performances; and gathering extensive photographic documentation. I was concerned that, because of my background as a professional actor, I might overemphasize the theatrical aspects of Plimoth, so, to compensate for this possible bias, I developed a questionnaire on the theatrical nature of this living history performance that was answered by both visitors and staff. I have reported many of the answers to this survey, verbatim, in chapters 5 and 6.

The chapters have been organized so as to give the reader a clear view of the whole evolution of the performance. The book begins with a description of an actual reenactment and concludes with an analysis of the theoretical questions provided by the contemporary performative re-creation at Plimoth. The first chapter introduces the basic Pilgrim story and surveys earlier performative modes used to represent it. Chapter 2 locates the roots of the living history performance in the costumed parade known as the Pilgrims' Progress and traces the development of the performance in the Pilgrim Village from the use of costumed tour guides in the 1950s to the presence of actor/historians in the 1980s. Chapter 3 offers detailed descriptions of the daily reenactments in the village of life in the year 1627, while Chapter 4 presents a survey of the special historical scenes that are re-created there over the course of a season (April 1 to December 1). Chapter 5 investigates the performers' backgrounds, training, and views concerning all aspects of their performance. Chapter 6 describes the audience, analyzes various aspects of tourism, and examines the ways in which the performers and audience interrelate, especially regarding the types of environmental staging employed in the village.

The final chapter focuses on theoretical issues, defining the cultural focuses that have shaped contemporary Pilgrim representation and analyzing it as the prototype of an emerging genre of cultural performance. For this concluding analysis, I have drawn heavily on the theoretical writings of several authors. From the field of anthropology, I have relied on some essential ideas from Milton Singer, Victor Turner and Clifford Geertz; from the history of religion, the concepts of Mircea Eliade; from folklore, the notions of genre theory developed by Dell Hymes and Roger Abrahams; from the study of tourism, the ideas of Dean MacCannell, Erik Cohen and Edward M. Bruner; from the study of postmodern culture, the critical thinking of Michel Benamou; from sociology, the theoretical constructs of Erving Goffman; and, finally, from my own field of performance studies, the theoretical and analytical writings of Richard Schechner, Barbara Kirshenblatt-Gimblett and David Cole.

I want to thank a number of people for the support and encouragement they have given me during the course of this long project.

I am especially indebted to the dean and faculty of the Graduate School of Arts and Sciences at New York University for a year-long dissertation fellowship, which made the initial writing of this text a much more agreeable task. My adviser, Richard Schechner, continuously offered valuable advice, criticism, and support. His own pioneering work as a performance theorist and theatre director has always served as a source of inspiration. Barbara Kirshenblatt-Gimblett gave steadfast encouragement. Her genuine interest in my topic was heartening, and her own course on tourist productions, offered by the Department of Performance Studies (spring 1985), helped me to look at my subject in a new light. Brooks McNamara's special seminar on documentary performance, given by the same department (spring 1986), was very helpful. I greatly appreciated being invited to sit in on the class discussions, many of which provided useful insights for my own work.

There are many people in Plymouth, Massachusetts, to whom I am also indebted. Caroline Chapin, former Curator of Manuscripts and Books at the Pilgrim Society, offered me invaluable assistance with my research on the historical background of the performative representations of the Pilgrims and helped me to locate many rare photographs. At Plimoth Plantation, James Baker, Vice President of Museum Operations, and Carolyn Travers, Director of Research, were always willing to answer my questions about the evolution of the living history program, even when skeletons sometimes popped out of the closet. Judith Ingram, former Director of Marketing, kindly provided me with information concerning the financial organization of the living museum. Anthony Pollard/Nanepashemet, Manager of Native American Interpretation at Plimoth, and Anita Nielsen, a Wampanoag teacher and interpreter, increased my understanding of the Native American perspective. I am grateful to the Media Services Department, especially Die Modlin Hoxie, for their assistance with the photographic documentation of the contemporary Pilgrim Village. Leonard Travers, former Director of Interpretation, and Paul Cripps, former Site Supervisor in the Pilgrim Village, were also helpful at many times and in many different ways. Dorothy Hale, Gerda Savery, and Henrietta Wolfenden from Visitor Services supplied me with many interesting details about the early years of the guides and hostesses. Ruth F. Trask, former Director of Financial Operations, also gave me insights about the beginnings of the museum, and John C. Kemp, present Manager of Colonial Interpretation, helped me to understand the new directions of the 1990s.

Cynthia Tokumitsu and Valerie Knight, my typists, were wonderfully conscientious; it was because of their diligence that I always made my deadlines.

My wife, Shelley Huffaker Snow, was constantly supportive, even in the most difficult moments. She also served as an excellent proof-reader and offered many valuable suggestions.

Finally, I want to thank my former colleagues on the interpretation staff of Plimoth Plantation—those creative, witty, exuberant, industrious, *underpaid* actor/historians, whose dedication, intelligence, and artistry I have come to admire.

Performing the Pilgrims

*One*

# Of Pilgrims and Performance

> Some day the Pilgrim Story will become the sub-
> ject of a Poet's song. . . . It contains every possible
> dramatic element: nobleness and baseness, bravery
> and cowardice, purity and impurity of life, man-
> hood and hypocrisy, gentleness and wrongheaded-
> ness. We very much fear, however, that (though
> Dramatic Poesy is the highest form of human
> expression) if that Song shapes itself into a drama;
> the Pilgrim Fathers will turn in their graves.
>
> Edward Arber,
> *The Story of the Pilgrim Fathers,* 1897

The corpse of Mary Brewster, wrapped in a winding sheet and covered with a shroud, is laid out on the large, canopied, oaken bedstead. The curtains are drawn open for those who wish to view
the dressed body. Mary died this three days past, on April 17, 1627.
Watching over her corpse are her husband, Elder William Brewster,
and her son, Jonathan Brewster. Both men wear the hats and beards
and cloaks of seventeenth-century English Separatists.

This is a "scene." It takes place in Elder Brewster's house at Plimoth Plantation, a "living museum" that re-creates the year 1627 in
the famous Pilgrim village. The performers fully embody these Pilgrim characters. They speak as if they *were* Elder Brewster and
Jonathan Brewster. Having been trained in seventeenth-century Separatist culture, they know that too great a display of sorrow in this situation would be historically inauthentic. In the Separatist world view,

a death in the family is but God's will; it is even an opportunity for rejoicing, since God, in his great mercy, has seen fit to take one of his children out of this wicked world. Here, however, the performers' faces remain somber, manifesting a controlled grief.

The small audience of a dozen or so that crowds the open doorway absorbs some of this sorrowful ambience. Their faces also become momentarily solemn. In another instant, though, one or two are brash enough to use their cameras. Jonathan Brewster's eyes flinch when the flash goes off. Until this moment, the scene had been lit only by the natural light from the doorway and by the fire glowing in the large open fireplace to the right.

This mise-en-scène indicates that Elder Brewster is a highly educated man. The shelves on the white, daub walls opposite the bedstead are lined with numerous leather-bound volumes in various sizes and shapes. An audience member steps forward and opens one of these ancient-looking books. He asks Elder Brewster a question. The sadness-filled silence is broken. The elder, speaking in a thick seventeenth-century English accent, answers the man's question.

Suddenly, the sound of a drum is heard. The spectators' turn toward the doorway. A tall young man, costumed in a handsome leather jerkin, enters. He is addressed as "Master Prence" by the elder. Master Prence requests that the audience leave the house, for the funeral procession is about to take place and the corpse must be prepared. As soon as they are out of sight and sound, Master Prence tells Jonathan Brewster to get the ladder down from the loft. Several Pilgrim women—the underbearers—enter the room, accompanied by a lad of about twelve. He enacts the role of the youngest Brewster child, Wrestling. Master Prence winks to this youngest performer, saying, "Run up there and give Jon a hand with hiding old Mary!" Make sure she's completely out of sight!" And the department store mannequin that has been used for many years to represent the mortal remains of Mary Brewster is quickly hoisted up and hidden in the loft.

The room is filled only with performers, now. It has instantaneously become a backstage area. In a moment of gallows humor, someone makes a joke about the absurdity of the "corpse" resting above. The other performers laugh. Their faces are more relaxed; there is even a sense of merriment in the air. They obviously enjoy performing this mock funeral. Master Prence proceeds to bang some nails into the empty prop coffin.

*Plate 1.* The mock funeral procession (Photo courtesy of Plimoth Plantation)

Outside, the drumming continues. A sizable audience of a hundred or more gathers in the street before Elder Brewster's house. One of the older performers, portraying Deacon Samuel Fuller, stands at the front gate. He holds a halberd, straight up in the air, directly in front of him. No one is allowed in the house. Finally, Master Prence reappears, followed by the Pilgrim women. They are dressed in their white coifs and dark cloaks and bear the prop coffin on their shoulders. Now, their faces are etched with pain and sorrow. To the sound of a dead march, the deacon leads the procession up the hill to the graveyard (plate 1). The audience follows at the rear of this little band of Pilgrim mourners.

The scene at the grave site looks like the latter part of act V, scene 1 of *Hamlet*, with a few exceptions. The characters represented here— these Pilgrim contemporaries of Shakespeare—were basically English yeomen, not the nobles of a Danish court. This funeral scene is necessitated not by the suicide of a young noblewoman but by the gracious passing of one of "God's elect." The present-day audience does not sit in comfortable auditorium seats but accompanies the performers to the site of the enactment, after the fashion of environmental theatre.

The performer playing the role of Governor William Bradford steps right up to the edge of the grave. He has a most austere physiognomy, perfect for the part. He says a few words of solace to the mourners, then steps back. Mary's teenage son, Love Brewster, now comes forward. He reads a short Christian verse that he has penned in honor of his mother. His hands shake as he reads. A gust of wind makes the air chilly on this April day. Love tacks his poem onto the coffin. The audience is visibly moved by this young Pilgrim's final gesture to his departed mother.

Next, Jonathan Brewster begins a "spontaneous" eulogy. Halfway through, he breaks into tears. Jonathan apologizes to his father for this unwonted show of emotion. His embarrassment at his own outburst of feelings seems real. His acting is good and believable. In the theatre, it would be called a "moment." And it is just that, here—a special piece of good acting that stands out. Finally, Jonathan regains his composure and concludes his brief extemporaneous speech. The coffin is lowered into the grave. As the audience begins to disperse, two young Pilgrim men, with rustic spades in hand, fill the new grave with earth.

The Brewster family returns to their house, where, for the rest of the day, they receive the condolences of many visitors, both the twentieth-century audience members and the "seventeenth-century neighbors." The Brewsters explain the facts of Mary's death and offer their guests ippocras (a sweet wine) and cake-bread. Like so many events at Plimoth Plantation, this occasion is both an opportunity for the historical education of the ticket-purchasing public *and* a full re-creation of a specific scene in Pilgrim history. At one point in the late afternoon, as Jonathan is teaching a few twentieth-century visitors about Separatist religious doctrine, his wife, Lucretia, and his sister, Mistress Patience Prence, are overcome with grief. They suddenly burst into tears, unable any longer to control their sorrow over the loss of their "mother."[1]

The funeral scene described above is undoubtedly a performance, but what kind of performance is this? Anthropologist Victor Turner locates the root meaning of "performance" in the Old French verb, *parfournir: par* ("thoroughly") and *fournir* ("to furnish") (1979, 82). Thus, "performance" suggests an act of complete embodiment. It is in this essential connotation that the performance at Plimoth Plantation corresponds to all ritual and aesthetic performances in which "spirits," be they animals, demons, gods, or ancestors, and dramatis personae are fully embodied. In all cases, costumes are worn, speech and movement imitated, historical/mythological scenarios reenacted, and impersonations actualized. Performance theorist Richard Schechner writes that "performance is a particularly heated arena of ritual, and theatre, script, and drama are heated and compact areas of performance: (1977, 52). As will be shown, the performance at Plimoth manifests aspects of a ritual of ancestor worship, produces actual dramas, and, at times, is highly theatrical. Ideally, its script is the perfect embodiment of the historical events of 1627 Plimoth. In actuality, its script is based on an interpretation of that history, constantly modified by the latest inventions of culture, and the performance itself is fundamentally shaped by a codification of behavior designed to please a large tourist audience. So, what kind of performance is this?

I call Plimoth a "living history" performance because it is part of a recent trend toward the reenactment and re-creation of historical events and milieus. Jay Anderson defines this trend as the "living history movement" (1985, ix). In his *Time Machines: The World of Living History* (1984), Anderson delineates the whole nexus of living history, including the other famous living museums, such as Colonial Williamsburg and Old Sturbridge Village; the acting out of historical texts as a research tool in archaeology and anthropology; and the amateur reenactments carried out by history buffs. Although he stresses the educational aspects of these simulations, Anderson is well aware of their performative characteristics. He writes: "Historical simulation is dramatic. It unabashedly uses our society's traditional mediums of cultural expression: ritual, ceremony, pageant, theater (including film, radio, television), games, sports, festivals, and celebration" (1985, 446).

Plimoth Plantation identifies itself as a "living museum" or a "living history museum." However, in his insightful, cross-cultural analysis, "Restoration of Behavior," Schechner has placed Plimoth Plantation in the same frame as other theme parks and restored villages that he defines as "large environmental theaters" (1981, 22). Schechner explains that "restored behavior" is the main characteristic of all performance and, here, it is the key element in creating the theatrical quality of this living museum. It is the attempt to restore the actions and events of 1627 that necessitates the production of illusions, with all the accompanying theatrical paraphernalia: costumes, props, dialogue, songs, dances. It is the improvisatory interaction between performers and spectators in the large and varied spaces of this outdoor museum that makes it an experience of environmental theater.

The plantation designates its costumed staff "informants" or "interpreters." However, many observers perceive these costumed role-players to be actors. In a pre-Thanksgiving *New York Times* article entitled "Pilgrimage to Plymouth," novelist James Carroll focused on the social significance of re-creating the Pilgrim past at that particular time of the year, commenting on the power of the illusion created by the performers in the 1627 village: "The 'Pilgrims' seemed serious about the pretense of their village. The *actors'* [italics mine] perfect balance between earnestness and playfulness is what enables us to suspend our disbelief, if only in flashes, that we've stumbled on another time" (1984, 34).

In his 1985 *Boston Globe* piece on Plimoth Plantation, free-lance writer and filmmaker John Engstrom described a scene in one of the re-created Pilgrim houses: "Seated on a heavy carved oak chair is *actor* [italics mine] Christopher Hall in the role of Miles Standish, the illustrious military commander of the colony" (1985, 12).

And in 1986, Boston *Patriot Ledger* reporter Lisa Rein recounted the struggle one of the costumed personnel was having with a new character recently added to the Pilgrim repertoire: "The 28-year-old *actor* [italics mine] and historian is tackling the formidable task of speaking broken English with a Polish and Dutch twang" (1986, 30).

At contemporary Plimoth Plantation, history has been taken off the page, down from the museum wall, and out of the glass exhibit case; it has become history *performed*. In recognition of its highly theatrical quality, I have entitled this performance of Pilgrim history "The Theatre of the Pilgrims." But is it really theatre? And how have the domains of theatre and museum become fused at present-day Plimoth? And why has such an antitheatrical culture been given a theatrical representation? All of these questions will be addressed in this study.

DRAMATIS PERSONAE: THE PILGRIM CHARACTERS AND THEIR CAUSE

Who exactly were the Pilgrims? They were people in the religious avant-garde of the late Elizabethan and early Jacobean Puritan movement in England.[2] As a whole, they were part of the group that has been identified as the "Left" of English Puritanism (Simpson 1955, 15). They were at the very front of the enormous social drama unfolding as a result of the Protestant Reformation in England. They were called "Separatists" because they had broken away from the Church of England, believing it to be tainted with popish corruptions. They wanted a pure and simple church based on a covenant between themselves and God, not on the king's law. So, in 1606, a number of the so-called "Pilgrim Fathers" formed their own church in Scrooby, Nottinghamshire. Their action was seditious. Since James I was extremely hostile to such religious rebels, they were, according to William Bradford, "hunted and persecuted on every side" (Bradford 1981, 9). In 1607, warrants were issued for the arrest of William Brewster, describing him as a "'very dangerous schismatical Separatist'" (Bartlett 1971, 71).

In 1608, 125 members of this Scrooby congregation escaped to Amsterdam. At that time, there were several other refugee Separatist churches in this Dutch city. The Scrooby group attached themselves to one known as the Ancient Exiled English Church at Amsterdam. In 1609, because of scandals and squabbles in that church, the future Pilgrims migrated to Leyden.[3] There they remained for the next eleven years, supporting themselves by laboring in the textile industry and in other humble trades. Poverty was constantly at their door. So, around 1617, fearing the approaching end of the truce between the Spanish and the Dutch, and having read reports of the newly established Virginia Company's successes, they decided to undertake the dangerous voyage to the New World. They were approached by a London businessman, Thomas Weston, with an offer to fund their voyage and plantation in return for nearly all the profits of their first seven years' labor. Weston's London partners, the Company of Merchant Adventurers, put up the money to hire the *Mayflower;* however, they demanded that some non-Separatists planters be taken aboard. These individuals came to be known as the "Strangers." They were "persons unknown to the Leyden Pilgrims or to their friends, who had to be taken along to please the Adventurers and increase the number of colonists" (Bradford 1981, 46 n.6).

After much delay and two false departures, the 180-ton *Mayflower* set sail from Plymouth, England, on September 16, 1620. It took sixty-five days to cross the Atlantic Ocean. On November 21, 1620, the *Mayflower* was safely moored in what is today Provincetown Harbor, at the tip of Cape Cod. About a month later, the Pilgrims sailed up the coast and settled at New Plimoth.[4]

The *Mayflower* left England with 102 passengers; four died before it reached New Plimoth. By the summer of 1621, only fifty-two persons were left alive. However, the Plimoth colony managed to survive. Other ships came, bringing more people: in 1621, the *Fortune,* and in 1623, the *Anne* and the *Little James.* By 1627, there were more than two hundred colonists. Mainly of the yeoman class, they came from many different parts of England. Most of the newcomers were related to the Separatists, but others were kith and kin of the Strangers. The Pilgrims had befriended the local Wampanoag Indians and, from time to time, these natives would visit the plantation. In the winter of 1626, the *Sparrowhawk,* headed for Virginia, was shipwrecked on the coast of Cape Cod. Its passengers were given refuge at Plimoth until the fall of 1627. Also during 1627, the Dutch, who had settled at Manhattos (present-day Manhattan), twice visited Plimoth.

All of these historical individuals who were present at Plimoth in 1627 are potentially dramatis personae for the living history performance at contemporary Plimoth Plantation. Every day of the year 1627 prescribes a possible script. However, ideally there should be documentation of the events of the day and who was present. For instance, there is little information on which Wampanoags were present in 1627 and when they came. The Dutch came only at two specific times. On the other hand, there are historical records that tell when the *Sparrowhawk* arrived and form the basis for some fascinating potential characterizations of its passengers.

The Scrooby-Leyden congregation formed the core of Plimoth Plantation, controlling both the government and the church. These are the people whom we call "the Pilgrims." They were passionately religious individuals. Like most Puritans, they were "fired by the sense that God was using them to revolutionize history, and committed to the execution of his Will" (Simpson 1955, 39). Their cause was one of religious freedom. In England, they had taken Puritan Nonconformity a step further and totally severed their ties with the Anglican church. Most Puritans wanted to reform the Church of England from within. The Separatists had put their lives on the line. During the reign of Elizabeth, John Greenwood and Henry Barrow had been hanged for "promoting schismatical and seditious opinions" (Stowell 1888, 195). In matters of religion, Separatists refused to accept the authority of the Crown. Consequently, they were cruelly persecuted by Elizabeth I, James I, and Charles I. The Separatists were at the forefront of the Puritan movement. As Edmund S. Morgan puts it: They were obliged to make decisions and think out the implications of Puritan principles before other Puritans did" (1965, 18–19).

The appearance of the Pilgrims on the coast of New England in 1620 was a manifestation of high social drama. They were riding the wave of an escalating political and religious crisis that would lead to the English civil wars. In a sense, they were the harbingers of the Puritan Revolution.

Victor Turner describes four phases that define the development of any social drama (1974, 38–42). The first phase is the *breach.* In the present case, the breach was the unwillingness of the Puritans to conform to the principles and standards of the king's church. The second phase, the *crisis,* was the widening rift between the Puritans and the Anglican church, whose head since the time of Henry VIII had been the king. James I and his son, Charles I, desperately tried to squelch the Puritan rebellion, but the crisis continually mounted. The third stage of this social drama, *redressive action,* culminated in the war between the monarch and the Puritan forces led by Oliver Cromwell. The ultimate forms of redress were the regicide and the temporary overthrow of English monarchical government. The fourth phase, *reintegration,* did not occur until the return of Charles II to the throne in 1660 and the gradual reintegration of the Puritans back into English society, during what has come to be called the Restoration.

Turner recognizes an alternative to reintegration in the final phase— *schism.* In the Pilgrim story, schism is significant. The early Separatists, the most extreme Puritans, were branded as "fantastical schismatics." It was their process of schismogenesis—separating from the church and fleeing their own country—that led to the founding of a new nation. Within a decade of their settling at New Plimoth, there was a massive migration of more moderate Puritans to New England. By 1630, the Massachusetts Bay colony had five times the population of Plimoth Plantation (Bradford 1981, 235 n.1). These later emigrants had also resolved their social drama by schism. Whereas in England, the Puritan social drama climaxed with the beheading of a king, in America, the seeds were planted for a revolution that would create a nation never to know a king.

I have tried to describe the dynamic aspects of the historical social drama of which the Pilgrims were so much a part. What is important for the present study is the way in which this historical social drama generates future performances. As Turner writes, "Social dramas are the raw stuff out of which theater comes to be created as societies develop in scale and complexity and out of which it is continually regenerated" (MacAloon 1984, 24). The establishing of a new nation is obviously an immensely meaningful moment in history. In the last chapter, I will discuss how the Pilgrim story even functions as an "origin myth." At this point, I want to show how the story has been embodied in several modes of performances, leading up to its theatricalization in the present-day living history performance.

PRECEDENTS FOR A THEATRICAL REPRESENTATION

It is a fascinating historical irony that the Pilgrims, in their own era, detested the theatre. During the late Elizabethan period, many Puritans wrote pamphlets and delivered sermons against the theatre. They cited the objections of Tertullian and St. Augustine, who saw the theatre as the devil's workshop. As Jonas Barish points out, paraphrasing William Perkins (a Puritan divine well known to the Pilgrim Fathers), the players were considered evil because "they try to substitute a self of their own contriving for the one given them by God" (1981, 93).

It has been documented that Elder Brewster's library contained two of the major antitheatrical tracts: "Th' Overthrow of Stage-Plays" by John Rainolds and "A Shorte Treatise Against Stage Playes" by an anonymous author (Echeverria 1971, 40).[5] The "Shorte Treatise," published in 1625, lists "the reasons which prove Stageplayes to be unlawful." In addition to pointing out the theatre's pagan origins and the Deuteronomical prohibition against transvestism (Shakespeare's boys dressing up as girls), it warns of the potential corruption of audience members who observe acts of evil (murder and adultery being common themes of Elizabethan/Jacobean drama), and attempts to discredit the actors. The treatise also focuses on the issue of "Time Misspent": "There is losse of pretious time, which should be spent in Gods service by those that are hired to be diligent labourers in his vineyard" (1625, 20). These few words express the essence of what has come to be known as the Protestant ethic. As Edward Norbeck relates: "America's forefathers believed strongly in the set of values known as the Protestant Ethic. Devotion to work was a Christian virtue; and play, the enemy of work, was reluctantly and charily permitted only to children" (1971, 48). This attitude persisted in Plymouth for a long time.

Peter Gomes, a Harvard theologian and Plymouth historian, has called the years between 1820 and 1920 the "Pilgrim Century" (Gomes 1985). During this period poems, songs, paintings (plate 2), and statues honoring the Pilgrims proliferated, and performances representing the Pilgrim story began to appear.

The first actual performative representation of Pilgrim history that I have been able to locate occurred on December 22, 1801. It was part of the Forefathers' Day celebration that had been inaugurated at Plymouth in 1769 to commemorate the landing of the Pilgrims on Plymouth Rock. On this particular occasion, "'an Indian, dressed in the habiliments of a Sachen, met Capt. Turner in the place where Massasoit was first discovered, and the emblems of peace and friendship, which were interchanged, brought into view, an interesting *scene* [italics mine], that existed soon after the arrival of our ancestors'" (Withington 1920, 236–37). This seems to be the first example of re-creating a famous moment in Pilgrim history. It is interesting that this first scene should depict the relationship between the Pilgrims and the Indians, for the Native American plays an important part in the Pilgrim story.[6] The Wampanoags, a coastal Algonquin tribe who lived in the vicinity of Plimoth in the 1600s, helped the Pilgrims to survive the first crucial year by teaching them how to plant the New World corn, maize, and how to catch the herring that ran in the local rivers. In 1621, the Pilgrims made a treaty with the Wampanoag leader, Massasoit. Friendly relations continued between these two groups for many decades, although today Native Americans sometimes equate the landing at Plymouth Rock with the beginning of the genocide of their people.

Most of the early nineteenth-century Forefathers' Days were accompanied by processions, banquets, and orations. The biggest was the bicentennial in 1820, which began the Pilgrim Century. At this celebration, Daniel Webster gave a three-hour-long oration in which he extolled the virtues of the Pilgrim Fathers and identified Plymouth

*Plate 2.* Edwin White's mid-nineteenth-century painting, *The Signing of the Compact in the Cabin of the Mayflower* (Photo courtesy of the Pilgrim Society)

*Plate 3. Tableau vivant,* 1921 (Photo courtesy of the Pilgrim Society)

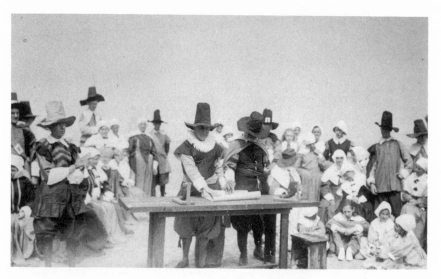

*Plate 4.* Scene from the Tercentenary Pageant, 1921
(Photo courtesy of the Pilgrim Society)

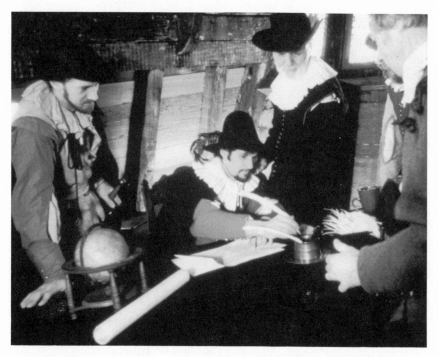

*Plate 5.* Actor/historians, 1980s (Photo courtesy of Plimoth Plantation)

*Above and opposite:* Four representations of the signing of the Mayflower Compact

as the spot "where the first scene of our history was laid" (1825, 9). However, although there were enormous celebrations in 1853 and 1870, it was not until the very end of the century that historical Pilgrim scenes were re-created and Pilgrims impersonated.

In 1896 and 1897, a "historic festival" entitled "Old Plymouth Days and Ways" was produced in Plymouth. It employed *tableaux vivants,* dances, and, possibly, "scenes acted in dumb-show" to portray parts of the Pilgrim story (Withington 1920, 260). One tableau showed the landing of the Pilgrims on Plymouth Rock while another depicted the treaty with Massasoit—the same scene that was portrayed in 1801.

*Tableaux vivants,* or living pictures, were to become an extremely important theatrical means for presenting the Pilgrim image. The well-known paintings that already represented the famous Pilgrim scenes could easily be copied by the placing of costumed individuals in a frozen pose. This sort of performance was enormously popular on the New York stage at the end of the nineteenth century.

As Jack McCullough writes: "The late 1890s blazed brightly with elaborate tableau vivant productions. The most successful variety managers of the day . . . all competed for audiences by means of tableaux" (1981, 131). In 1896, Margaret MacLaren Eager of New York brought her expertise in this mode of production to Plymouth. According to Withington, "She arranged the tableaux, selected the persons, determined the costumes, and had the entire responsibility for the preparation of the scenes, and acted as stage manager" (1920, 259). By this time, theatre had managed to penetrate the antitheatrical prejudice of the Puritan progeny in Plymouth, Massachusetts.

During the Plymouth Tercentenary, actually celebrated in 1921, *tableaux vivants* productions were performed at the beginning and at the end of the mammoth year-long commemorative event. Both productions were done on the proscenium stage of the Old Colony Theatre, which had opened in downtown Plymouth in 1914.

On April 15, 1921, an evening of tableaux was presented in commemoration of the departure of the *Mayflower* on that day three hundred years earlier. The performance began with a "Chorus of Pilgrim Maidens" dressed in Pilgrim costumes and singing Schubert's arrangement for the twenty-third Psalm. Frederick W. Bittinger describes this tableau performance:

Part two of the program was a series of ten tableaux, beautifully staged representing incidents and events in the Pilgrim story. This elaborate work was under the direction of Mr. Hugh Dowling, assisted by Mrs. Henry Royal, Miss Rose Briggs and others. . . . There were vocal interludes during the display of the tableaux and Bryant's Pilgrim hymn was sung with spirit by chorus and audience. Rev. Arthur B. Whitney read the prologues impressively and the evening's exercises closed with the singing of America, as the last picture, "The Pilgrim Heritage: Civil and Religious Liberty," was displayed. (1923, 34)

This evening, along with a similar evening of tableaux presented on September 6, 1921, seems to have been the first fully realized theatrical representation of the Pilgrims.[7]

The living pictures performed on these occasions were dramatic stagings of the most significant scenes of Pilgrim history and had titles such as "The Signing of the Mayflower Compact" (plate 3), "The Landing of the Pilgrims," "The Treaty with Massasoit," and "The First Thanksgiving." Many of these moments had already been portrayed in oil paintings. For example, compare plate 3 with Edwin White's famous mid-nineteenth-century painting *The Signing of the Compact in the Cabin of the Mayflower* (plate 2). During the 1921 Tercentenary, this celebrated scene would be re-created in yet another form—the historical pageant.

On twelve evenings during July and August of 1921, a gigantic pageant honoring the three-hundredth anniversary of the landing of the Pilgrims was presented in a 10,000-seat amphitheater especially constructed for this performance, near the site of Plymouth Rock. It was a prodigious event. Thirteen hundred local people were costumed as Pilgrims; some were trained to enact the roles of specific Pilgrim characters. A chorus of three-hundred, backed by the Gallo Symphony Band of Boston, sang such works as "The Return of the Pilgrims" (words by Robert Frost; music by John Powell). The most sophisticated lighting technology of the period was used to illuminate this nighttime production.

This pageant, entitled *The Pilgrim Spirit,* appeared at the height of what Brooks McNamara has called "The Pageant Era." Pageants were mushrooming all across the United States. As McNamara explains: "Although they were not always associated with larger festivals, most celebrated some myth or historical event of some importance to Americans" (1975, 60). The Plymouth Tercentenary pageant was certainly no exception. It was a spectacular and glorified presentation of the Pilgrim story. It also contained an element of ancestor worship, as "the actors in the spectacle, which was one of the largest events in pageantry ever attempted in this country, were many of them, descendants of the old time peoples, they portray" (Bittinger 1923, 43).

The director or "pageant master" of this enormous production was George Pierce Baker, a leader of the American pageant movement, who was already famous for his 1910 *Peterborough Pageant*. Baker was also a pioneer in the field of theatre education.[8] He saw the pageant as a very promising theatrical form:

> "Pageantry," says Professor Baker, "seems likely to be for us in America a combination of the Chronicle-Play and the Morality, a free dramatic form which teaches, though not abstractly, by stimulating local pride for that in the past which makes the best incentive to future civic endeavor and accomplishment. Already in the communities where it has been tried, it has quickened patriotism, strengthened civic pride, and stimulated or revealed latent artistic powers." (Withington 1920, 291)

As *The Pilgrim Spirit* is, without a doubt, the most colossal theatrical performance of Pilgrim history ever produced, it will be worthwhile to make a brief survey of exactly what it presented.

Each of the evening performances began promptly at 8:30 P.M. with Plymouth Rock, like an ancient Greek oracle, directly addressing the audience. Bittinger, who witnessed the performance on July 20, 1921, describes this moment:

> The pageant opened with a dark stage, save for the stars and the moon, and the seating space also dim as the stage or field, for the whole is acted upon solid earth with no more accessories in scenery than an old Greek theatre. Out of the darkness was heard a fanfare of trumpets which slide into a chord suggestive of some grand hymn. This ceased and from Plymouth Rock, that old glacial drift boulder which was close at hand, came a powerful voice, The Voice of the Rock. (1923, 46)

After this prologue, Episode I unfolded in eight scenes representing all the early explorers' visits to Plymouth, even going back as far as Thorwald, the Viking. These were mostly portrayed in pantomime.

Episode II contained five scenes that depicted the great Puritan social drama described in the previous pages: the Protestant Reformation in England; the martyrdom of the early Separatists John Barrow and Henry Greenwood; King James's persecution of the Separatists; the decision of the Pilgrims to flee England; and, finally the escape to Holland. Many of these scenes were acted out with dialogue. For instance, after a grand parade representing "The Progress of King James," a scene unfolded in which a Puritan leader presented the king with the famous Millenary Petition. Both characters had speeches. At the end of the scene, King James recited his celebrated threat to the Puritans: "I shall make them conform or I will harry them out of this land." The conflict between the king and the Puritans was further expressed in an antiphonal choral number, "The Harrying Chorus."

Some scenes showed large crowds of Pilgrim characters involved in re-creating a historical moment. For example, Baker's script for the pageant described the moment just before the escape in 1608. Episode II, scene 5 began:

> The lights reveal on the whole Field a group of forty women and children and twenty men and youths. Most of the children are clustered in a group near Town Brook, eagerly watching something hidden from sight. There are a few women with them. Some youths are at front, left and right as if standing guard. (1921, 58)

With a cast of thirteen hundred, every character in the Pilgrim saga could be portrayed.

Episode III began with another huge parade, the "March of the Dutch Cities," around the pageant field. Following this, a scene with dialogue depicted the Pilgrims making their momentous decision to voyage to America. Then one of the amateur actors portraying the Pilgrims' pastor, John Robinson, recited a pastiche of Robinson's well-known letters, as though it were a farewell oration. The voyage of the *Mayflower* was represented by a musical interlude. Episode IV showed seven famous scenes of the Pilgrims in America. Many of these were simply more elaborate versions, sometimes with dialogue, of the same scenes represented in the tableaux performances already mentioned. For example, in the pageant, "The Signing of the Mayflower Compact" (plate 4) had many more people in it, the figure of Elder Brewster read the compact aloud, and a scene with dialogue followed. At the end of these seven vignettes, Governor William Bradford was shown in tableau, writing down his history, *Of Plimoth Plantation,* by the light of a candle. The figures of Lincoln and Washington stepped out of the shadows and each said a few lines. Then the chorus of three-hundred sang "The Return of the Pilgrims," as forty-eight young women bearing the flags of the forty-eight states paraded onto the pageant field. As the "Voice of the Rock" made its final proclamation, the pageant came to a close:

> The lights are full on the Mayflower, the Pageant Ground and the harbor are ablaze with light, and great searchlights are sweeping the sky. As the last line is sung the Field darkens quickly till there is light only on the Mayflower. . . . As the light fades in the Mayflower, the PAGEANT ENDS. (Baker 1921, 136)

Bittinger called this pageant "the greatest stage production ever known in this part of the world" (1923, 96). Somewhere between five-thousand and ten-thousand people saw each of the twelve performances. Each production lasted for two hours. On August 1, 1921, President Warren Harding reviewed *The Pilgrim Spirit,* heralding it as a spectacular demonstration of "how much we, of today, owe to that sturdy Pilgrim spirit which the first founders of our nation brought with them across the seas" (Bittinger 1923, 86). This grand pageant was a fitting climax to the Pilgrim Century.

In terms of the development of a theatrical representation for the Pilgrims, a significant advance in the 1921 pageant was the fact that the tableaux had been brought to life. At the beginning of his pageant script, Baker wrote that the first "five tableaux are to be played in pantomime to music" (1921, 9). It is obvious that, in these "tableaux," the actors moved about. These living pictures no longer consisted of stationary, painterly poses; they had become moving pictures. The Pilgrim Fathers had stepped out of the paintings onto the stage, remained frozen for a while, and then begun to act out their drama.

As the Pilgrim Century came to a close, the Pilgrims were represented in another form of moving picture—the silent film. In 1923, silent film actor Charles Ray spent much of his fortune on a movie production based on Longfellow's poem "The Courtship of Miles Standish." The stills from this film reveal a delightfully romantic and melodramatic portrait of the famous Pilgrim lovers John Alden and Priscilla Mullins. Unfortunately, the film was a flop, and Ray went bankrupt. The American public's fascination with the Pilgrims was by now beginning to dwindle, and the film simply faded out of existence.[9]

*Two*

# The Development of a Performative Representation of the Pilgrims at Modern Plimoth Plantation

> Dozens of skilled actor/historians enact the roles
> of the real settlers and you can walk among them,
> chatting here with Mistress Hopkins while she
> weeds her garden, and there with Governor
> Bradford while he prepares to hold a session of
> his court.
>
> James Carroll, *New York Times*, 4 November 1984

After the extravagant production of the Tercentenary pageant, there were few public performances representing the history of the Pilgrims. Those interested in the Pilgrims could go to see their relics at the Pilgrim Hall Museum. In the words of the late George C. P. Olsson, a former president of Plimoth Plantation, Inc.: "When I first came to Plymouth, I felt the Pilgrim story was not being told. In fact, I don't think any real effort had been made since the 1920 Tercentenary. For more than 25 years there was only the Pilgrims' Progress tableau which took place every Friday in August" (Plimoth Plantation 1983).

What is the "Pilgrims' Progress tableau"? It is a remnant, still in existence, of the Tercentenary celebrations. It is significant as a transitional mode of representing the Pilgrims, connecting the early tableau performances to the development of living history performance at

*Plate 6.* George H. Boughton's 1867 painting, *The Pilgrims Going to Church*
(Photo courtesy of the Pilgrim Society)

Plimoth Plantation. Like the tableaux in Baker's pageant, it is also a moving tableau. The Pilgrims' Progress re-creates the famous scene of the Pilgrims marching to their Sabbath day service at the Fort-Meeting House. This procession was described in detail by an eyewitness to the event in 1627.[1] The subject of George H. Boughton's well-known 1867 oil painting, *The Pilgrims Going to Church* (plate 6), this scene was one of the tableaux productions given at the Old Colony Theatre during the Tercentenary.

In 1921, the town of Plymouth instituted the Pilgrims' Progress as part of its Tercentenary commemorations. It was probably influenced by, but separate from, the formal production of *The Pilgrim Spirit*. Rose Briggs, one of the Progress marchers, writes: "The idea of the Pilgrim Progress was suggested by a passage in Daniel Webster's oration at the 200th Anniversary, in which he exclaims how moving it would be if one could see for a moment the Pilgrims as they lived" (1970, 1). Here, then, is the seed for the development of a performative re-creation of Pilgrim history.

In this 1921 Progress, townspeople were costumed as specific Pilgrim characters: the historical personages who had survived the first horrible winter in Plimoth. To the sound of a drum, they marched up the street that covered over the original main street of the historic Pilgrim village. Then they proceeded up the hill where the Pilgrims them-

*Plate 7.* Pilgrims' Progress, 1940 (Photo courtesy of the Pilgrim Society.)

selves had marched (although, by 1921, it had become a cemetery) to the site of the original Fort-Meeting House. There, a short service was held in which psalms from the original Pilgrim psalter were sung and extracts from authentic Pilgrim writings were read aloud. Altogether a simple ceremony, it has continued in this basic form, every year following, up the present. Today, the Pilgrims' Progress is performed in Plymouth every Friday afternoon in August at five o'clock and also on Thanksgiving Day.

What is particularly relevant, here, in regard to the evolution of a theatrical representation of the Pilgrims is that, over the years, the Progress began to involve a kind of role-playing. James Baker, a lifelong resident of Plymouth and presently Vice President of Museum Operations at Plimoth Plantation, recalls that, back in the 1950s, local people started to become identified with their roles in the Progress. Other townsfolk would say, "Oh, that's Elder Brewster" or "That's Myles Standish" (Baker 1985a). This probably came about because these individuals played the same part year after year. Rose Briggs states that "the role of Myles Standish was sustained for many years by Mr. Adrian Whiting" (1970, 2).

There is another significant link between the Pilgrims' Progress and the emergence of a theatricalized embodiment of the Pilgrim story. Two of the 1921 Progress marchers, Edwina Dittmar and Rose Briggs, were to become the first costume designers at Plimoth Plantation. Dittmar says:

> For the early picture taking for postcards, publicity and special events [for Plimoth Plantation] we borrowed costumes from the Pilgrim Progress. These Progress costumes were used during the Town's celebration (1921) for its 300th anniversary of the landing of the Pilgrims. Miss Rose Briggs had done a great deal of research at that time for costumes for the Pageant and with her foresight has kept the Pilgrim Progress going. The costumes used in the Progress needed to be repaired and replaced from time to time over the years, and this is where my knowledge of Pilgrim costumes was learned working with Miss Briggs. (Dittmar 1967, 1)

So here is a point of convergence between the Pilgrims' Progress and the first years of the living museum. The costumes worn by the marchers in the Progress during the 1940s and 1950s (plate 7) show up again on the early costumed employees of Plimoth Plantation, Inc.

The Progress, along with the 1921 pageant, had definitely established a precedent for Pilgrim impersonation in Plymouth. The impulse toward living history was evident in the desire of local people to continue the annual reenactment of this famous historical scene— "The Pilgrims Going to Church." In terms of the development of a theatrical representation of Pilgrim history, a series of transformations is discernible: the scenes depicted in paintings become *tableaux vivants,* which become moving tableaux, culminating in the Pilgrims' Progress. As the living museum at Plimoth Plantation evolves, this series continues: costumed guides who lecture on Pilgrim scenes that are represented by wax mannequins in tableaux are replaced by "actor/historians" re-creating Pilgrim history through the total environmental theatre reenactment of the year 1627 in Plimoth (figure 1).

THE ORIGINAL IDEA FOR A PILGRIM VILLAGE

It wasn't until after the end of World War II that a new plan for a much larger reenactment of the Pilgrim story came about. In December 1945, Henry Hornblower II convinced his father, Ralph Hornblower, to donate $20,000 to the Pilgrim society in order "to acquire land and prepare preliminary plans for a Pilgrim Village" (Plimoth

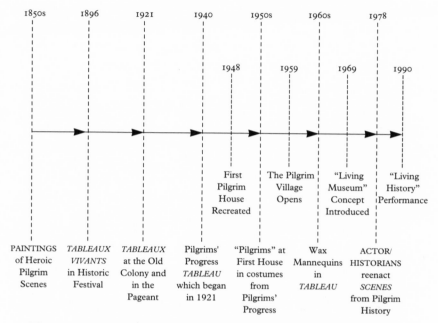

*Figure 1.* A progression of the various modes for representing the Pilgrims, from the 1850s to the 1990s

Plantation 1983). Ralph Hornblower was one of the six richest men in New England, and his son, an avid and skilled amateur archaeologist who had studied at Harvard and Berkeley, had a particular fascination for Pilgrim culture and history. The Hornblowers had been summer residents of Plymouth for many years.

There were existing models for Henry Hornblower's idea of a re-created historic village: Henry Ford's Greenfield Village, which opened in 1929, and Colonial Williamsburg, built by John D. Rockefeller, Jr., and mostly completed in the mid-1930s. Another model closer to home was Old Sturbridge Village, which had been in the works since the late 1930s and was finally opened in 1946 (Wallace 1981, 80–81). Old Sturbridge Village—like Colonial Williamsburg, still flourishing—was designed to re-create a New England village as it existed at the beginning of the nineteenth century. Located in Sturbridge, Massachusetts, this restored village includes an excellent, functioning period farm. Costumed staff demonstrate regional folk activities including blacksmithing, tinsmithing, spinning wool, and sheepshearing. All interpretation is done in the third person except for special events, such as the re-enactment of a "town meeting," in which costumed staff completely embody their roles as village folk (Anderson 1985, 88–89).

On October 2, 1947, Plimoth Plantation was incorporated, and its purpose was clearly stated in the Articles of Incorporation:

> The creation, construction and maintenance of a Pilgrim Village as a Memorial to the Pilgrim Fathers; the management and operation of the same and generally the restoration or reproduction of antiquarian houses and buildings, implements, tools and facilities; the historical education of the public with respect to the struggles of the early Settlers in the Town of Plymouth, the expansion of that settlement and the influence of the Pilgrim Fathers throughout the world. (Plimoth Plantation 1948, 8)

This statement indicates that the aim was mainly an educational one, although a note of "ancestor worship" ("Pilgrim Fathers") is also present. As with the Ford and Rockefeller villages, the emphasis was on reconstructing the historical milieu by means of the "reproduction of antiquarian houses." Now the question remained: who was to portray the original residents and how were they to be represented?

In September 1949, work began on the replica of a typical "first house." It was located on the land that had been cleared for the Tercentenary pageant grounds, adjacent to Plymouth Rock. The design was rendered by Charles T. Strickland, an architect well known for his restoration of the Old North Church in Boston. Before the First House was completed in 1949, townspeople were costumed as Pilgrims and stood by to answer questions and collect donations. Again, their costumes were designed by Rose Briggs, who was also the curator at the Pilgrim Hall Museum. Many photographs from this year show family scenes. These are probably promotional shots, as the First House was basically a "promo" for the Pilgrim Village-to-come.

In 1953, a replica of the Fort-Meeting House was constructed on the waterfront near the First House. Again, photographs from this period depict scenes such as "Pilgrim Family Leaving Church." These scenes were probably just tableaux, set up for photographic purposes. In 1955, a "1627 House" was erected next to the First House. Public interest in the Pilgrim Village was steadily growing. Even in its first year, 390,000 people visited the reproduction of the First House.

THE FIRST REENACTMENT: THE SECOND COMING OF THE *MAYFLOWER*

Numerous plans were made for Plimoth Plantation from its inception. The 1948 Program for the Pilgrim Memorial mentions such projects as the reproduction of "the First Street," with twelve houses, the "Common Store House," and the "Governor's House"; the building of a "Village Green" where actual historic houses might be preserved; the construction of an amphitheatre where pageants depicting the Pilgrim story could be performed; and the re-creation of an "Indian Village" campsite. One of the foremost undertakings was to be a complete reproduction of the *Mayflower*. The 1948 Program states:

> The story of the Pilgrims is not complete without the inclusion of the ship that brought the Pilgrims to the New World. A reproduction of the Mayflower would make a very desirable addition to the project. . . . It is planned to build a full-sized replica, completely rigged, which will be anchored in Plymouth Harbor so that visitors may go aboard. (Plimoth Plantation 1948, 22)

Within a decade after the incorporation of Plimoth Plantation, the proposal for the re-creation of the *Mayflower* was realized. Dr. R. C. Anderson of Greenwich, England, had already given a model of the *Mayflower* to Pilgrim Hall. In 1949, the plantation asked naval architect William A. Baker to make designs for a full-scale replica. These plans were published and caught the attention of an Englishman named Warwick Charlton. He and his business partner founded what came to be known as "Project Mayflower." They started working toward their goal after receiving a substantial initial gift from Felix Fenston, a wealthy Londoner. These men proposed to have the ship constructed in England, based on Baker's designs, then sailed across the Atlantic and presented to Plimoth Plantation (Colby 1970, 100). They hired Stuart Upham of Brixham, in Devon, to build the ship. His family had been in the business of building wooden ships for some two hundred years. Mr. Upham's craftsmen worked carefully for fifteen months (July 1955 to September 1956) to construct the ship in the ancient manner. For instance, they made the "tree nails" (wooden pegs used to hold the beams together) out of wood from some cider vats that were over 130 years old (Charlton 1957, 47). On July 4, 1955, Commander Winslow, an English descendant of one of the most famous of the Pilgrim Fathers—Edward Winslow—"laid the keel"

(Villiers 1958, 8). Captain Alan Villiers, an Australian sea captain and one of the few men who still knew how to sail a square-rigger, offered his services to navigate the completed vessel. On April 20, 1957, the *Mayflower II* set sail from Plymouth, England, the same place from which the Pilgrims had embarked for America three centuries before.

In actuality, the voyage of *Mayflower II* was not a complete reenactment. The Pilgrims were not impersonated aboard the ship, nor was the original route across the sea precisely followed. But what is important in relation to the living history performance that later developed at Plimoth Plantation is that role-playing and "acting" did, in fact, take place on board the *Mayflower II*. Though partly planned, this situation also resulted from the desire of the crew to simulate the experience of the original seamen and passengers. On Sundays, for instance, the crew dressed up in Elizabethan seafaring attire and heard prayers read from a three hundred-year-old prayer book (Villiers 1958, 38).

There were dangers to be found in attempting to replicate certain conditions on the reproduction of a three-hundred-year-old ship. The crew often discussed how Elizabethan sailors might have carried out a particular nautical maneuver. Captain Villiers had read in William Bradford's narrative of the original voyage how the seventeenth-century seamen took in the sails during extremely high winds. The *Mayflower II* was faced with just such a situation off the coast of the Carolinas toward the end of its journey. Captain Villiers had his crew reenact the procedure used by the original crew: "After the perilous task of taking in the sails, they hove to and waited anxiously. Villiers remembers: '... Indeed it was amazing. I reflected that the Pilgrim Fathers, who tossed through many such a wild night in Atlantic storms, at least knew tranquility in great gales'" (Anderson 1984, 115).

The voyage of the *Mayflower II* took thirteen days fewer than the original did, but its company had many experiences similar to those of the Pilgrims. As the first mate told Captain Villiers, "This lively little ship is altogether too historically correct for my liking" (Anderson 1984, 114). Finally, on June 13, 1957, the *Mayflower II* crossed Cape Cod Bay from Provincetown, just as the Pilgrims had done in 1620, and, with its crew dressed in their Elizabethan costumes, "tied up to a buoy off famed Plymouth Rock, where the Pilgrims landed" (Villiers 1958, 46).

With the exception of brief excursions to New York, Washington, and Miami during her first year in America, *Mayflower II* has been moored at the state pier in Plymouth, Massachusetts. In accordance with the 1948 plan, this re-created ship serves as an open exhibit for the general public. The performance that takes place today aboard the *Mayflower II* will be discussed in chapter 4.

GUIDES AND HOSTESSES: THE "OLD STYLE" INTERPRETATION

The reenactment of the voyage of the *Mayflower* brought Plimoth Plantation international attention. The guiding force of "Project Mayflower," Warwick Charlton, was an economic and industrial public relations man and was adept at getting media coverage for the event. One of his tactics involved convincing many English companies to send samples of their merchandise across the sea in treasure chests stored in the bowels of the re-created vessel (Charlton 1957, 39). The crossing of *Mayflower II* inspired almost as much excitement as Thor Heyerdahl's famous *Kon-Tiki* voyage.

At the same time the reproduction of the *Mayflower* was going on, Plimoth Plantation acquired land for the proposed Pilgrim Village. The original idea was to re-create the village on a piece of property located next to the Plymouth Country Club. That land was never obtained; however, in 1956, Hattie Hornblower, Henry Hornblower's grandmother, gave fifty acres from the family's summer estate to Plimoth Plantation. The land was about three miles southward from the site of the original Plimoth and had a remarkably similar landscape to that of the real Pilgrim Village. Adjacent to the Eel River, it offered a magnificent view of Plymouth Harbor—a vista probably very like the one that the Pilgrims had from the top of Leyden Street in 1620. This is the current site of Plimoth Plantation.

With acquisition of this property, work began on re-creating the houses of the first village. Descendants of the original *Mayflower* passengers were approached for funds to reconstruct their ancestral homesteads. The Howland Society responded first and a reproduction of John Howland's house was begun in 1957. In 1958, the Fort-Meeting House was moved from the waterfront to the Eel River site. By 1959, the houses of William Brewster, Richard Warren, and William Bradford were also re-created, and Plimoth Plantation had its first full season as an outdoor museum (Colby 1970, 104).

Inside these earliest reproduced houses were placed "guides" and "hostesses" who answered the visitors' questions about Pilgrim history. They were dressed in Pilgrim costumes—stereotypical polyester

versions with starched white collars and cuffs and the historically incorrect but traditional buckled shoes and hats—but these townsfolk
did not represent any particular historical characters. They spoke
in twentieth-century American accents, from their own twentieth-
century points of view. Basically, the guides and hostesses were a carry-
over from the First House on the waterfront. These local men (guides)
and women (hostesses) were trained by Arthur Pyle, a Plymouth High
School history teacher, who, according to Jim Baker, was the first
employee at Plimoth Plantation (1985b). The first director of education, Mr. Pyle wrote the original training manual for interpreters and
developed the first style (the "old style") of interpretation. Jim Baker
describes this:

> Mr. Pyle believed in what he called the "conversational approach,"
> which was different from a lot of museums. He didn't want set
> speeches by people. He thought it was unnatural and off-putting.
> And so he got it so you got a lot of information. You got suggested
> ways of talking and he did a lot of educational materials, too. But
> the whole things was a natural presentation of information, based on
> what the visitor was heading towards or interested in. (Baker 1985b)

At this time, all the museum's employees worked on a part-time basis,
since the season only lasted approximately four months.

The old style of interpretation remained in effect for most of the
next decade (1959–69). Carolyn Freeman Travers, head of research at
Plimoth Plantation and daughter of former museum director David
Freeman, calls the old style the "sainted ancestors bit." She started
working as a hostess in 1968 when she was thirteen years old and
recalls the performance of the old style interpretation that was given in
the village houses (eleven of which were completed by 1969): "I'd sit
in the house and listen to the same rap: '. . . the house in which you
are standing represents the home of Governor William Bradford, who
was the second governor of the Old Colony, and if I may direct your
attention to the tableau on your left . . .'" (Travers 1985). At this
point, the guides and hostesses had to share the setting with mannequins that were set up in various tableaux inside the re-created houses
(plate 8). It was the interpreters' responsibility to inform visitors about
the house and the scene that a particular tableau represented.

Of course, this overall style did not remain static during the entire

*Plate 8.* A hostess and a wax mannequin inside a re-created Pilgrim house in the Pilgrim Village, early 1960s (Photo courtesy of Plimoth Plantation)

period. Just as the historical accuracy of the architecture improved as time went on, so did the costumes that the guides and hostesses wore. Gradually, more active exhibits were added, such as candle dipping and basket making for the women, and the saw pit and the musket drill on top of the Fort-Meeting House for the men. Although there are many photographs from this era portraying scenes from Pilgrim life, such as "Pilgrim Cooking Lesson," "Bible Reading," and "Pilgrim Family Dinner," they are, again, not so much reenactments as promotional shots resembling those taken at the Pilgrim House by the waterfront.

MANNEQUINS TAKE CENTER STAGE

In 1956, on a trip to the Virgin Islands, Henry Hornblower II, founder and president of Plimoth Plantation, met Cyril Marshall, director of the St. Croix Museum. Marshall was an artist, a sculptor, and a craftsman in both wood and metal. Harry Hornblower convinced him to come to Plymouth in order to design the mannequins that were to be used as exhibits on the *Mayflower* and in the Pilgrim Village. For a number of years, Marshall divided his time between Plymouth and St. Croix. Finally, he stayed on as exhibits director.

Ruth Trask, retired Director of Financial Operations at the plantation, recollects that the original mannequins came from De Stephano's, a company in Boston that made "mannequins for all the big department stores to put in their windows" (Trask 1985). Jean Poindexter Colby writes: "Made of papier mache with plaster coating for faces, they were embellished by Mr. Marshall with personal features, wigs of human hair and appropriate clothing. Details for this project came from studying paintings and prints of the period. . . . Mr. Marshall's mannequins were indeed works of art before he finished them" (1970, 110–11).

For over a decade, these mannequins were the centerpiece of the historical exhibition at Plimoth Plantation, used to depict many scenes of the Pilgrim story. One of the oldest of these was called "Pilgrim Maids Cooking." Another famous tableau in this style showed Deacon Samuel Fuller, the village surgeon, working on the leg wound of a Pilgrim patient in the re-creation of the Fuller House (completed in 1960). One of the favorites in the village was the Pilgrims at their worship service in the Fort-Meeting House. Colby describes the dramatic impact of this tableau: "The Fort-Meeting House is a center for demonstrating the deep significance to them of religion. Seeing the group of lifelike mannequins listening intently to their preacher and hearing the old Pilgrim hymns sung with gusto (a professional recording) is a moving experience for visitors" (1970, 108).

During the 1960s, this mode of representing the Pilgrims was enormously popular with the general public. As Jim Baker explains, these mannequins had an "aura of antiquity," while the local people in their polyester Pilgrim outfits seemed terribly "modern" and were perceived as such by the visitors (1985a). Usually, the guides and hostesses would interpret a specific composition of Pilgrim mannequins in the same way a museum guide would interpret a great painting. Ruth Trask, however, tells the story of one man who liked to play a trick on the visitors; he would sit perfectly still among the mannequins in the Fort-Meeting House and then suddenly get up. "People nearly had a heart attack!" she says. (1985).

The last of the mannequins was removed from the Pilgrim Village sometime in the early 1970s. However, the mannequin scenes stayed aboard the *Mayflower II* until 1980. To this day, some people say that they prefer this means of representing the Pilgrim story above all the others that Plimoth Plantation has offered to the public. Currently, this method of representation has been taken over by the Plymouth National Wax Museum, which boasts the ironic motto: "Where your Pilgrim heritage comes alive."

THE SIXTIES: BEGINNING TO DEBUNK THE PILGRIM MYTH

With the arrival of the sixties, a whole new atmosphere began to develop at the plantation. Around 1959, a young man named James Deetz, who was getting his doctorate in anthropology at Harvard, appeared on the scene. According to Jim Baker, it was James Deetz who set Plimoth Plantation on its "scholarly footing." Deetz felt that with the serious scientific investigation of archaeological and historical evidence, a truer picture of the Pilgrims' daily life could be brought to light. After he started teaching at Brown University, he had his students come down to Plymouth for archaeological digs and to search through the massive files of Pilgrim wills, inventories, and court records. As Deetz says in his article "The Reality of the Pilgrim Fathers": "In researching its history and culture in depth, it is possible to set straight a host of misconceptions that most people hold of the 'Pilgrims' and their seventeenth-century descendants" (1969, 32).

As Deetz, who became assistant director of the museum, and his team of researchers began to explore the available data more deeply, a new image of the physical environment of the first village began to emerge. The existing re-created village, with its picturesque oyster-shell walkways, rose bushes, and charming Elizabethan glass windows, was, by this point, seen to be a falsification of history (plate 9). As Deetz says: "To create a neat, apple pie orderly community is simply not in accord with known historical fact" (1969, 39). By the late sixties, a radical new scenography was evolving at Plimoth Plantation.

In 1969, these developments culminated in a crisis. In fact, the day before the opening of the 1969 plantation season is looked upon by many old-timers around Plimoth Plantation as a "day of infamy." Historical research had shown Deetz that much of the furniture in the village houses was inauthentic; so with his assistant, Kathy Gates, he went down to the village and removed it all, until the houses looked

*Plate 9.* A historically inauthentic Pilgrim house, mid-1960s
(Photo courtesy of Plimoth Plantation)

appropriately barren. When museum director David Freeman got wind of this, he went down to see the village for himself. Ruth Trask, who was in the administration offices that day, reports: "David Freeman went down to the village. He came back and his face looked like a boiled lobster. I knew when I saw him walk in that door that he was absolutely furious. He got hold of Jim Deetz and told him that *that* village was not opening the next day until he restored all of the things in it" (Trask 1985). However, because Deetz had Harry Hornblower's imprimatur for this action, the furniture did not get replaced.[2] Soon, most of the mannequins would be removed as well.

The movement during the sixties was definitely away from the "sainted ancestors bit" and more toward an accurate portrayal of history. As the views on the material culture shifted profoundly in this decade, so did the conceptions of the Pilgrim world view and psychology. Kathy Gates, who had an M.A. from Radcliffe in seventeenth-century English history and literature, revised the training manual that had been used by the guides and hostesses. A new Pilgrim was soon to

*Plate 10.* Edward Winslow's house in the Pilgrim Village, 1985
(Photo by Stephen Snow)

appear in a more authentic environment. Deetz wrote: "Having created a village of simple frame houses, and furnished them according to the best research data available, it remains to populate the village with trained interpreters who give the appearance of seventeenth-century Pilgrims" (1969, 42).

By 1969, the guides and hostesses had become "interpreters" who used the village and all it contained to engage the visitors in discussions on various aspects of the specific seventeenth-century English culture of the Pilgrims. However, these interpreters still spoke of the Pilgrims in the third person.

The important changes in scenography and portrayal of the Pilgrims taking place at the plantation were, of course, part of the larger pattern of debunking American myths that occurred in the sixties. The youth of the counterculture undoubtedly looked upon the Pilgrim Fathers as negative authority figures. The old Victorian heroic images of the Pilgrims were being demolished. Deetz recalls that, at that time, the plantation staff consciously recognized that they were eroding the romantic myth of the Pilgrims (1987). Many of the older generation were alarmed by the new presentation of the forefathers. As Carolyn Travers put it: "Some people never forgave us for becoming real people instead of sainted ancestors" (1985). During the late sixties, the purpose of re-creating history became "telling it like it was" which meant showing slave cabins in Colonial Williamsburg; and, at Plimoth Plantation, taking the Pilgrims down from their pedestals and revealing what they really were—hard-working farmers.

The new styles of performance erupting in the sixties—multi-media events, happenings, conceptual art, environmental theatre—also helped to shape the new way of presenting the Pilgrims. In 1969, Deetz could speak of the Pilgrim Village in terms of Marshall McLuhan's concept of "cool media": "The village is cool media. All senses are appealed to, and structured information content is relatively low. Signs, labels, and other written information are almost nonexistent. Nothing is displayed or demonstrated simply for the sake of display or demonstration, yet by inquiring and conversing with any of the many interpreters in the village, information is easily obtained" (1969, 39).

THE SEVENTIES: DEVELOPMENT OF THE "NEW STYLE" INTERPRETATION

During the late sixties, the concept of the living museum had become a burning issue on the open-air museum circuit. Plimoth Plantation had been a leader in this field, removing its static exhibits and replacing them with costumed interpreters who actually performed seventeenth-century village tasks. The point was to do what the Pilgrims did in their daily lives, not just talk about it. As Cary Carson sees it, the concept at Plimoth had become: "Take us as you find us and make whatever sense of things you can" (1981, 28). By 1974, the emphasis was on a working village. The "Villagers" taught the culture of the Pilgrims by doing their chores and engaging in musket drills, prayers, feasting, dancing, and singing. Now, the focus of interpretation was on activity.

This new approach was balanced with a fairly disciplined attention to historical information. In the early seventies, director of education Robert D. Ronsheim demanded that all his interpreters know the whole history of Plymouth Colony, from 1620 to 1692. Difficult examinations were given to interpreters on a regular basis. They were required to know accurate information, just as Deetz had re-created an accurate Pilgrim environment. Ronsheim expected the interpreters to be able to elucidate specific themes for the visitors. Such topics as religion, Dutch influence, and the military were expounded upon in particular houses. For instance, Brewster House was the location for a discourse on religion. Jay Anderson, who worked in Foodways at the Plantation at this time, recounts that the interpreters called their little lectures "sermonettes" (1985).

The early seventies were the height of the hippie era, and many older visitors and townsfolk complained that the Pilgrim Village now looked like a hippie commune. There was a great uproar when the *Mayflower* descendants arrived in 1970 for the 350th anniversary of the coming of the *Mayflower*. Jim Baker recalls how they cried out in dismay: "It's full of hippies! Where are all those nice ladies in neat costumes, sitting with collars and cuffs. . . . We want our romantic village!" (1985b). In fact, many of the older hostesses who formerly staffed the village had left after the crises of 1969.[3] The Pilgrim Village was, at this point, inhabited by young, long-haired people going around barefoot. Assistant director Deetz had given his permission for such behavior with this historical justification: "The Plantation's personnel can go barefoot if they desire, as have farming folk for all ages in warm weather" (1969, 39). The seventies Pilgrims were allowed to wear much less clothing; both men and women could wear loose-fitting cotton shirts with breeches or skirts on warm summer days. With these new style costumes, a new mode of interpretation, a new McLuhanesque village—which did not include the signs with *Mayflower* family names that had previously hung on the Pilgrim houses—it is no wonder that many *Mayflower* descendants felt at a loss to distinguish their seventeenth-century ancestors from twentieth-century hippies. The photographs taken at the plantation during this period (1969–79) indicate that the counterculture had made a significant impression upon the interpretation of Pilgrim history at Plimoth Plantation. Yet as Deetz has pointed out (1987), there actually was a remarkable similarity between the cultural styles of the Pilgrims and the hippies. The Pilgrims were also a countercultural force: they were the protestors of their own age. The hippies' impulse to build communes was like the Pilgrims' desire to form their own congregation. Of course, the pot-smoking, guitar-strumming youth who now inhabited Plimoth Plantation would have been abhorrent to the Pilgrim Fathers in many ways. But it is a fascinating coincidence that the hippie movement and the re-creation of the Pilgrims' historical culture should converge at this time.

The look of the Pilgrim Village was now accentuated by a palisade constructed all the way around it in 1970 by prisoners from the Plymouth County jail. This enormous paling, covering several acres, defined the village as a special area, separate from the quotidian reality of the twentieth-century world. In 1969, the year 1627 had been designated as the specific year to be represented inside the Pilgrim Village. It was chosen for several reasons: the joint stock company that had financed the initial voyage and supported the Plimoth Colony for most of its first seven years was liquidated in 1627; subsequently, land and cattle were divided among individual households in that year; an important census was then drawn up; and, finally, the most detailed description of Plimoth Plantation by an outsider—the Dutch merchant Isaack de Rasieres—was made at that time. From 1969 on, the scenarios played out by the interpreters within the confines of the palisade have for the most part been based on historic texts from 1627.

Since the early 1970s, the village has stayed pretty much the same. A few new houses have been reproduced, more animals brought in, and the saw pit moved from place to place. But, with the exception of a few minor changes that have occurred when better information on the material culture has become available, the general ambience has remained the same. The whole thrust has been toward creating the illusion of the daily life of a seventeenth-century New England farming community. In the words of Deetz: "The village is presented as a living community, where people perform the routine tasks involved in the life of the time" (1969, 36).

One important aspect of the living museum that developed in the seventies is the Native American Program. It grew out of a protest made by about two hundred Native Americans on Thanksgiving Day, 1970: "Various Indian organizations staged a series of symbolic protests over the treatment and plight of the Indian. The most spectacular events—casting sand on Plymouth Rock and momentarily taking over Mayflower II—made pictures across the Atlantic" (Plimoth Plantation 1970). Of course, an Indian Village had been in the original 1948 plans for a Pilgrim Memorial and had been constructed simultaneously with the Pilgrim Village. However, it wasn't until 1973 that the Wampanoag Summer Campsite was staffed with persons of Native

American descent (see chapter 1, note 6). By this time, the need to portray more honestly the Native American version of early New England history was clearly recognized.

## THE EMERGENCE OF FIRST-PERSON INTERPRETATION

As the plantation moved into its third decade as an operating outdoor museum, a whole new form of interpretation emerged—"first person." What might at first appear to be a leap into a new technique—the total impersonation of the Pilgrim characters—had actually been developing all along. In the Tercentenary pageant, in the Pilgrims' Progress, and, at moments, in the reenactment of the voyage of the *Mayflower,* people had begun to role-play with the Pilgrim characters. However, during the first ten years of Pilgrim Village, the costumed employees did not represent specific characters; they told the Pilgrim story in the third person. Sometime in the early 1970s, certain guides began to experiment with speaking in a seventeenth-century English dialect. William Pine, George Newcomb, and Robert Marten began to study period linguistics on their own and occasionally would play with it in the village. Dorothy Hale, a hostess at the time, recounts these early experiments with dialect:

> They would go down there—this is when two of them were just kidding around. We'd hear them and we'd just kind of listen and chuckle. And the visitors would kind of like stand there and—"Are these guys for real?"—you know. And then they would come up to us up in the movie building and say: "Who do those people think they are kidding down there?" It did not go over well when there were only one or two of them doing it! (Hale et al. 1986)

These first attempts at dialect were still not in the first person, but things were moving more and more in that direction. By 1971, the guides and hostesses were periodically presenting mini-dramatizations of different historical scenes, such as the trial of Reverend John Lyford and Mad Jack Oldham that took place in Plimoth in 1624. These scenes were performed for visitors and marked the "inauguration of role-playing" at the plantation (Plimoth Plantation 1971). Deetz's new program, with its focus on activity, also induced the interpreter to identify more closely with his Pilgrim role. As Deetz explained to me, it was quite natural for people who worked hard all day on building a

Pilgrim artifact to say "*I* build this or that" rather than "This is the way *they* (the Pilgrims) did it" (1987). Or, as Carolyn Travers puts it: "A reproduction village with reproduction furniture sort of calls out for reproduction people" (1985).

Many people had an impact on the development of the first-person program at Plimoth Plantation. Certainly one of them was James Deetz. Deetz also mentions the brainstorming sessions held by Thomas A. Young, then Director of Exhibits, along with Laurie Downing, Catherine Gates Marten, and Robert Marten. By 1977, full-fledged characterization of and intentional identification with the Pilgrim role was an idea whose idea had come. It was the next step in a logical progression that led from the living museum environment to living history performance.

One of the most important figures in this evolution was Robert Marten. Jim Baker says that Marten took first-person role-playing further than anyone, during the experimental stage in the early seventies. Baker recounts how Marten used to dye his hair for the role of Myles Standish, who had red hair, and says that Marten was a "natural actor—a natural mimic" (1985b). Marten had started working at the plantation in the early 1960s and had either witnessed or experienced all of the various changes in the interpretation program over the decade. He had spent a good deal of time researching the authentic seventeenth-century dialect of the Pilgrims and by 1977 had developed methods for training other interpreters in both dialect and first-person role-playing technique. Marten was thus instrumental in the plantation's implementing its first full regular season of first-person role-playing in 1978.

By this time, there had been a kind of caesura in the administration of the plantation. Most of the older officers had gone. Arthur Pyle and Cyril Marshall had retired, David Freeman died in 1976; and, in 1977, James Deetz had left to become director of the Lowie Museum of Anthropology at Berkeley. In this gap, the new approach to interpretation encountered little resistance. Young, the recently appointed assistant director, who had been sympathetic all along, gave his approval, and first-person interpretation moved in full force before the unsuspecting public. As the 1983 Plimoth Plantation Annual Report states: "Visitors no longer met with 20th century instructors in Pilgrim attire, but 'informants' portraying William Bradford, John Billington, John and Priscilla Alden and others. Living history took on its present form." The general public responded enthusiastically to this new way of representing the Pilgrims. In an interview, Jim Baker explained his feeling that this positive reaction was due to the refocusing on the people in the Pilgrim story. Visitors enjoyed being able to address the famous and not-so-famous characters of Pilgrim history.

However, this transition into first person was not easy for all the interpreters (also known during this time as "cultural informants").[4] Caroline Chapin, formerly Curator of Manuscripts and Books at Pilgrim Hall and an interpreter at Plimoth Plantation during the 1977 and 1978 seasons, found the first-person mode to be very demanding. She remembers that the seventeenth-century English dialect was not easy for her. She feels that if acting does not come naturally to a person, then the first-person approach can be extremely difficult. She says: "I didn't feel like I was an actress. I wasn't hired to be. I was more interested in delivering the information and learning about the folkways" (1985).

Is first-person interpretation really acting? This is one of the most important and complicated questions to be addressed in this book. For if it is acting, then what kind of acting? The core of my thesis that this living museum has been transformed into a type of environmental theatre hangs on this question. Although the matter will be explored in depth in chapter 5, I want at this point to establish some basic premises for this discussion.

What is acting? In the traditional theatrical sense of the term, acting is creating the illusion of being a character other than oneself through the performance of actions dictated in a script that usually tells a story set in another time and place. Most commonly, acting is role-playing in a fictional setting. This type of dramatic acting requires special training in voice, movement, characterization, and the particular stage conventions of a given ethnohistorical context. Thus, a fifteenth-century Japanese Noh actor would have to learn how to work with a very delicate mask and a specific set of movements in order to portray the ghost of a noblewoman. A sixteenth-century English actor would have to know breath control and the rules of rhetoric to perform the speeches written by Elizabethan dramatists. In both these cases, the main goal of the actor is to embody a character within a given set of imaginary circumstances.

In the early twentieth century, the history of the theatre and of acting was drastically altered with the systemization of the principles of
creative and natural acting by the great Russian actor and director
Constantin Stanislavski. As pointed out in the notes to the preface,
the Stanislavskian or Method approach to acting is particularly conducive to a naturalistic style of performance. It developed in a period
when naturalistic and realistic styles of playwriting and production
were becoming more and more predominant. The old histrionic
modes of oratory and declamation were in decline. Stanislavski's mission was to identify those universal laws that could help the actor
become more natural, genuine, and truthful in his or her portrayal of a
human being. To this purpose, he developed a series of "inner techniques," such as the famous "emotion memory," that helps actors
make use of their own psychological instrument in an organic and creative way. As Lee Strasberg, perhaps Stanislavski's major American
interpreter, has said:

> Theatres and actors of great variety and diversified form have cre-
> ated outstanding works on the basis of the training acquired by the
> use of Stanislavski's principle. The works created are never copies or
> imitations of one another but are original creative achievements.
> That is the purpose of Stanislavski's idea. It teaches not how to play
> this or that part but how to create organically. (Cole 1955, 16)

Another way to say this is that when the good Stanislavskian or
Method actor is acting, the audience does not see the effort of the
attempt to enact the role because the actor has so seamlessly, organi-
cally, naturalistically "become" the character.

According to Jim Baker, Robert Marten had studied Stanislavski
and considered himself to be a Method actor. I do not know to what
degree Marten had investigated Stanislavski or whether he truly had
any professional training in the Method, but that he aligned himself
with this approach to acting is fascinating and puzzling in light of the
fact that he vehemently denied that first-person interpretation is in
any way connected to dramatic acting. The Stanislavskian approach to
acting has certainly been utilized in every conceivable style of production, from Shakespeare to expressionistic drama to ultra-realism. How
could Marten, one of the originators of Plimoth's method of first-
person interpretation, identify himself as a Method actor while at the

same time denying that the performance given by interpreters in the Pilgrim Village is a form of acting?

I think that Marten's ambivalence on this issue is revealing and can be explained in two ways. First, I think he equates dramatic acting with overacting or "ham" acting. In his paper "Plimoth Plantation Interpretation Defined" he writes:

> We shun an approach toward characterization other museums (some-what unsatisfactorily) have used in attempting "living history", namely the dramatic theatrical approach. . . . Our impostors do not act out or play their character roles, because if they do so, in our experience, the visitors, sensing the presence of the conventions of drama, would tend to settle back (mentally and emotionally) to observe the entertainment. Learning progress through entertain-ment has severe limitations and we note other museums which have benefited little from the seemingly appropriate theatrical approach. (1977, 5–7)

The essential fear expressed here is that if the interpreters really act out their parts, they will alienate the visitor-spectator with their overly dramatic behavior and ruin the opportunity for historical education to take place. I think Marten is expressing an anxiety shared by many persons at Plimoth Plantation that too theatrical an approach to enactment will jar the attempt to create the illusion of another time and place. Marten, the Method actor, describes his ideal interpreter as one who creates a complete characterization, speaks in an authentic dialect, interacts naturally with the visitor-spectator, and blends per-fectly into the re-created seventeenth-century milieu. This interpre-ter's performance is seamless and never gives the audience any reason to doubt that she or he is, indeed, a seventeenth-century Pilgrim. Is this acting or not?

Marten's prescription for an optimal first-person interpretation per-formance certainly sounds like a good example of Stanislavskian, nat-uralistic acting in which the audience is unaware of the actor's tech-nique—only the character is present. Of course, the difference, and it is an important one, is that the interpreter interacts, in role, with the visitor-spectator and is not separated from his or her audience by a stage platform or a proscenium arch. In fact, both performer and spectator dwell in the domain of the stage environment. Perhaps this is what motivates Marten to call his method of first-person interpretation "character imposture." He relates the Plimoth Plantation interpreter more to the con artist type of imposter than to the dramatic actor, for, like the imposter, the interpreter must pass him- or herself off as somebody he or she is not through *interactions* with other human beings. We might refer to this as the Goffmanian approach to acting, since the sociologist Erving Goffman has demonstrated that most human beings are capable of this kind of dissembling, and much of everyday social interaction is very cleverly stage managed (1959, 1967, 1974). Once the con game has begun, the imposter must simulate the speech, behavior, thoughts, and actions of another person in order to survive. Marten's point is that the first-person interpreter does the same thing. In order to educate the audience, he or she perpetuates a playful game of imposture. There is certainly some justification for Marten's position, since most of the interpretation staff are not trained professional actors. Still, their aim is to convince their audience that they are characters living in another time and place. Is this acting or not?

Perhaps the real question should be: is this really the art and craft of acting? Each Plimoth Plantation interpreter is paid to put on a costume, simulate the gestures and speech of a seventeenth-century individual, and interact with others as if she or he actually lived in another time and place—to inhabit a scene different from that interpreter's actual reality. All interpreters enact actions based on the historical script of what happened in New Plimoth in 1627, elaborating on this through their improvised interaction with the visitor-spectators. Even Marten identifies this elaborate performance as an art. He writes: "In order that he or she enrich the visitation experience by practice of this *art* [italics mine], he/she is required to master . . . a special body of information necessary to enliven his characterization" (1977, 4). Obviously, education is Plimoth Plantation's primary purpose. But to accomplish this goal, both the entertainment and aesthetic value of the role-playing have become extremely important.

How can it be denied that the kind of role-playing which, since 1978, constitutes first-person interpretation at Plimoth Plantation is anything other than the kind of naturalistic character acting so common in contemporary theatre and film? At times, in his writing, Marten lets this slip out. In a 1981 newspaper interview in which he is asked how the roles of the Pilgrims are cast each season, he says: "We're looking for the 20th-century counterparts of 17th-century people. . . . John Billington was a rogue, a con man. So we'll find someone who's capable of being in this role. Usually he's played by a character actor who could sell a man his own shoes" (Schechner 1981, 24). Isn't this type casting? And notice the terminology: "role," "played," "character actor." By 1981, the language of the theatre had certainly invaded the domain of the living history museum.

THE EIGHTIES: THE AGE OF THE ACTOR

"You play your role beautifully." "You ought to be on Broadway!" "Are you members of the Actors' Guild?" These comments, and many more like them, are ones that I overheard during the two seasons, 1984 and 1985, that I worked as an interpreter at Plimoth Plantation. By the eighties, the general public had come to consider the cultural informant to be an actor. And, to some degree, the interpreters themselves share in this perception. For example, during August of the 1984 season, no fewer than five interpreters from Plimoth Plantation auditioned for a new professional theatre associated with the League of Regional Theatres that was opening in the Plymouth area. Indeed, there is a good deal of theatrical activity among the members of the interpretation staff. Some have professional acting experience; others have performed, and continue to perform, in local community theatres; a few have backgrounds in academic theatre or theatre education. Almost all have some performing experience, ranging from appearances in Lincoln Center to college theatre productions to semi-professional singing groups. As we will see, the dressing room at the interpretation department definitely has the "feel" of a theatrical greenroom.

Further validation of the notion that the interpreters are actors (an issue hotly debated among themselves), appeared in the pages of the *New York Times* (4 November 1984). Novelist James Carroll wrote: "Dozens of skilled actor/historians enact roles of the real settlers and you can walk among them, chatting here with Mistress Hopkins while she weeds her kitchen garden, and there with Governor Bradford while he prepares to hold a session of his court." As Carroll explains in his article, these actor/historians are very serious about keeping up the illusion that their village *is* 1627 Plimoth. The more completely the Pilgrim story becomes embodied, the more people perceive the process of embodiment to be the art of acting.

The former hostesses who now run the visitor services program at Plimoth report that 99 percent of the public think that the interpreters are, in fact, actors. When they return from their tour of the Pilgrim Village, the first question the visitors ask is: "Are these people actors and actresses?" (Hale et al. 1986) Even Deetz, just before he left the plantation, started to look at interpretation as a form of acting and at the new mode of representing the Pilgrim story as a kind of improvisational theatre (1987).

How and why have theatre and museum become fused at this time? This issue will be completely analyzed in the last chapter. At this point I will simply state that I see the situation at Plimoth as the result of a general blurring of genres and forms that has taken place in the arts and sciences in the past decade. In 1980, Clifford Geertz wrote his noted essay on this subject, pointing out how the "drama analogy" had has a powerful impact on the thinking of social scientists in recent years (1980). Undoubtedly James Deetz was one of those social scientists. Jerome Rothenberg has cited a parallel phenomenon in the performing arts: "There is an unquestionable and far-reaching breakdown of boundaries and genres: between 'art and life' (Cage, Kaprow), between variously conventionally defined arts (intermedia and performance art, concrete poetry), and between arts and non-arts (*musique concrete,* found art, etc.). The consequences are immense" (Benamou 1977, 13).

The consequences are, indeed, immense. The cultural vectors effecting this blurring of genres have helped to reshape the presentation of American history and given a people who detested the theatre—the Pilgrims—a form of theatrical representation. The performance of living history now given at Plimoth Plantation has been spawned by the postmodern overlapping of genres in both the social sciences and the arts. At Plimoth, the traditional modes of presenting history in the museum setting have merged with the presentational techniques of theatre. Actor/historians now perform the Pilgrim story (plate 5). Of course, the impulse toward a theatrical representation of Pilgrim history has been with Plimoth Plantation since its inception. Even in 1948, an amphitheatre where the Pilgrim story could be dramatically portrayed was in the planning stages. Ideas such as total theatre, environmental theatre, and audience participation during the 1960s surely influenced the present-day performance in the Pilgrim Village. As we have seen, the cultural style of each era has left its imprint on the presentation of history at Plimoth Plantation. In the 1980s, museum methods conjoined with those of the theatre, and history became history *performed.*[5]

In 1981, Bob Marten was fired for refusing to obey orders from then-director David Case not to talk to the media about a controversy that had developed at Plimoth Plantation. That spring, Marten had hired a young black man to play a Pilgrim, justifying this action by his own interpretation of a certain historical document. When the consensus of historians disagreed with his interpretation, Marten refused to back down and was consequently dismissed from his job.[6] Marten's assistant, Len Travers, then took over as head of interpretation and held this position until 1987. Along with Travers, Paul Cripps, Donna DeFabio, and Lisa Whalen—all experienced first-person interpreters—serve as supervisors and oversee the performance in the Pilgrim Village. This regime, which is so steeped in the first-person mode, has extended the theatrical aspect of the living history performance. In the eighties, more and more reenactments were added to the season's program, including funerals, weddings, court days, Governor's council meetings, musters, and what is affectionately known by the interpreters as "D-days"—a three-day-long reenactment of the historic visit of Isaack de Rasieres, the Dutch secretary from Fort Amsterdam (modern Manhattan), to Plimoth Plantation in 1627. This is the culminating performance of the season and is scheduled to coincide with a re-creation of the traditional English harvest feast (the prototype of our Thanksgiving). During the 1980s, professional New York actor Toby Tompkins performed the role of de Rasieres.

As the reenactments have proliferated, more and more role-playing skills have been required of the interpreters. In turn, the supervisors have often had to become directors and critics. Although the re-created historical scenarios are usually produced with improvised dialogue, sometimes they are scripted. In 1984, Len Travers wrote a play called *The Evidence Before Us* (later adapted by Toby Tompkins), which was produced by the plantation with the help of a grant from the National Endowment for the Humanities and performed by the men on the interpretation staff (the cast is all male). In 1986, Tompkins prepared another playscript for the interpretation staff. This drama concerns the Quaker troubles at Plimoth and is set in a later period (circa 1660). Both plays have been performed by interpreters, outside of their regular working hours, in the Pilgrim Village and in a traditional theatrical style.

The interpretation program seems to be moving in a theatrical direction all the time. As Caroline Chapin says: "I see it getting more and more theatrical. . . . I think it's fine if there's enough information and documentation to support what people are saying" (1985). This is what Jim Baker means when he says that the interpreters' performances often need more "body"; that is, characterizations need to be fleshed out with details that can be verified in the historical records. The first-person style without accurate content is an empty performance. Here, James Carroll's term "actor/*historian*" seems to make sense. Verifiable information compensates for the "fictiveness" of the role-playing and justifies the overall performance. As Jay Anderson has written regarding living history performance, the acting—the simulation—is used as a tool for "interpreting the realities of the past more effectively" (1984, 12). In Baker's words, the performance at Plimoth "uses a theatrical method just as an orator uses a rhetorical method to get his points across" (1985b).

As its charter states, the primary purpose of Plimoth Plantation is to educate the general public about the Pilgrim story. In the 1980s, an equally important task became the maintenance of the illusion through which that story is re-created. As Schechner has pointed out, this living museum is, today, an environmental theatre (1981, 22). Like theatres everywhere, Plimoth Plantation creates the illusory scene of another time and place through the manipulation of an environment and the impersonation of the dramatis personae who inhabit it. Contemporarily, the interpreters at Plimoth have become actor/historians who build their characters from a script that synthesizes the available historical information. Using many of the techniques of acting, they labor to make their staged reality consistent; to keep the delicate seams of their illusory scene from breaking; and to convince the audience of the truth of their characters' existence.[7] Today, when one enters the palisade walls of the Pilgrim Village, one enters the Theatre of the Pilgrims.

# Three

# Within These Palisade Walls

## A Pilgrim Playhouse

> What about the job made me feel I was an actress?
> Every morning at 8:30 I was getting into a cos-
> tume; at 8:45 I was starting to think in dialect; at
> 9:00 I was starting to talk in dialect; at 9:15 I was
> in a set—an environment very different from that
> of the twentieth-century; and by 9:30, I was acting
> or believing or, for some reason, not acknowledg-
> ing anything after the seventeenth-century. Now,
> either I was acting or I was crazy!
>
> Nancy Mindick, 1985

In the darkness before the first light of dawn, a cockerel's cry sets off a chain of crowing, up and down the hill of the deserted Pilgrim Village. A dog barks in the distance. The sound of waves lapping against the shore of Plymouth Beach disappears as the light grows brighter and the stars slowly fade away. In the stillness of daybreak, the low hum of automobiles being driven along Route 3A—a paved roadway that covers over an ancient Indian trail—becomes barely discernible. At this hour, the Pilgrim Village resembles a ghost town. There is no sound of human voices—only the bleating of sheep and the wind in the trees outside the palisade walls. The mist that commonly comes off the Atlantic on these spring mornings adds to the ghostly effect. The village has looked like this for most of the winter. Now, the light of an April dawn gradually penetrates the mist, and the phantom houses begin to take on a more solid appearance, as though they might be inhabited by humans.

The great door of the northern flanker gate slowly swings open, and a man half-dressed as a Pilgrim, with a nylon windbreaker covering his doublet, enters. He waves to the night watchman to bring in the truck. The sound of the pickup's horn sets the cocks crowing again. The headlights look eery in the mist. Bill Mullin and George Chapman, two of the older interpreters, begin to get the village set up. Doors to houses are unlocked; newspaper is put by the fireplaces to help the twentieth-century Pilgrims start their morning fires; firewood is unloaded from the pickup and placed near the doorsteps of the various Pilgrim families. Bill, a retired high school principal and former history teacher, is known around the plantation as the weather expert. He scrutinizes the sky to the east and makes his prognostication. George, an ordained Congregational minister with a sardonic sense of humor, makes a wry comment on Bill's prediction. They have been fellow travellers in these early morning hours at Plimoth Plantation for several years now.

It is eight o'clock and, above, at the "movie building" (the name most commonly used by the plantation staff for the orientation center)[1], the interpreters have begun to arrive. They usually go directly to the interpreters' lounge, a large room on the second story of the old carriage house—once part of the Hornblowers' summer estate—that has been converted into the orientation center. On the first floor is a large exhibition area and an auditorium, where the visitors see a multiprojector slide show that orients them to the seventeenth-century culture of the Pilgrims. The orientation center is about two hundred yards from the front portal of the palisade. It is the last stop in the twentieth century before a visitor enters the village.

Hank Roach and Mike Merritt are sitting on one of the large sofas in the interpreters' lounge, having a smoke. As usual, they are among the first to arrive. Hank and Mike are both three-year veteran interpreters. They both sport great Pilgrim beards, but their present attire distinguishes them as modern men. Hank has on black, lace-up boxing boots, red suspenders holding up his dungarees, and an earring with a little feather hanging from it. Mike wears a bright green Hawaiian shirt that looks as though it might glow in the dark. They are discussing the goings-on at a local community theatre where Mike has worked as an actor and where Hank is contemplating joining the scenery and prop crew.

At a table in the kitchen, adjacent to the interpreters' lounge, Joff Spaulding is reading a book by Kierkegaard. He has come in early this morning, since his three-year-old son, Joffrey, Jr., got him up in the middle of the night and he couldn't get back to sleep. Joff was, at one time, an actor in Hollywood. He is presently writing a book and is having difficulty finding the time, between the demands of his family and the responsibilities of being a Pilgrim. He is a great storyteller. He once had a nightclub act in which he performed as an Irishman— "Willy"—and told stories and recited poems. When Mike comes into the kitchen to see if the coffee is ready, Joff stops him and tells him the story of how "little Joff" knocked on his door at three in the morning and asked Daddy to come and play with him. He acts out all the parts for Mike. Although Joff looks a little tired, he has the perennial story-teller's twinkle in his eye. This is his first season working as an interpreter at Plimoth Plantation.

The other interpreters have been slowly trickling in (the cast usually numbers about 36, but only about 25 are "on" during any given day of the season). Eric Marr has brought in donuts for everybody; people are getting coffee and going into the lounge. Some carry parts of their Pilgrim costumes over their shoulders or under their arms. The room is filled with laughter and a kind of giddiness. Richard Pickering enters, having made a long drive from Braintree, and he tells everybody in the lounge about a play he saw last night in Boston, about how awful the leading lady was. He does an imitation of her, à la Bette Davis. Everybody laughs. Regina Porter, who has long red hair, bounces in, describing how her car broke down, again, last night on Route 3 on her way home to Marshfield. Somebody starts telling a joke about a particularly dense visitor who was in a Pilgrim house the day before. People laugh. The old-timers nod and wink to each other. Plimoth Plantation has only been open to the public since April 1, so during the month of April interpreters are just starting to get used to their Pilgrim characters, costumes, and speech. This is especially true for the first-year interpreters, who spend a great deal of time in front of the large mirror that covers one whole wall of the lounge and in trying out their dialects on one another.

By half past eight, there is great commotion in the interpreters' lounge, with people coming in and out of the men's and women's dressing rooms, just off the lounge area, in all varying stages of dress.

One female interpreter is trying to borrow an apron to match her outer skirt. A young male interpreter is complaining that his doublet is too tight; he can't swing his arms properly to chop wood. One of the veteran male interpreters is asking the assistance of his "wife" in putting on his collar. He speaks mockingly to her, in his Pilgrim dialect: "Waif, wouldst thee kindly gi' me a hand, here, with me collar?" She dutifully obliges, at the same time muttering something about women's lib. The preparations for entrance into the seventeenth century are disturbed for a moment. Donna DeFabio, one of the supervisors, sticks her head into the main doorway that leads to the lounge and announces that a Japanese film crew will be in the village this morning, and that "everyone not involved should just ignore them."

There is more hustle and bustle as nine o'clock approaches. Chris Hall, another veteran interpreter, rushes in, as usual, at the last minute. Chris carries an old cardboard file box with a handle on it for his briefcase. He is drinking a bottle of Moxie and reading a book about early explorers of the New England coast. Chris is known by everyone to be a genuine eccentric. He wears an old sweater over his Pilgrim shirt. To make himself ready for the role of Captain Myles Standish, he must replace his old sneakers with the proper seventeenth-century boots (actually, Frye boots that have been altered to look like seventeenth-century footgear). Paul Cripps, another supervisor, comes into the lounge, warning; "Five minutes, folks," just as a stage manager would call out the time till "curtain." The interpreters' lounge resembles a theatre's greenroom.

The men go into the musket closet to collect their firearms and their quota of black powder for the day. Women take down their baskets from the shelves that are next to the exit from the second story of the orientation center. Usually, these baskets contain foodstuff, along with instructions on how it is to be prepared, for this particular day. On the other side of the exit, directly across from these shelves, is the doorway to a large kitchen, where all the seventeenth-century foodstuff is stored. Some of the female interpreters will, in the last few minutes before entering the village, go to Lisa Whalen, the supervisor in charge of Foodways, and ask her advice on how to prepare certain Pilgrim dishes or beg for a little extra milk or butter.

The latecomers, including John Kemp, hurry up the steps and rush down the long hallway to the interpreters' lounge. John has just driven from Cedarville, a small township down the coast, already dressed for his role as Jonathan Brewster. A Ph.D. in English literature from the University of Pennsylvania, John plays the role of Elder Brewster's peculiar son—the village alchemist. Rushing up the steps right behind John is Regina Martin, who plays one of Elder Brewster's daughters. She chides her "brother," making a joke that relates his tardiness to his alchemical practices. They both scurry to the dressing rooms to put away their things and get ready to punch in.

In the hallway just outside the interpreters' lounge is a time clock. At nine o'clock, a long line of Pilgrims punches in, one after the other. Then they make a procession down the hall to the stairway that leads to the ground level. Everyone is now fully dressed in Pilgrim costume, so there is something formal, almost ritualistic, about this march (indeed, it can look a bit like the Pilgrims' Progress described earlier) into the seventeenth century. On this spring day, there is a little nervousness and excitement in the air as the group makes its way to the gate that separates the parking lot by the back of the orientation center from the main grounds of the plantation. Bill Mullin assures everyone that it is going to be a fine, sunny day, despite the present mist and low-hanging clouds. As they pass out the gateway, the interpreters wave to the women from visitor services, who stand, in their official maroon jackets, by the main exit from the orientation center. They smile and wave back, wishing everybody a "good day." As already mentioned, many of these women once worked in the village as hostesses.

There are two paths that lead from the orientation center to the village: the one on the left (as one faces the Atlantic) slopes down to the northern flanker gate; the one on the right rises up a little incline to the top flanker gate, near the Fort-Meeting House. Depending on where in the village an interpreter's house is located, one or the other of these pathways is chosen. From the hillock that leads to either of these little roadways, the thatched roofs of the Pilgrim houses can be seen over the top of the palisade—houses that will soon be inhabited for the day by these twentieth-century incarnations of the Pilgrims.

THE PLAYHOUSE(S)

As already stated, the site of the re-created village is quite similar to that of the original village, described by de Rasieres in 1627:

*Plate 11.* A bird's-eye view of the Pilgrim Village
(Photo courtesy of Plimoth Plantation)

New Plymouth lies on the slope of a hill stretching east towards the sea-coast, with a broad street about a cannon shot of 800 feet long, leading down a hill; with a [street] crossing in the middle, northwards to the rivulet and southwards to the land. The houses are constructed of clapboards, with gardens also enclosed behind and at the sides with clapboards, so that their houses and courtyards are arranged in very good order, with a stockade against sudden attack. (James, Jr. 1963, 76)

The present hill is not quite as high as the one at the original site and the actual Fort-Meeting House was probably further back on the hill. The original palisade (de Rasieres's "stockade") was certainly quite a bit larger. But the view from the top of the hill was probably pretty much the same: a gorgeous vista of the Atlantic, all across the eastern horizon. About three miles directly out to sea is Saquish Neck, which appears to be a large island (though, actually, it is a long peninsula connected to Duxbury on the northern shores of Plymouth Harbor). Hidden behind it is Clark's Island, which the Pilgrims, in 1620, had considered as a possible site for their plantation.

From a bird's-eye view, the twelve-foot-high palisade that encloses the village takes on the shape of a diamond (plate 11). Entering the top or western flanker gate, a visitor sees the main street stretching out in front, leading all the way to the bottom of the hill and the flanker gate closest to the sea. At about the middle of the hill (just as de Rasieres related), there is a cross street, extending from the northern flanker gate to the southern. Thus, the streets form a cross. The houses are located only on either side of the main street (known as Leyden Street). Back in the late 1950s, the lots for these houses were laid out according to William Bradford's description of the original village.[2] At the present time, there are seven reproduced houses (including the Store House and the Common House) on the southern side of the main street and eight on the northern. In all, with the Fort-Meeting House at the top of the hill and the palisade surrounding it, the village replicates a "colonial bastide fortress" that had antecendents in earlier English frontier settlements (Plimoth Plantation, *The Training Manual,* vol. 1, "Fortification," 2).

The present-day Pilgrim Village has an aura of antiquity because of the rough-hewn, weathered appearance of the cedar and pine that covers its buildings. Since Deetz introduced the realistic look in the late 1960s, the village is only picturesque in a weather-beaten sort of way. In the bright sunlight, it appears ramshackle and unkempt, and visitors often refer to the houses as shacks, huts, and cabins. It looks like a rough-and-tumble place to play. In fact, nothing in the village is irreplaceable. There are no priceless antiques; all the objects and artifacts are reproductions. The village is really only so much sand, clay, mortar, wood, and thatch. Historically, it might be viewed as the analogue of a poverty-stricken Third World village (and many visitors from Third World countries recognize this); but, in contemporary America, the village as a whole can be seen as a playground and the houses that compose it as so many playhouses.

In fact, many forms of play have taken place in the Fort-Meeting House, which stands near the top entrance to the village. The large hall on the ground level, where *The Evidence Before Us* was presented in 1984, has also been used as a movie set. Reenactments of court trials and the governor's council have been produced in it. It is often the site of the interpretation staff's after-hours parties. Reproduced to represent the Pilgrims' first blockhouse, it was moved from the waterfront to the village in 1958. In the fall of 1986, the Fort-Meeting House was remodeled in a more historically accurate style.

The ground floor of this edifice is where the Pilgrims held their worship services; it is a large square space, containing a few wooden benches, a pulpit, and a few scattered barrels. It is very dark, since the tiny openings for light are only big enough to put a musket through. Light may also come from a trapdoor in the ceiling. When this door is opened, a beam falls directly down into the center of the room. Ironically, this hall is hardly ever used for its original purpose; the re-creation of the Pilgrims' eight-hour-long Sabbath-day service has not proven to be much of a crowd-pleaser.[3]

Presently, there are thirteen reproductions of Pilgrim family houses: Winslow, Standish, Alden, Cooke, Bradford, Allerton, Billington, Brewster, Hopkins, Howland, Fuller, Warren, and Soule. Basically, these are very simple one- or two-room, box-frame houses, clad with planks or clapboards that cover over the wattle and daub walls. They all have at least one chimney and a loft. They represent the somewhat temporary cottages that the Pilgrims had constructed by 1627. There are few differences in construction styles that might indicate an individual's regional background or position in the social hierarchy. Although the buildings reflect continuous improvement in the matters of historical authenticity, they still contain inaccuracies. There are too many shingled roofs, and the houses are overly fenestrated; the massive cobblestone chimneys (constructed by local Portuguese masons in the late 1950s and early 1960s), although very handsome, are historically incorrect. Because such inauthentic architectural components are part of the scene, the contemporary Plimoth Plantation *Training Manual* often recommends that the interpreter divert the visitor's attention with some obfuscatory tactic. Regarding the cobblestone chimneys, it states:

> The massive cobblestone chimneys which were built in so many of Plimoth Plantation's re-created dwelling houses are particularly unfortunate.
>
> [Interpretive note: In the meantime let us excuse the stone chimneys as having been built by East Anglican emigrants (who are more accustomed to building with round stones) who brought the necessary ingredient for mortar (lime) with them. They arrived in the Fortune (1621) and left the colony during the Lyford dispute. We do not remember their names.]
>
> *The Training Manual,* vol. 1, "Architecture," 11–12)

This half-truth is served up to the public in the interest of keeping the illusion of historical authenticity. Today, the reproduced houses constitute an environmental theatre in which maintaining such an illusion is of paramount importance.

Although the Fort-Meeting House is often used as the stage for "special events" such as court trials, the main stage for the representation of the Pilgrims' daily lives is each house itself. Here is where the major interactions with visitors and fellow interpreters take place. Situated as they are on either side of the main street, the reproduced houses resemble booths at a fair. As Patricia MacKay pointed out in her article, "Theme Parks," in *Theatre Crafts:* "Theme parks, amusement parks . . . are all variants of the classic amusement environment design: bounded or confined spaces composed of small individual areas or units devoted to entertainment, performance, display or vending through which spectators may wander" (MacKay 1977, 72). The reproduced antiquarian house through which the visitors wander on their stroll through the village is the essential environmental unit of performance at Plimoth Plantation.

Winslow House is a good example (plate 10). Construction on it began in 1961. It is a re-creation of the dwelling place of one of New Plimoth's most prominent citizens, Edward Winslow. As visitors come down the main street after entering the western gate at the top of the hill, it is the first house on the right. It has one of those spurious cobblestone chimneys in the center of its shingled roof. The exterior of the house is a little odd, since each side exhibits a different style of architecture: the left side (as a visitor enters from the main street) is covered with vertical planks and the right side with horizontal clapboards. This is because the second half of the house was completed at a later date when a different concept of historically accurate architecture was in effect.[4]

The wooden exterior of Winslow House is so weathered that it has a dark hue; some of the clapboards are broken and splintered. Two great stepping-tones lead to the front door; past that entrance are door-ways to the two sides of the house. This is a basic two-room, box-frame construction. To the left is John Winslow's side. John is Edward's brother and recently married. His chamber is sparsely furnished: a few barrels, an oaken chest, a simple hempen chair, a feather mattress on the floor (no bedstead), and an oaken Bible box (a small, rectangular chest) on top of one of the barrels. Birch brooms, muck baskets, and various seventeenth-century farming tools are scattered about. The room has four windows, either covered with dirty linen or shuttered. The window in the back wall, when opened, offers a beautiful view of the Atlantic. Inside the fireplace, which is in the western hall, hang trammels, with sundry pot hooks and cooking pots. A large brass kettle, completely charred on the outside, hangs from one of the pot hooks. In the hearth are a fire shovel and an iron skillet.

The other side of the house contains the chamber of one of the community's wealthiest men, Edward Winslow. His father was a landowner and a gentleman in Worcestershire, England, and, of all the Pilgrims (with the exceptions, perhaps, of William Brewster and Myles Standish) Winslow comes the closes to being gentry. There are many items in this room that reveal his social status: the pewter, the glassware, the brass bed warmer, the beautiful hand-carved table and chair, and, most of all, the great, canopied, oaken bedstead in the southwest corner of the room. On the table are quill and ink pot, for Edward Winslow serves as one of the assistant governors and as magistrate to the Court of New Plimoth. In the eastern wall is a large fireplace, containing andirons with a spit across them, a trivet with a skillet on it, and several large cooking pots. There is a barrel in the northwest corner. It supports the Bible box in which Master Winslow keeps his Geneva Bible, psalter, and other precious books. Winslow is also one of the most educated men in the village; he is known to have attended the Latin School at Worcester Cathedral. Another barrel, between the fireplace and the entrance, serves as a counter. It holds a mortar and pestle, bottles of wine, vinegar, and olive oil, and a cone of sugar. In the back wall of Edward's chamber is a door that leads out to his wife's garden. The whole house functions as the stage on which the Winslow family act out their daily lives (examples of their performance are described in the next section).

Behind every house in the village is a traditional Elizabethan English garden containing both herbs and vegetables. These gardens are rectangular raised beds sided with clapboards. This is the women's territory; in the seventeenth century, men had nothing to do with the gardening. The female interpreters, therefore, are required to become familiar with the medicinal properties of many herbs. By midsummer, the vegetables from these gardens are being served up in "sallets" and "pottages" for the families of the various women interpreters. There has always been a keen interest in seventeenth-century horticulture at Plimoth Plantation, and, today, the museum has its own horticultural-ist, Darlene Baeauvais, who keeps a careful watch over what plants go in and how they are tended.

Since the aim has been to re-create a living, seventeenth-century farming community, the animals and the areas where they are kept are an integral part of village life. There are goats, sheep, pigs, oxen, cows, chickens, and cats. Every house has a chicken cote, and there are sev-eral pig cotes about the village. On the top of the hill to the left (as one enters the western gate) is a small pasture for the sheep. Below that, on the other side of Edward Winslow's backyard, is a long, fenced-in area where the cows can graze. At the middle of the village, near the northern flanker gate, is an area with several small thatch-roof sheds for the sheep. Near the southern flanker gate is an enormous cow barn with a great conical-shaped thatched roof. At the bottom of the hill, behind the Store House, is a wooden goat shed and a grazing area for the goats. During the day, the interpreters tend to the animals' basic needs—providing food, water, and fresh straw, milking, cleaning cotes and sheds—but the animal program is supervised by the curatorial services staff who look after the welfare of all the property and live-stock within the Pilgrim Village. In 1981, a rare breeds program was established at Plimoth Plantation, and attempts are being made to obtain archaic breeds that more nearly resemble the kind of livestock the Pilgrims would have had in 1627 and to keep these animals repro-ducing. This program is overseen by Jon Haskins, an expert in animal husbandry. Though constituting an exhibit in themselves, the animals also become part of the illusion-creating process of the overall perfor-mance as a result of the interpreters' attentions. Seeing the costumed actor/historians tend to the feeding of a strange, ancient breed of pigs helps to convince visitors that they have, indeed, entered the seven-teenth-century reality of the Pilgrims. One is reminded of Marianne Moore's definition of real poetry, in which the poet must:

> present
> for inspection, "imaginary gardens with real toads in them"
> (Moore 1961, 41)

There are certainly many "real toads" to be discovered within the pal-isade walls that enclose the illusory world of the 1627 Pilgrim Village.

Once inside the houses, the interpreters begin their daily routines with certain set tasks. The men start the fires, using matches and newspaper, and the women begin to sweep the dirt-tracked floors with twentieth-century brooms. The streets of the village are earthen, sand-filled road-ways that quickly turn into mud when it rains, so the floors of the Pilgrim houses are perpetually dirty. At this hour, a little after nine o'clock, before any visitors have come, there is usually a bit of backstage banter among the members of a household: jokes, gossip, speculations on the visitor turnout for the day. This conversation may be partially in character. For instance, interpreters may speak in seventeenth-century dialect about matters pressing to them in their twentieth-century lives. (Once in the village, most interpreters speak in dialect continuously, even when no visitors are present.) After the fires are lit, the men fetch water in the large blackened kettles that will sit over the fires during the day and be used by the women for cooking and washing dishes. At this time, everybody disguises or hides any remnants of the twentieth century. Watches and rings are put in pockets, cigarette packages stealthily concealed in pouches, newspapers thrown up in the loft (where the public is not allowed), and paper coffee cups and plastic wrappings burnt in the fireplace. A few male interpreters will already be out in the main street, dragging great birch branches over the tire tracks left by the truck earlier this morning. This odd-looking ritual erases the last, flagrant signs of twentieth-century life.

In the midst of all these preparations, a drum sounds. It is the call to morning meeting—a daily gathering of the interpretation staff in the center of the village to discuss the business ahead for the day. The head interpreter, Len Travers, who has been beating the drum, stands in the middle of the street. He is dressed in twentieth-century garb. Len has some important news, and people gather around him to listen. He fills everybody in about the Japanese film crew that is going to be making a short documentary film on Plimoth Plantation today. The main location will be Allerton House. He explains who will be involved with this project and directs everybody else to go about his or her business as usual, pretending that the cameras aren't there. Someone makes a crack about being "used to that." There is a little grumbling about television union rates. Many of the interpreters have been on local or national television in their Pilgrim roles and usually receive no extra pay for these appearances. Paul Cripps says, "You knew what you were getting into when you signed on." There is a little muttering, a sarcastic aside or two; a few people shrug their shoulders. At this point, Donna DeFabio hands out the "psalm of the month." It is Psalm 3, as translated and arranged by Henry Ainsworth, a contemporary of the Pilgrims. It has a dirge-like melody and militant lyrics. Ted J. Curtin refreshes everyone's memory by humming the melody through once. Suddenly, two of the interpreters break into a rendition of the "Volga Boatman," using psalm-like, seventeenth-century phrases and heavy Russian accents. Everybody laughs. Ted continues with the choral direction of Psalm 3 and gives everybody a note. Almost all the interpreters have to read the words off the photocopied sheets that Donna has handed out, but John Kemp has already memorized the lyrics. When he gets to the last verse, he points to his teeth to remind himself of the strange phraseology:

> Arise thou-up, save me my God, o Jah:
>> for, all my foes though smitest on cheek bone:
>> breakst wickeds teeth, to Jah salvation:
> thy blessings, on thy people be Selah.
>
> (Ainsworth 1617)

Again, everybody laughs.

Suddenly there is an interruption. David Hobbs, at six feet six inches the tallest Pilgrim, yells out: "In coming!" All heads turn toward the top of the hill. The first visitors of the day have entered the top portal, about one hundred yards away. Psalm sheets are quickly returned to Donna DeFabio, who hides them under her apron or in the basket she carries. People head back to their houses. The street has now been cleared of all tire tracks, twentieth-century brooms are thrown way back into the lofts, and interpreters begin their seventeenth-century labors: the men chopping wood, riving, and adzing; the women preparing food, sewing, and tending gardens. Specially assigned tasks for the day, such as daubing a wall or building a chicken cote, are begun, and dialect is projected a little louder than before, for the benefit of these first visitors.

The first visitors this morning turn out to be a family of Mormons from Utah: a mother and father in their mid-thirties, and a boy and girl, twelve and ten, respectively. They have come all the way to Plymouth especially to see the Pilgrims. The father has recently discovered that he is a direct descendant of Richard Warren, one of the original *Mayflower* passengers. They have been waiting in the parking lot since eight o'clock, so eager are they to see their "forebears." First, they enter the Winslow House. They discover Master Edward Winslow seated behind his great oaken table, quill in hand, thinking over the next words he will set down on the paper before him. These are polite visitors; they knock before they enter the chamber. "Come in, come in, if it please ye," says Master Winslow, from his seat. "Good morrow to thee," chimes in Mistress Susannah Winslow, who is busy at the hearth making a port pottage for the noonday meal. The father of the Mormon family apologizes for interrupting Master Winslow's concentration. These visitors are a little bashful, as is often the case when visitors come singly into a house and are not part of a crowd.

"Nay, nay," says Master Winslow, with a wave of his hand. "I just be writin' here a letter to my brother, Gilbert. He come wi' me on th' *Mayflower*, ya know, but he never favored it here. He's back home in Droitwich, now. Back in Worcestershire, in the family salt trade, agin."

"How long does it take a letter to get to England?" asks the Mormon father.

Master Winslow laughs. "Oh, it might well take a year or more. For it could take the ship, carryin' the letter, oe'er three months just to get to London, and, after that, the post in England is very slow. It might be, then, two years before I get a reply back from my brother."

The visitor father laughs and shakes his head, saying, "Nothing changes." Pointing to his two children, he asks Master Winslow, "Could you show Bruce and Jennifer how you use the quill pen, sir?"

Master Winslow obliges and reacts with great surprise when little Jennifer says that she knows how to write. He explains that women are not educated in seventeenth-century England and that only a few women here, in this first New England village, "know their letters." Mistress Winslow adds that a woman has no need to read as her husband can read scripture to her. The eyes of even this Mormon mother flinch at this seemingly anti-feminist remark. The father quickly changes the subject and asks Master Winslow if he knows of a Richard Warren. Little does he know that he is asking the interpreter who played Richard Warren during the previous season. Master Winslow describes the Warren family background in detail, to the delight of the Mormon visitors, and then accounts for Master Warren's absence, this day, by saying he is "off wi' th' fishin' partie, to Cape Anne, for a fortnight (in reality, the role of Richard Warren has not been cast for this season). Looking a little dejected, the visitor tells Master Winslow that he is a descendant of Richard Warren. Master Winslow looks the man over quizzically, and says, "Well, I don't see how that could possibly be, goodman, for Master Warren's eldest is not yet even wed!"

At this moment, Captain Myles Standish enters the Winslow House, barking out in gruff voice, "God bless this house." All heads turn to the doorway. Captain Standish is fully appareled in helmet, gorget, breastplate, and cape, with a rapier hanging in its scabbard from his waist. He has an auburn beard (the interpreter, Chris Hall, has bleached his hair to achieve this effect). "Good morrow to thee, Master Winslow, Mistress Winslow," sputters Captain Standish. The visitors are about to witness a "scene."

"It might be a good morrow," says Mistress Winslow, sotto voce, "if someone's sheep had not gotten out and run rampant all about the village, this last night."

The Captain is stung and snaps back, "Is not a wife's place to hold her tongue before her husband speaks? I have come here on sartain business concerning *Master* Winslow. Not his wife!"

The visitors are fascinated by this display of "real" emotion. Historically, Captain Standish was the sole owner of the sheep in 1627; in actuality, the sheep *did* get out the night before and destroyed most of the young lettuce in the women's gardens. In this scene, the interpreter who portrays Susannah Winslow, Ann Angell, is transferring her real anger at curatorial services to Captain Standish/Chris Hall.

"Aye, sir," says Mistress Winslow, "mayhaps it were best that one keeps about a business they have some knowledge of than one they seem to have no control o'er."

The captain's feathers are duly ruffled. "Hast thou no control o'er this woman's tongue?" he demands of Master Winslow.

Winslow responds, "Sir, if the truth be known, thou shouldst hear much worse from many wives o' this village, whose tender herbs your sheep have entirely devoured."

The cantankerous captain begins to boil; asking, "And who will press charges first? Who will press charges agin me?"

The sanguine Master Winslow raises a hand to calm the growing fury. "Now, Captain," he says, "thar's no need . . ."

The visitors are delighted by this scene, which seems very real to them since the dialogue, all improvised on the spot, flows naturally from the lips of these Pilgrim characters. More visitors enter the chamber and interrupt the scene to ask what happened. The Mormon mother explains the background of the scene to a Jewish woman from Brooklyn. The Brooklynite immediately sides with Mistress Winslow. "Give it to him, honey!" she joins in. None of the visitors knows of the real events that have created the subtext of this scene; they only perceive the moment within the context of the illusory historical environment. In this case, the suspension of disbelief has been greatly enhanced by the "real toads" (the sheep) in this "imaginary garden" (the illusory historical setting).

"Sir!" says the choleric captain. "I have come to speak with *thee* on matters pertainin' to the militia. Your squadiron shall be called out this day and I expect every man in full armor and all *those* with swords to wear them. By the sound of the drum, then Master Winslow, make yourself ready!"

"Aye, sir," responds Master Winslow. "I shall." Standish turns about abruptly. His cape snaps against the barrel by the door as he exits. Master Winslow turns to the audience that has now gathered in this room, shakes his head, and says, "Th' man was born under Mars, for he thinks of nothin' but matters military." Everyone laughs.

Master Winslow gets up and crosses to the oaken chest in front of his great bedstead. On top of the chest sits his breastplate. As the visitors watch, he picks it up and puts his arms through holes in the blackened metal armor, pulling it all together about his chest by tightening a little leather belt at the level of his abdomen. "Susannah, wouldst thou gi' me a hand wi' that gorget?" he asks his wife. She quickly fetches that gorget from the beam where it hangs and carefully fastens it at the front of his neck, being heedful that the sharp metal does not tear her husband's collar. "Thank 'ee, wife," says Winslow. Now he picks up his musket and explains to the visitors that it is a snaphance and works by means of a mechanism of flint and iron rather than a match (the seventeenth-century term for a small piece of cord with a burning tip). He puts the point of a small bent nail into the touch hole of his musket in order to clean it. Finally, Master Winslow places his bandoleer over his shoulder and sets his black-felt hat on his head. He is ready. As soon as the drum sounds, he exits quickly, jogging down the hill to the drill that is about to take place.

From many of the houses, now, men are beginning to hasten into the street. Almost all have some piece of armor: a breastplate, gorget, a "pot" or helmet. The drummer is standing in the center of the village, near the redoubt (a small fortification, about ten feet by ten inches, containing four small scattershot cannons known as *petereros*), beating out the alarum. Seven or eight men line up at the center of the cross streets and about thirty visitors gather around them. It is a slow day, so far. In the middle of summer, there could be four or five hundred spectators for this event. The Japanese film crew has set its cameras up on the lower side of the main street. Suddenly Captain Standish bursts through the semi-circle of visitors on the upper side of the street. "Make way! Make way!" he shouts to the crowd. "Lieutenant!" he shouts to the giant Pilgrim in the line. "Inspect these men's firearms!" David Hobbs, who plays Goodman Edward Hollman, is, in fact, the specialist in charge of muskets and armor. It is his job every day, as a staff member, to check over the muskets and distribute the black powder. In his role as Lieutenant Hollman, he passes down the line of Plimoth militiamen, making jests and criticizing the condition of each man's musket.

Captain Standish inquires, "Has Beavun gone ta fetch fire, yet?" Lieutenant Hollman nods his head and explains that the servant lad is presently getting the match lit in the Brewster house. "Then, let us have a prayer," says Standish. "Deacon Fuller, if you wouldst be so kind?"

Bill Mullin, who plays Deacon Samuel Fuller, offers up one of his wonderful alliterative invocations: "Dear Lord, thou hadst protected us from persecution, pestilence and plague, all these many years; thou hast seen us safely across the seas, and secured a place for us in this great wilderness; for all these thy many blessings, we lift up our hearts in thanks to thee." As the deacon continues, all the Pilgrim men have set themselves in some pose of prayer: the Church of England men have their heads bowed; the Saints have their heads lifted to the heavens. Bill Mullin ends his prayer with "And, Lord, give us a volley that will put fear into the hearts of any enemy, be they French or Spanish or Naragansetts. Amen."

After the "amen" echoes throughout the militia, Captain Standish begins to bark out his orders: "Unshoulder your piece! Pose your piece! Take up your piece and prick out the touch hole!"

With these commands, the men begin to charge their muskets, somewhat raggedly, as befits men who are farmers and not professional soldiers. Standish complains bitterly about their slowness in completing his orders. He threatens that the last to finish will be given extra watch duty. When all the men are finally charged and have reshouldered their muskets, the captain shouts: "Winslow! Hopkins! Pratt! Come forward one pace!" They do so. "Now, to the right face, turn!" There are now two lines of men heading down the hill, with the drummer out in front. Standish yells to the crowd and the Japanese cameramen, "Make way, there. These men are trained militia, if you do not move yourselves, they will march over you!" The crowd laughs and scatters. The Japanese film crew picks up its equipment and scurries to the side of the road. "Drummer, make ready!" The drummer beats out a slow, solemn, militant march. "Prepare to march. And march!" shouts Standish. "Close up your ranks!" orders Hollman, marching in line with the other men.

A group of grade school children come running through the northern flanker gate and follow the procession down the hill. The captain brings the militia to a halt. To a drum roll, the muskets are prepared for discharge: the matches set and screwed in, the flash pan opened. A child has momentarily run out onto the field of fire. Standish screams at the child to get out of the way (even though only paper wadding is used in these muskets, there is still an element of danger). When all is safe and ready, Captain Standish raises his sword high above his head and then suddenly brings it down, exclaiming: "Give fire!" A thunderous report echoes across the village, and the crowd, now at mid-morning composed of some fifty visitors, applauds this display of military skill.

Standish comes behind the men, ordering "About face!" He asks who did not fire, and Robert Bartlett sheepishly raises his hand. Standish mockingly berates him as being "a better cooper than a soldier." The young militiaman hangs his head. Standish says a few words to the men about the next drill in a month's time (historically, these drills occurred once a month or so, but since they make such good public spectacles, they are performed twice a day at modern Plimoth Plantation). Finally, Standish asks Master Winslow to say the thanksgiving (the concluding prayer). Master Winslow says he would be honored and, lifting his eyes to heaven, begins:

Almighty and Merciful God, as Though dost sit upon Thy throne in Heaven, we do lift up our hearts in thanks to Thee, knowing that it is only from Thee that we receive our strength and succor. We are here but a small band of men in this great wilderness, yet Thou hast shown Thy guiding hand amongst us and raised us up against many great obstacles. For was it not Gideon of Old, who with but a few, like ourselves, did smite the mighty host of the Mideonites? Let us, Thy humble creatures, rejoice in Thy great mercy and praise Thee for Thy many blessings unto us. In the name of Thy Son, our Lord and Savior Jesus Christ. Amen.

Captain Standish caps this little show with a final proclamation: "In the name of God and Charles, king of England, Ireland, Scotland, Wales, Virginia, Bermuda, etc., the squadiron of the northern flanker of the New Plimoth militia is dismissed!"

The women interpreters have been relieved for a short time during the morning drill. With the visitors' attention focused on the militiamen, the women have had a chance to catch their breath and to get some cooking done with no one watching them or asking them questions.[6] By late morning, the village has begun to fill up with visitors. In the spring and fall, this can happen very quickly. Thousands of schoolchildren are bused in from all over the East Coast. By eleven o'clock, there might be two or three hundred visitors wandering through the houses. The style of interpretation changes when larger groups enter a house. Interactions among Pilgrims, such as the one described earlier in the Winslow House, become more difficult to enact. Interpreters have to become more like teachers, educating the visitors on different aspects of Pilgrim life, but still staying in character: "Aye, indeed, I have planted two acres of Indian corn, placin' an alewife in each hill, jist as the Indians of these parts ha' showed us when we first come." Often, they must explain away situations that are patently false in relation to the realities of seventeenth-century farm life. For example, rarely would adult men have been home in the middle of the day in such a community (for this reason, it is difficult to find justifiable activities within the village context for male interpreters). A wily visitor will sometimes ask why so many men are at home in the daytime. An interpreter must quickly come up with a credible excuse: "I've been out i' th' field since first light, sir. E'en a horse deserves a bit o' rest. Do ye not think so?" or "I'm expectin' my brother to be returnin' with the fishin' partie from Cape Anne by th' noon hour, an' I must give him a hand wi' his portion o' th' catch." A good interpreter can usually gain the visitor's confidence and go on with his role, completing the task he has been working on in the house. The house, after all, is the main stage where the action must take place.

A group of university students and their professor, on a field trip, come for a visit with Jonathan Brewster. They find him at home alone in Allerton House (his dwelling in this particular house is so much historical conjecture, but it does provide a proper setting for one of New Plimoth's most fascinating characters). The single square room that constitutes Allerton House is very dark, since the windows are tiny; the floor is made of dark packed-down earth; there is no great cobblestone chimney, only a little open fire in one corner. The hearth is also earthen, and the smoke rises up an open daub flue. It is damp in the house today and Jonathan sits by the fire, warming his hands (plate 12). He wears a thick black woolen cloak over his doublet and a great, wide-brimmed, black felt hat. It takes a moment for the students' eyes to adjust to the dimness of the room. (The following dialogue is based on the transcription of a tape recording made by Barbara Kirshenblatt-Gimblett on 12 April 1985. I have interpolated some actions. After this, the reference to any taped dialogue in this text will appear at the end of the cited material.)

JONATHAN BREWSTER

Good day to thee.

WOMAN VISITOR

Hi. Hi . . . Who are you?

JONATHAN BREWSTER

Jonathan Brewster.

WOMAN VISITOR

(putting a long antenna-like, professional field microphone near Jonathan's head in order to record this conversation)
I hope you've no objection to my using this.

JONATHAN BREWSTER

Well, I was just wonderin' if this were a sign of some sort.

*Plate 12.* "Jonathan Brewster" warms his hands by the fire.
(Photo by Alan Duffield)

WOMAN VISITOR

Oh, it's a sign of great interest.
   (laughter among the students)

JONATHAN BREWSTER

Oh, indeed? Well, you're welcome to carry whatever you like here-
abouts. Unless it's a cross.

WOMAN VISITOR

Well, ah . . .

JONATHAN BREWSTER

We'll not tolerate that.

WOMAN VISITOR

Why?

JONATHAN BREWSTER

That's a . . . sort of superstition and we do not allow that here.

WOMAN VISITOR

Well, you believe in Christ, don't you?

JONATHAN BREWSTER

Oh, indeed.

WOMAN VISITOR

So what's wrong with the cross?

JONATHAN BREWSTER

That's a superstition.

WOMAN VISITOR

He didn't die on a cross?

JONATHAN BREWSTER

Oh, well, he did die on a cross, but to be worshipping *that*—that is
ideology.

WOMAN VISITOR

Oh, I quite agree, I quite agree. It's also very depressing

JONATHAN BREWSTER

It's some of the issues which have come up with the Church of England folks—they don't see the cross anywhere in our meeting house
and they say we must put one up before they would go to worship
there. There's nothing in the scripture that says you should in any-

way worship before the cross. They're making too much of it. That's
where it seems to be a sign of the danger of it.

WOMAN VISITOR

Yes, I quite agree.

JONATHAN BREWSTER

Well, I'm glad to hear that.

John Kemp is a master interpreter. In this case, he has transformed
what could have become a conversation about the ridiculous anachronism into a lesson on the "plain style" of the Church of the
Saints (a term the Pilgrim congregation applied to themselves, since
they tried to live a "sanctified" life). He has used the absurd presence
of twentieth-century audio technology in a Pilgrim house as a pretext
for discussion of one of the most dynamic underlying social/political
issues in the village: the differences between the Saints and the Strangers
(the epithet usually applied to those villagers who are not members
of the Church of the Saints, though, historically, it should be applied
only to those non-Saints who were passengers on the *Mayflower*). This
scene goes on for another ten minutes, while Jonathan Brewster explains further about the religion of the Saints and describes his father,
Elder Brewster, who is their religious leader—the teaching elder of the
village. Though the students might be tempted to make John Kemp
break out of character by engaging in what is known among the interpretation staff as "Pilgrim-baiting," the breadth of his knowledge of
seventeenth-century English culture is too great for them; it is evident
that he can transform any ploy into an elucidation of some aspect of
the Pilgrims' lives.[7] The students are charmed by Kemp's characterization, and their professor thanks him wholeheartedly as they leave
the house.

After the noon hour, many Pilgrim families settle down to their midday meal. This is the reenactment of the Pilgrim dinner, which always
took place in the middle of the day and was the biggest meal. The
food that the women have been preparing all morning is served up.
Interpreters are not required to eat the food that has been cooked on
the open hearth, but in fact, most of the female interpreters become
very skilled in seventeenth-century culinary arts. This daily reenactment of dinner equals a free lunch for the interpreters. Rarely is the

whole family at home for this meal (it is rare that a whole family is cast for a season). Today is an exception, for both Master Edward Winslow and his brother, Goodman John Winslow, are "back from their morning's labor i' the field." Their wives, Mistress Susannah Winslow and Goodwife Mary Winslow, are also home for the noonday meal.

The table has been set with some of the finest linen to be found in New Plimoth. Only a patrician Pilgrim family like the Winslows would have such a fine cloth for their board. Pewter plates, glass goblets, a horn spoon for the master, and even monogrammed napkins adorn the Winslow table. As a final sign of this family's social status, Goodwife Winslow sets a bottle of fine "Rhenish" wine, imported from England, by the master's place. Everyone in the family now sits.

The room is filling up with visitors—twenty or more—who are fascinated to watch this seventeenth-century gustatory ritual. Master Winslow offers up a grace and a few of the visitors respond with "amen" when he concludes. Then, the women begin to serve the men. The pork pottage is placed steaming in a great wooden bowl on the table. Mistress Winslow scoops some out onto a trencher (a small square wooden platter) and serves it to her husband. Master Winslow has thrown one of the long white linen napkins over his shoulder so that it falls down on either side of his torso. From time to time, he wipes his hands on it. Mary Winslow places a round loaf of bread that she baked the day before in the outdoor beehive oven on the table. "Wouldst thee kindly pass me the butter, Susannah?" asks Master Winslow. All the while, brother John is engaged in a conversation with a visitor about the wars in the "Germanies" in the year 1627. Goodman Winslow is very knowledgeable about seventeenth-century geography and military history (in fact, this is interpreter Eric Marr's favorite subject).

A visitor asks Mistress Winslow if this is a typical meal for this time of the year. Mistress Winslow explains that the present victuals are the last of the winter's pork and must be eaten up while the meat is still good; pork pottage has been a constant part of the family diet throughout the winter months. She goes on to describe how she pickled the cabbage in a salt brine, concluding her recitation by saying how glad she is that "the time o' the year for good fishin' has come."

Master Winslow elaborates on the bounty of the waters at New Plimoth.: "Turbot, scote, haddock, pollack, mackerel, bluefish, and the herrin', or what we calls 'alewives,' that be runnin' up the streams, here, since the end o' March." John adds how sick the family will be of alewives by the summertime. The visitors laugh.

Mistress Elizabeth Howland suddenly pops her head in the door and informs Goodwife Winslow that she'll "be goin' to my husband i' th' field at one o'clock." This is a code, commonly used among inter-preters, that lets the goodwife (Barbara Austin) know that the young woman who plays Mistress Howland (Kathleen Hall) will be going out on her break at one o'clock, so that they can keep their luncheon date. After Mistress Howland leaves, Master Winslow asks the goodwife to say the thanksgiving, and she offers up a very sincere, heartfelt prayer. Since Barbara Austin is a devout Roman Catholic, she has been able to project her real Christian faith into her fictive Pilgrim persona (even though the Pilgrims, of course, were vigorously anti-papist). Good-man John Winslow gets up from the table first and says he is going to the common muck heap to get some good muck for the Winslow wives' garden. Mary excuses herself, saying she must journey to the Common Store House for some thread. As this dinner comes to a conclusion, Master Winslow converses with some visitors and finishes his wine, while his wife boils the water that will be used for doing the dishes.

Every interpreter gets an hour off for lunch, but these breaks are necessarily staggered from about eleven o'clock to two o'clock, so that all the houses of the village are properly staffed. If the village is too sparsely populated, the illusion is broken, and the visitors complain. Usually, at least one interpreter is left behind to "cover" a house while colleagues go "out to their fields."

Interpreters on break exit up either of the dirt roads that lead to the orientation center, smiling and nodding, bidding "good day" to the visitors who are entering. Once beyond the fence that hides the stair-way to the interpreters' lounge, people bring cigarette packs out of aprons and breeches and indulge in a kind of mocking laughter, just at the relief of being back in the present world for a few minutes. Jokes are told about the "crazy" visitors who have been encountered during the morning. One female interpreter tells about a Japanese camera-man making a pass at her. Having punched out and returned to the lounge area, women pull off their coifs (linen bonnets) and men toss their Pilgrim hats like Frisbees onto the various couches and chairs.

"Master Hopkins" asks if anyone is going to the museum cafeteria—
he would like a bowl of chili. "Bess Haybell" and "Lucretia Brewster"
are going out to Friendly's for ice cream and ask if anybody else wants
some. One interpreter has his nose in a newspaper, reading out loud
the latest report on the Boston Celtics and giving all within earshot his
opinions on their play-off chances. Joff Spaulding is absorbed in his
volume of Kierkegaard again. Richard Pickering has taken a paper
titled "The Theology of John Robinson" out from the interpreters'
library that is located in the supervisors' office. Chris Hall, cooking up
some soup in the interpreter's kitchen, explains to Richard that history
would have been much different if Robinson (the pastor of the Pilgrims' congregation in Leyden) had ever actually made it to New Plimoth. Pam Smith, Lorna Kent, and Richard Rogers are headed for
Burt's, a local twentieth-century pub just on the other side of Route
3A, a stone's throw from the bottom flanker of the Pilgrim Village.
They still wear their Pilgrim costumes; the management of Burt's is
used to the Pilgrim presence after all these years. Pam and Lorna are
both actually English, and they are carrying on with typical English
humor a parody of a terrible verbal spat. Richard Rogers laughs now
and then asking what certain phrases ("don't get your knickers in
a twist, love") mean. Unwittingly, he continues to talk in his own
recently learned seventeenth-century English dialect, which sounds
very different from the real accents of the two English interpreters
(there were four in the village during the 1985 season).

Once their break is over, the interpreters punch in again and head
back down to the village to relieve their housemates. During the
spring, when there are large groups of schoolchildren or in August,
when there are two or three thousand visitors a day, these breaks can
be desperately needed. If an interpreter is left alone in a house for a
long period at such a time, he or she can burn out very quickly. In
August, because of the intense heat and the huge number of visitors,
interpreters will often be found just sleeping in the lounge during their
breaks. But today the cool spring air is refreshing and the interpreters
look forward to going back to work. Perhaps some spontaneously invented scenario will liven things up in the afternoon.

In fact, a plot has been set afoot. This morning, Edward Holman, a
single man (there are many more young men than young women of
marriageable age in the 1627 village), gave some ribbons to two of the

young servant maids, Elizabeth Haybell and Edith Pitts. Bess has been flaunting her ribbons in front of Edith and boasting that Edward gave her the prettiest ones, because he likes her better. She has brought poor Edith to tears with her gibes and taunts. This scene has caught the attention of many visitors and has become part of the village gossip for the day. The historical authenticity of this improvised scene might be questioned—would this have really happened in New Plimoth in 1627? This particular scenario has evolved because of interpreter David Hobbs's spontaneous decision to bring the ribbons to these two young women. There is no historical account of such an event.

From time to time, however, the interpreters get inspired and want to do a little historical playwrighting of their own. A chain reaction is set off, since every character in the village must respond to the event from his or her own point of view. If this event becomes a hot item, then the visitors will hear about it in every house they enter. It will have a kaleidoscopic effect on the visitors' experience of the village: they will encounter the reactions of all the different Pilgrim personalities that are represented on a given day. The visitors also become involved in such a scenario. In this particular instance, Master Winslow goes to speak with Bess about her un-Christian-like cruelty toward Edith. As one of the upstanding members of the Church of the Saints, he feels it is his duty (again, the interpreter's choice) to speak to this servant girl about morals, for her own master is away on the fishing voyage. After he finishes sermonizing the lass, Bess spontaneously breaks into tears before a house packed with visitors. Several of the visitors begin to question Master Winslow. What right did he have to instruct this young woman about her behavior? Was he not himself being cruel to her? Master Winslow is put on his mettle. The interpreter comes up with a biblical quotation to justify his character's actions. Master Winslow speaks humbly of the need for proper moral conduct on the streets of New Plimoth, and of how it is the masters' duty to tutor their servants in religion, just as they would their own children. Even if this scene is a little off the mark in terms of historical authenticity, it fascinates and moves the many visitors who witness it.

By mid-afternoon, there are a hundred or so visitors walking about the village, questioning the Pilgrims about their activities, their lives, their culture. John Winslow is splitting wood in front of Winslow House. John Alden is fitting some clapboard onto the frame of the new Cooke House. Master Stephen Hopkins is cleaning his musket, sitting on the bench in front of his own homestead. Stephen Tracy (Jon Haskins from curatorial services) is taking the oxen, Swan and Turk, back out to the field; he speaks quietly to them, swatting them gently every now and then with the birch rod in his hand. By the northern flanker, several Pilgrim women are waiting for their bread to bake in the outdoor oven. It is the replication of a scene from the normal daily life of a seventeenth-century English farming community in America, reenacted for the benefit of anyone who would come to see. Yet the interpreters perform their various tasks so naturally, in such a relaxed manner, that it seems as though the activities would go on even if there were not a single visitor present. It is a powerful illusion, and the visitors are easily seduced into suspending their disbelief.

As shadows begin to fall in the late afternoon, the illusion grows even stronger. In the governor's house, where the maidservant, Edith Pitts, washes the pots by the dim light of the hearth, the scene has a ghostly aura. It is as if a Rembrandt painting of a Pilgrim setting had suddenly come to life. The appearance of the governor's chamber is very natural, and the chiaroscuro lighting effects are perfect. This living picture is aesthetically pleasing, and a visitor may even feel transported into another dimension. But the feeling of realness in this scene comes mainly from the presence of the interpreter—the actor/historian. Edith is vivacious. She is chattering away about the governor, who is not present (in fact, he is rarely present; thus, his maidservant has a great many opportunities to talk behind his back). A woman visitor asks Edith a question about her religion, and it is revealed that Edith is a member of the Church of England, serving in the household of one of the most prominent Saints.

WOMAN VISITOR
Did you go to church in England?

EDITH PITTS
'Corse, we did, Now, you asked me did I go to church. We went to church and tha's just what we said—"I is goin' to church." We went for half the day and then we would come home and tend to our family responsibility. Now, heuh, ya can't even say, "I is goin' to church." You've got ta call it the "meetin' house." The folks wi' the Church of the Saints, they say, they say: "We is the church. The people is the church."

MAN VISITOR

Isn't it uncomfortable for you, being in the Church of England, in the governor's house? He's the chiefest of the Saints, isn't he?

EDITH PITTS

I know it. I know it. I ain't sayin' nothin'. In truth, most of the time, I don't speak my feelin's about it. If my master was in the house, I wouldn't be sayin' it. That's the reason that there's all different kinds of truth. There's the truth when your master's in the house and the truth when he's out of it.

(laughter among the visitors)

Indeed, now, if he was in the house and if someone said, "What do ya think of the Church of the Saints?" I'd say, "Oh, they is godly folks. They is godly folks. I favor 'em." But if he is out of the house, I'd say, "You've got ta be a 'saint' to live amongst 'em."

(more laughter)

MAN VISITOR

You don't think you'll become a Saint, yourself?

EDITH PITTS

Nay, tha's what my mistress says: "Oh, Edith, mayhaps some day you'll see the light" and such.

MAN VISITOR

What is Mistress Bradford like?

EDITH PITTS

Oh la! Do you mind if I labor while we talk? I got ta get this dun.
(Edith continues washing dirty pots in a great basin set on the bench in front of the governor's hearth)

MAN VISITOR

Is she a kindly lady?

EDITH PITTS

In truth, now, she's got a good heart actual. She comed heuh a couple of years ago. She didn't come over on th' *Mayflower*. My master, his first wife, Dorothy, comed over on th' *Mayflower*, but she fell off the ship. That's the reason he sent for this other woman to come— Alice. And then they married once she got heuh. In truth, she is a very lovin' woman. She treats me almost as a dottah. Sometimes though—I ain't sayin' nothing—but the problem *is* sometimes she puts too much pepper in our soup and such.
(Snow 1984c)

And so the small group of three or four visitors in the Bradford House, in these last moments of the afternoon, is treated to some entertaining, although at times apocryphal, anecdotes about Governor William Bradford's second wife. The interpreter, Nancy Mindick, has utilized one of the oldest traditions of the stage servant: she has made the audience her confidant. (In fact, Mindick spent a good deal of time studying the servants in Elizabethan and Jacobean plays in preparation for her role as Edith.) In her well-crafted performance as a servant maid, she creates a point of view for one of the unknown, lesser figures of Pilgrim history, much to the delight and appreciation of the visitors.

The day is coming to a close in the Pilgrim Village. Animals are fed, tools put away, fires extinguished. There are only a few persistent visitors around in this last half hour; they are still asking questions, trying to get their money's worth. At the beginning and end of the plantation season, this is a peaceful time of day. Some contraband tea (the Pilgrims did not have tea in 1627 Plimoth) might be shared among housemates. Treats of different kinds that have been carefully hidden in the most unexpected places during the day are brought out: cookies, wine, beer, candies, and, once in a while, marijuana (the partaking of which is grounds for immediate dismissal).

Interpreters peek out of doors to see if anyone is coming. At this time, they can sneak a smoke or share a little conversation with their colleagues. The usual topic is village gossip—news and rumors about the real goings-on among the twentieth-century staff members. A few minutes before five o'clock, Donna De Fabio comes around, in the role of Priscilla Alden, and tells the few remaining visitors that the village gates will soon be closed, as the villagers must now "bring the cows back from the pasture." This is the code phrase used to make all the interpreters aware that it is closing time. Chris Hall, as Captain Standish, is still passionately involved in a dialogue with two Egyptian visitors. He is discussing some esoteric aspect of biblical geography with them. Len Travers, in street clothes, walks behind the two Egyptians and, so only Hall can see him, puts his hand under his chin in the old broadcasting "cut off" sign. Chris concludes the points he was making and tells the two visitors he must "fetch in the cows."

The spring twilight is clear and lovely. Bill Mullin was correct in his prediction: it has been a beautiful, sunny day. Now, in the dusk, with most of the visitors gone beyond the palisade wall, the interpreters begin to make their way up the hill. A few of the women quietly begin to sing Psalm 23, just because they feel like it. One or two of the men join in. Amidst the sounds of awakening life all around—birds, crickets, peepers—the singing seems sweet and unaffected. There is also laughter in the air, but unlike the nervous giggling of this morning, it is relaxed and calm. The day's performance is over, and the actor/historians can now return to their dressing rooms.

As the interpreters come to the bottom of the stairway that leads to the interpreters' lounge, they find some notes posted by the women from visitor services. These are the statistics for the day, general comments on the overall performance of the Pilgrims, or, sometimes, special compliments for specific interpreters: "Phillipe Delanoye is excellent and most informative," "Jonathan Brewster is outstanding," "Mistress Alden is incredibly knowledgeable," "Bravo for Edith Pitts. We hope she finds a husband!" These little notes serve as capsule reviews that let the interpreters know how the public is receiving their performance.

Everyone has punched out. The dressing rooms are filled with much mirth and horsing around. At a quarter after five the day is over. It is time to relinquish the Pilgrim persona; it is time for the interpreters to let down their hair. In the men's dressing room, Ted J. Curtin says, "I've got a joke for you guys" and he proceeds to tell a story about a rabbi's son who converts to Christianity, much to his father's distress. The troubled rabbi goes to see his best friend, another rabbi, to discuss his tragedy. To his amazement—and here Curtin imitates a thick "Jewish" accent—his friend tells him, "You know, my son has also made a conversion to Christianity." Ted Curtin has captured everyone's attention with his act. He goes on with the story: next, the two rabbis decide to seek out the advice of the head rabbi, only to discover that he has suffered the same fate. "What shall we do?" they ask him. He says that they should go immediately into the synagogue and pray to God. Curtin concludes, "So after they pray for a few minutes, the ceiling of the synagogue opens and a thunderous voice answers, 'You know something? My son, he has become a Christian *too!*'" Curtin delivers the punch line with great skill. Nearly everybody in the room laughs.

The joke is typical of the kind of humor that occurs in the dressing room, especially at the end of the day. These jests most commonly refer to the Pilgrims' "other": blacks, Jews, Catholics ("papists"), eroticism, high technology, twentieth-century nihilism (one interpreter used to punch out saying, "God is dead after five o'clock"), dirty jokes, anti-religious jokes, black humor—anything that is far removed from or that contrasts with Pilgrim culture (or, in many cases, the stereotypical images of Pilgrim culture). But this humor can also be very lighthearted. For instance, today David Hobbs does a wonderfully ridiculous imitation of Elvis Presley as a Pilgrim. Chris Hall and Eric Marr, only half-dressed and in their bare feet, dance around like a couple of country yokels, singing "Life is Like a Mountain Railroad." People are getting back into their street clothes.

All of this fooling around—the jokes, the pranks, the satire—is part of the "cooling down" period that comes at the end of a long day of reenacting the lives of the Pilgrims. How some of this functions as symbolic inversion (Babcock 1978) will be discussed in chapter 5. This time is surely the same as the cool-down process that Richard Schechner has described for performers all over the world.[8] The kidding around that takes place is a way for the interpreters to distance themselves from the roles they play eight hours every day, five days a week. It helps them to begin to reenter their own reality. Some will now go home to their wives and husbands and families. Some will go out for a beer with friends. Others will hang out in the interpreters' lounge a little longer, only gradually giving up their Pilgrim identity. For most, tomorrow will be another day, living and working in the Pilgrim Village.

# Four

# Scenes from the Theatre of the Pilgrims

> More typical (as became apparent in the course of
> numerous visits during this past spring, summer
> and fall) are the special events, which occur at reg-
> ular intervals during the plantation's eight-month
> season and range from a visit of the Dutch am-
> bassador to reenactments of weddings and trials
> (a recent press release declared, "PILGRIM GOES
> ON TRIAL FOR SMOKING IN PUBLIC") to the inevitable
> (and nostalgic) recreation of the first Thanksgiving.[1]
>
> John Engstrom, *Boston Globe Magazine,*
> 24 November 1985

Without a doubt, much of latter-day Plymouth is what Dean MacCannell would call a "tourist attraction" (1976) and what Barbara Kirshenblatt-Gimblett and Edward Bruner would characterize as a "tourist production." The co-authors write: "Tourists take in tourist sites, not in isolation but as nodes in a network of attractions that constitute the tourist itinerary and recreational geography of a region" (1989, 249). As the largest township in Massachusetts, Plymouth certainly constitutes such a "region." The performance at Plimoth Plantation, which I refer to as Theatre of the Pilgrims, is nested in a complex network of tourist attractions related to Pilgrim history and legend. In order more fully to understand the cultural performance that has emerged at Plimoth Plantation, one must know how the surrounding "recreational geography" has affected the special scenes that are produced in this living museum.

*Plate 13.* One of the many Pilgrim images in downtown twentieth-century Plymouth
(Photo courtesy of the Old Colony Memorial)

Everywhere a visitor turns in contemporary Plymouth, the Pilgrim
image is imprinted: from T-shirts to souvenir dolls to local business
logos. Signs and billboards advertise Pilgrim Animal Hospital, Pilgrim
Beauty Parlor, Pilgrim Autobody Shop. On the roof of the John Alden
Gift Shop sits a giant bust of a stereotypical Pilgrim Father (plate 13).
All of these words and images are "markers," in MacCannell's sense of
the term, and demonstrate what MacCannell calls "sight sacralization" (1976, 41–48). Plymouth is an enormous tourist production and
numerous markers name it, frame it, and enshrine it as a world-class
attraction. From the Pilgrim Hall Museum to the Plymouth National

Wax Museum, everything elevates the central attraction—the Pilgrims—and their image is reproduced ubiquitously.

This profusion of complex modern touristic phenomena, with the simultaneous attempt genuinely to reconstruct Pilgrim history, creates what Kirshenblatt-Gimblett labels "surreal juxtapositions," which "precipitate profound doubts about the status of what is experienced, about 'appearance' and 'reality'" (1988, 61). Schechner describes such experience as "the postmodern thrill at the mix or close coincidence of contradictory categories" (1981, 26). This "thrill" factor is important in the success of the overall environmental tourist production that includes both Plymouth and Plimoth Plantation. For example, within this total "recreational geography," tourists can experience Pilgrim impersonation in four different categories: at the annual Pilgrims' Progress, they can witness townspeople dressed up as Pilgrims for the day: at the chamber of commerce information booth, they may encounter local women attired in stereotypical Pilgrim dress; at the wax museum, they can still find costumed mannequins set in famous scenes of Pilgrim history; and, of course, they can take in the first-person role-playing performance at Plimoth Plantation. "Surreal" seems an apt description of such kaleidoscopic experience.

Of paramount importance in all this are the economic considerations; for in modern-day Plymouth, Pilgrims have become big business. At least 50 percent of all commercial endeavors in the township are related to the tourist trade (Lonardo 1987). Because of the formidable economic structure of the overall tourist production, massive numbers of visitors must be attracted to its network of sites, including Plimoth Plantation. Thus "special events" must be held, with all the accompanying machinery of public relations.

Certainly one prototype for such special events was the reenactment of the crossing of the *Mayflower* in 1957, a major media event that attracted international attention. Today, the *Mayflower II,* which plays a role in the Theatre of the Pilgrims, continues to evoke an aura of historical significance. The living history scene aboard this replica of the famous ship is also produced by Plimoth Plantation. The *Mayflower II,* moored at a dock near the center of "Historic Downtown Plymouth," serves as a marker for the Pilgrim Village and reflects a high degree of sight sacralization, since it is only a stone's throw from the enshrinement of legendary Plymouth Rock.

Coming down from the center of twentieth-century Plymouth to the waterfront, one discovers a row of little shops dedicated to the tourist business: Tastee Freeze, knick-knack stores selling the Pilgrim tourist fare, and restaurants with names like The 1620 and The Pilgrim Inn. Two recreated Pilgrim houses constructed in 1948 and 1955, still standing in a little grove to the right of the state pier, now serve as retail outlets for the plantation's gift shop. On the pier itself are several other gift shops and Captain John's Whale Watching Tours. On the south side of the pier is a maze-like structure of screens leading up a ramp to the *Mayflower II*. These screens constitute an exhibit that introduces visitors to the story of the *Mayflower*. The general layout of this exhibition and the reconstructed ship create problems for the interpreters of this part of the living museum. Unlike the village, the *Mayflower II* is not sequestered from its twentieth-century surroundings. Since the reenactment of its seventeenth-century voyage, it has been docked at this public wharf in the modern commercial harbor of downtown Plymouth. From its deck, one can still see the Tastee Freeze and the Governor Bradford Motor Inn. For this reason, the illusion of another historical reality is harder to maintain aboard the ship. Walking up the gangplank to the main deck, the visitor enters a staged performance.

Steve Kocur, the supervisor on board the *Mayflower II*, positions his cast at certain set stations on different parts of the ship. At the sound of an hourly bell, the actor/historians change stations. The cast represents both the ship's crew and a few of the Pilgrim passengers who might have been aboard on the day that is being re-created: February 21, 1620.[2] Historically, most of the passengers who survived (thirty were already dead by this date) would have been living ashore in temporary shelters by this time. However, so that a variety of character interpretations could be provided, history had to be reshaped a bit: Pilgrims who would have been on land helping to build the plantation are anachronistically situated on the ship. For visitors, wandering about the ship can be a more intimate experience than tramping around the Pilgrim Village. The cast (usually about eighteen in all) aboard the *Mayflower II* has a family atmosphere. Many in this group have stayed with the job for four or five years and have become very skilled interpreters.

For example, Ted A. Curtin has played Christopher Jones, the master of the *Mayflower*, for a number of years. Curtin is a retired navy submarine commander. With his white beard and slightly gruff voice, he gives a wonderful impersonation of a salty old seventeenth-century English sea captain. Here is his explanation of his relationship to the Pilgrims to a group of visitors standing on the half-deck:

MAN VISITOR

Is this where you signed the famous compact?

MASTER JONES

Nay, I had naught to do with that. That were the doin' of the governor and all of 'iz. Most of the men of the passengers did sign of that agreement. When they come to Cape Cod, 'ere, they decided they'd stay in Newe England and they had no right to be 'ere by law, ya see. Their charter doth call for Virginia. We were takin' 'em to Virginia—the northern edge of Virginia. Aye, by Hudson his river. But havin' decided to stay 'ere, the indentured folk amongst 'em said they'd not be bound by any law, then, for their indenture had called for Virginia. So they'd be on their own to do as pleased. But the governor and the like of 'im said, "Well, they'd better 'ave some sart of arrangement or we'd all perish if they'd not work together." So, most of the men did sign of that agreement they 'ad.

(pointing to his little cabin)

No, this 'ere's my cabin. They were doin' that down below in my great cabin. All their plottin' and plannin' took place down thar.

(he turns to some visitors who have just come aboard)

Good day to thee, folk. 'Av a look in this place if you'd like.

(again, pointing to the smaller cabin, just below the poop deck)

Make yourselves at home.

VISITORS

Thank you.

MAN VISITOR

So, I take it you don't favor these people?

MASTER JONES

The passengers? Aye, well, the sooner thar off my ship the better I like it! I be on my way home. No, I've had no quarrel with 'em. These ones that do call themselves Saints appeared a bit strange to me to be namin' themselves as such. 'Tis the Church that decides who's a saint, I always been taught. But I must say they be of saintly behavior. All they been through and never a complaint out of any one of 'em. The rest of the passengers—that's another half of 'em that's ordinary Englishmen—they see somethin's wrong and they'll complain about it if somethin's not to their likin'.

MAN VISITOR

I heard that one of your crew members used to curse the Saints all the time.

MASTER JONES

Aye, well, the sailors had great sport with 'em. Most any sailor would have sport with a landsman—they all begin turnin' green as soon as we do weigh the anchor. But that be one amongst 'em that had a harder mouth than most. It's true. And he were the first one to die. 'Ere 'e wuz, sportin' 'em about and sayin', "Well, ya be green, now, you'll soon die and we'll feed ya to th' fishes and my mates and me we'll divide up what ya left behind!" But 'e were the first one to be fed to the fish, so to speak. So that put the fear of God into the rest o' the crew for a while. But only for a while—you'll not keep a sailor quiet for long!

MAN VISITOR

So, how do you think they will fare here in this country?

MASTER JONES

Ah, I'll not give ya much for their chance to succeed 'ere. That's too many of 'em that died already. We're 'ere but tree months, a month at Cape Cod and two months in this harbor, and one third of 'em's died. An, indeed, five of my crew 'as perished since we come 'ere to this godforsaken, wild place. No, I be hired to get 'em 'ere and I'm losin' money every day I stay 'ere idle. But I'll not be able to sail now if I 'ad to, for half me crew is sick. Five of 'em perished and ten more is sick. So, I pray God I've got enough 'ands to sail the ship when th' time comes to go home.
(Snow 1985c)

Thus visitors are introduced, through first-person interpretation, to the perspective of the man who transported the Pilgrims from England to America.

Many such moments are improvised on the boards of the *Mayflower II*. There are also a few regular reenactments. Every day at noon, Master Jones summons his crew to the main deck. From the poop deck, he makes a little speech; then the Pilgrims say their prayers and sing psalms before partaking of the noon meal. This scene, like the daily reenactment of the musket drill in the Pilgrim Village, is an attempt to create a sense of the everyday routine of the Pilgrims' lives.

*Plate 14.* A media event interrupts the daily performance aboard the *Mayflower II.*
(Photo courtesy of Plimoth Plantation)

Finally, as in the Pilgrim Village, there are special visits by foreign
dignitaries. For example, in October 1985, His Imperial Highness
Prince Naruhito of Japan toured the Pilgrim Village (Engstrom 1985,
12). On October 8, 1984, Britain's ambassador to the United States,
Sir Oliver Wright, came aboard *Mayflower II* and presented a repro-
duction of a seventeenth-century ship's bell to Master Christopher
Jones. A special ceremony was held on the deck (plate 14). The *Boston
Patriot Ledger* (October 9, 1984) reported:

> As startled tourists watched, a Pilgrim trumpet sounded, a whistle
> blew and a loud cannon was fired to welcome Wright aboard the ship.
> "We've got a new bell brought from home, from England," an-
> nounced "Master Christopher Jones," the bearded interpreter who
> portrays the *Mayflower's* captain. "As long as *Mayflower* lies here in
> the harbor of New Plymouth, this bell will be the voice of England."

Such goings-on are not uncommon in relation to the special events
produced by the Living Museum of 17th Century Plymouth. Indeed,
these special scenes are created and timed to attract the largest pos-

sible tourist audience. Today, this requires the response and assistance of local and national media. The anchorperson of a major network news program will suddenly appear at Thanksgiving time to cover the story of the first Thanksgiving. One year, the food writer Craig Claiborne was invited to sample "the delights of the first Thanksgiving" (1991). Beautifully photographed images of Pilgrim interpreters and recreated artifacts frequently appear in national magazines and newspapers. Sophisticated television commercials are broadcast from Boston stations, advertising coming attractions at Plimoth Plantation.

Both on the *Mayflower II* and in the Pilgrim Village, the reconstruction of history is shaped by the force of this need to produce a tourist attraction. Sometimes, historical events have to be glamorized a bit or historical dates shifted a little, and some poetic license is allowed by the producers of this historical re-creation. Not all such special scenes are developed as media events, but certainly many are created with an eye on the box office.

SPECIAL SCENES IN THE PILGRIM VILLAGE

During the course of the season, many specific historical scenes are re-created in the Pilgrim Village. These "special events," which include out-of-the-ordinary episodes such as marriages, funerals, court trials, and musters, reflect the ritual aspect of Pilgrim life, especially rites of passage, seasonal celebrations, and ceremonies relating to the community's social dramas. As Maurice J. Moran, Jr., says, "Many special events continue the theme of historic reenactment" (1978, 68). These re-creations are usually based on historical records but are enhanced in order to be more interesting to the general public.

For the biggest special event of the summer, the reenactment of the historic 1627 wedding of Mary Warren and Robert Bartlett, the interpreters receive photocopied pages of the following commentary, entitled "Rationale for a Festive Wedding":

> In order to present to the public an event that is truly deserving of the description "special," the wedding of Robert Bartlett and Mary Warren will be celebrated somewhat more lavishly than is probably proper to the time and place we portray. A marriage in early New Plimoth would have been quiet, simple and unlikely to have been marked by any special activity . . . . Were we to re-enact the most plausible marriage celebration for 1627, it certainly would be small and not especially exciting. (DeFabio 1985a)

Here, historical reality is dismissed in favor of creating a "hook" that will attract public attention. These special events correspond to what in the amusement park business would be called a "wienie."[3] The fact is that Plimoth Plantation is a business, and it pays for 90 percent of its general operating expenses from sales and the "take" at the gate. In order to survive, it must bring in the crowds.

However, the plantation does attempt to balance these special events with presentations of certain special scenes that are well-researched and historically appropriate. For instance, during the 1985 season, a new type of scene was developed for the second special event of the year (the first being the annual reenactment of the funeral of Mary Brewster, described in chapter 1). Commonly referred to as the "Doorstep Wedding," these two occasions were "The Wedding of Mary Chilton and John Winslow" on April 27 and "The Wedding of Juliana Morton and Manasseh Kempton" on May 12. These simple wedding scenes were conceived as a counterbalance to the overdone, lavish "Festive Wedding" that always takes place at the height of the tourist season. Since I served as the magistrate for the April 27 wedding, I will describe the happenings of that day.

The cast list and scenario were posted a few days before April 27. The intention was for this re-enactment to be as faithful as possible to the historical descriptions of Separatist civil weddings. The Saints did not view marriage as a sacrament but performed their weddings as civil ceremonies (something they learned from the Dutch). This was to be a marriage in one of the most prominent Separatist families of New Plimoth. The notes for this day state:

> We will not observe any colorful customs, sportings or other activities so typical of festive English weddings of the period. There will only be a few friends and neighbors attending the ceremony and subsequent marriage dinner. Those who are not a part of this ceremony will look to their daily business as usual. A casual, but not disinterested, attitude should prevail. (DeFabio 1985c)

This particular wedding scene was to reflect what has often been called the "plain" style of the Saints.

Early in the morning, the various characters involved in this scenario began to prepare themselves. Master Edward Winslow and his wife, Susannah, dressed in their finest attire. Master Winslow was to serve as the magistrate for the marriage ceremony of his youngest brother, John, to Mary Chilton. Edith Pitts, who played Master Winslow's maidservant (just for this day), helped her mistress to get the wedding feast ready. John and Priscilla Alden, along with Joseph Rogers, were to be the wedding guests. Each prepared a gift for the bride and groom. John and Mary took over an hour to dress themselves. Suspense mounted as a crowd of fifty to sixty visitors gathered to see the young couple appear on the doorstep of Winslow House, where the simple civil ceremony was to be staged.

At 12:30 P.M., Master Winslow came out onto his front step, which served as a small raised platform, and announced that the ceremony would begin. The bride and groom came out and stood before him, and the visitors formed a semicircle around the wedding party. Then Master Winslow addressed the couple (plate 15), reading from a formal document:

MASTER WINSLOW

Do you freelie and without Constraint or perswasion of any, acknowledge and declare that by Hand and Mouth you have intered into engagements of Espousall and Marriage?

(here the couple responds)

And to this Ende do you, John Winslow, by these presents give thy Faith and fealty to Mary Chilton, acknowledging, holding and taking her for your Lawfull wife and Spouse?

JOHN WINSLOW

I do.

MASTER WINSLOW

In like manner, do you, Mary Chilton, in virtue of these promises, give your Faith and fealty to John Winslow whom you take, hold, and recognize as your Spouse, Lord and Lawful Husband?

MARY CHILTON

I do.

(DeFabio 1985d)

After the pronouncement of marriage, the couple kissed, the crowd cheered, and hugs were exchanged among family and friends.

At one o'clock, the wedding party retired to the large back chamber of Winslow House, in order to enjoy the bridale, or bridal feast. This was shown to be a solemn, intimate family gathering. Master Winslow said a brief grace; then, as Edith Pitts began to serve up the dinner, he

*Plate 15.* A "Doorstep Wedding," April 1985
(Photo courtesy of Plimoth Plantation)

read a passage from the Holy Scripture for the benefit of his brother and new "sister-in-love."[4] A little humor was introduced with the recitation of several seventeenth-century English riddles. Finally, a psalm was sung and the groom asked his bride to offer up a prayer. Mary Chilton, now "Goodwife Winslow," gave such a sweet, honest, innocent prayer that it brought tears to the eyes of Master Winslow.[5]

One important historical moment that is annually reenacted is the meeting of the governor's council that took place on May 22, 1627. (Since the year represented by the village is 1627, most of the special events roughly correspond with a date in that year.) In the history of Plimoth Plantation, several significant social dramas were coming to a head at this time. During the spring of 1627, Isaac Allerton returned from England with a new agreement that he had drawn up in London with some of the remaining members of the Company of Merchant Adventurers. Bradford wrote that, because of several financial and political crises ("losses and crosses"), the company had dissolved in 1625: "For the Company of Adventurers broke in pieces hereupon, and the greatest part wholly deserted the Colony in regard of any further supply or care of their subsistence" (Bradford 1981, 189). Therefore, the original contract of 1620 was now considered null and void. Allerton returned with a new arrangement in which the Adventurers proposed to let the planters buy them out for "the sum of £1800 of lawful money of England." This proposal created a new situation for the Pilgrims. Questions of vital importance to every member of the community had to be answered in the May 22 council meeting. How were the land and cattle to be divided? Who would now receive shares of the common stock? How was this great debt of £1800 to be paid? The old conflict between the Saints and the more economically motivated colonists—the major social drama of the village—also surfaced in this scenario. Bradford wrote:

> Now though they had some untoward persons mixed amongst them from the first, which came out of England, and more afterwards by some of the Adventurers, as friendship or other affections led them—though sundry were gone, some for Virginia and some to other places—yet divers were still mingled amongst them, about whom the Governor and Council with other of their chief friends had serious consideration how to settle things in regard of this new bargain or purchase made, in respect of the distribution of things both for the present and future. (1981, 208)

What should they do about these "untoward persons"? This council meeting offered the perfect opportunity for finding a way to cut out the unsavory characters among them.

Whether or not such a plan for cutting out the untoward persons was actually discussed at the historical meeting of the governor's council in 1627 is not known. However, for the May 22, 1985, reenactment of this event, Ted J. Curtin, a lead interpreter in the village (and son of Ted A. Curtin, master of the *Mayflower*) devised a script that included such a discussion. Curtin's scenario for this event was handed out to the participating interpreters a few days before May 22. The historical characters to be represented were Masters Bradford, Winslow, Prence, Standish, Alden, and Hopkins. The interpreters met once to go over the scenario, but there really was no formal rehearsal. The script basically gave suggestions for topics of discussion, with a little additional dialogue. For example, the scene concerning the subject of untoward persons read as follows:

GOVERNOR BRADFORD AND MASTER WINSLOW
(Those who have been troublesome should have their just reward. Discuss cutting out "untoward persons.")

MASTER ALDEN
(Agrees that it is a good idea, but is it possible?)

CAPTAIN STANDISH
(Grudgingly doubts if we can manage defense with fewer men.)

MASTER HOPKINS
(Warns of trouble if non-church members are eliminated.)

MASTER WINSLOW
(And that not only here but at home—the Council for New England, Church of England, etc.)

MASTER ALDEN
(And their share in troubles must buy them something if nothing else does.)

GOVERNOR BRADFORD
(wearily)
Six and a half years of this! I fear that this body general could not bear any more strife and contention. If it would make for general peace and contentment, I would even give more than their due.
(General Discussion)

GOVERNOR BRADFORD
(Moves for an equal division amongst "Freeman.")
(Curtin 1985)

Thus words are put into the mouths of historical personages who lived through this particular episode by the actor/historians who play it. In fact, the whole scene has the feeling of a one-act play. It is performed in the morning, and continued in the afternoon. The council gathers around a table at the back of the Fort-Meeting House, with visitors sitting, in an audience-like fashion, on the benches in front of this table. While the governor and his council discuss the matters at hand, people do not usually interrupt them to ask questions. The atmosphere is that of spectators watching a play.

Although the dialogue for this scene is almost entirely improvised, the decision that the governor's council makes are based on historical facts. At the end of the session, it is concluded that every head of a household will be allowed to purchase one share for each member of his family who lives with him; that single men in their majority can purchase one share for themselves; that the land will be allotted in the *near* future; and that the cattle will be divided immediately. As no one owns land in 1627 (except for the few acres allocated to each family in 1623 for the sole purpose of growing corn) and all things have been held in common up to this point, these decisions are momentous. They will affect the interpretation of every character in the village for the rest of the season. In fact, the announcement of the cattle division is actually posted on the redoubt wall the next day, for all the interpreters to come and read. The scene of this meeting and its consequences affords another excellent example of how history is *performed* at contemporary Plimoth Plantation.

Several times during the season, court trials are staged in the Fort-Meeting House. These are the oldest and perhaps most traditionally theatrical of all the reenactments. On each occasion, a few interpreters are specifically cast for the day in the necessary roles: magistrate, guard, clerk, plaintiffs, defendants, and witnesses. Over the years, certain stock cases have been set: "The Drunkard," "The Poore Slaggard," "The Night-Walker" (a person who has broken the village curfew). Mostly these scenes are improvised, but there have been instances in which lines had to be memorized, just as in a play.

These "Court Days" are a wonderful diversion for interpreters and visitors alike. For the interpreters, such courtroom dramas break up the routine and give them an opportunity to identify with some of the problems of Plimoth social life, as well as to investigate various aspects of seventeenth-century English jurisprudence. As a matter of fact, the "crimes" are usually based on those found in the *Records of the Colony of New Plymouth: Court Orders, Vols. I and II, 1633–1651* (Shurtleff [1855] 1968). They are adapted from this later documentation of moral and legal transgressions at Plimoth. Some of the offenses are some-what sordid, so visitors get a chance to see a bit of the seedy side of Pilgrim life. For instance, during the first "Court Session" of the 1985 season, on June 23, John Kemp (who normally played Jon-athan Brewster) was cast as the notorious Master Fells who, according to Bradford, was suspected of keeping a maidservant "as his concu-bine." In this reenactment, Fells and the young woman, Joan Newton, were brought before the court on accusations of "uncivil carriage." However, the charges had to be dismissed because Fells's other ser-vants refused to testify against their master (an interpolation of Brad-ford's historical account). At this time, only titillating gossip was sparked. Suspicions were raised, but these would have to be played out in another scenario (the maidservant eventually becomes preg-nant, at which point she and Master Fells run away together) on another day.

During the morning on a "Court Day," the constable, John How-land, goes about the village handing out summonses to the various "defendants." Gossip quickly circulates among neighbors, and visitors are able to hear many different points of view about any given case. Around midday, a drum is sounded in the center of the village and the two magistrates (English law of the period required that there always be two), the constable, the clerk, the guard, and others make a formal procession up the hill to the "courtroom." This consists of the great oaken table, set up with ink pot and quill, on a raised platform at the back of the Fort-Meeting House; the benches placed in rows at the front (as in the "Governor's Council" scene); and visitors, inter-spersed with costumed interpreters, sitting and standing all about. At this point, the courtroom is abuzz. The magistrates bring the court to order and the clerk calls the first defendant before the bench.

Often, the cases presented in these quarterly court sessions have an entertaining, comic quality. For example, here is part of the scenario for "The Case of the Drunkard":

MAGISTRATE
Have the accused come forward.
(the constable does so)
The clerk will read the charge.
(charge is read)
There is witness to this?

CLERK

Aye, Mistress Prence.

MAGISTRATE

Let her be brought forward.
(witness comes forward)
Let the witness be sworn.
(clerk swears witness)
Please say unto the court what you did witness concerning this matter.
(witness gives her story)

MAGISTRATE

Thanks for your witness; you may sit.
(to the culprit)
Well, Clement Briggs, thou hast heard the charge against thee and
the witness of this woman of honest reputation. What say *you*?

CULPRIT

That I have been falsely witnessed against
(a glance at witness)
by one who don't know "drunken" from "merry." 'Twas not my
intent to become affected; 'twas a hot day and I drank to slake my
thirst. I knew not 'twould affect me.

MAGISTRATE

Thou seem'st to make a distinction 'twixt "merry" and "drunken";
pray explain to me the difference.

CULPRIT

Uh . . . Well . . . "drunken" . . . uh . . . when one is *drunken,* he is so
full of drink that he cannot stand up; and . . . uh . . . when he is but
*merry* . . . uh . . .

MAGISTRATE

He *can* stand up?

CULPRIT

(brightening; he thinks his point has been made)
Aye! That's it, your worship!

MAGISTRATE

(standing)
Am I merry now?

CULPRIT

(confused)
Indeed, your worship, you do not seem so.

MAGISTRATE

Yet, I stand.

CULPRIT

(really confused)
What . . . means your worship?

MAGISTRATE

Only to demonstrate the ill logic of thy argument. Thou sayest in thy defense that thou wast but a *little* drunk—very well, "merry"—and that this should excuse you. By this reasoning, a maid three months pregnant with child may argue that she is but a *little* pregnant!
(culprit snickers; icy stare from magistrate stops him)
Sin is sin, Clement Briggs, whether gross and broad blown or small and unnoticed, and it separates us from the grace of God.
(Travers 1984a)

I have inserted the names "Mistress Prence" and "Clement Briggs" here, as these were the characters portrayed in this scene on September 22, 1984. However, this is a stock scenario and various Pilgrims can be substituted for the standard roles on different occasions. Although the main joke in this scene is a little tired, the visitor/audience invariably finds it amusing. It represents another instance of comedy in the Theatre of the Pilgrims.

These courtroom drama scenes often require the best acting skills that an interpreter can muster. Some interpreters are much better than others at depicting the heightened emotions brought on by the intensified situation of a court trial. For example, when the character played by one especially talented young actress/historian, Teresa Mason, was found guilty of breaking the village curfew, Mason spent her entire two hours "in the stocks," sobbing real tears and ingenuously promising contrition. Her playacting brought pity to the eye of many a visitor and cogently demonstrates the dual function of the actor/historian. Indeed, many of the interpreters really are very good actors.

FUR TRADING: A SCENE PLAYED WITH A NATIVE AMERICAN INTERPRETER

Several times during the spring and early summer a scene is enacted depicting the fur trading that went on between the Pilgrims and the local Indian tribe. Not a great deal is known about this activity except that it definitely occurred, and that, by the year 1627, beaver pelt had become a trade item highly sought by the Pilgrims. Since this commodity fetched a very good price in London, the Pilgrims hoped to pay off their enormous debt (which by 1627 had mounted to £2,400) to the remaining stockholders of the Company of Merchant Adventurers by shipping massive quantities of this fur back to England. The notes for the 1985 scenario of the trading reenactment state:

> During the next six weeks, we will engage in occasional fur trade with a few of our Pokanoket neighbors. Unfortunately, there isn't much evidence of exactly how, when and where local trading took place in 1627. Thus, we are going to "interpret" 6 trading sessions— spread around the village for our convenience of staffing and scheduling (and not because there is any evidence that such trade *was* spread around the village). (Kemp 1985)

"Pokanoket" was the term used by the Pilgrims to designate all of the Wampanoag Indians, a nation that inhabited southeastern Massachusetts and eastern Rhode Island. Wampanoag literally means "eastern people."

Since 1973, Plimoth Plantation has included a Wampanoag Summer Encampment staffed by Native American interpreters as part of the Living Museum of 17th Century Plymouth. Today, the reenactment of fur trading constitutes the basic point of contact between the Pilgrim interpreters and the Wampanoag Indian Program. This program is separate from the Pilgrim Village and is organized very differently. Since the Native American interpreters for the most part no longer employ the first person role-playing technique, I will not discuss the Wampanoag presentation beyond the description of this one scene, which constitutes an exception (see chapter 1, note 6).

The main Pilgrim characters represented in the fur trading scenario are Edward Winslow, Stephen Hopkins, and Myles Standish. All of these men were known to have some familiarity with the Wampanoag language. At the beginning of the season, the interpreters who play these roles are given a manuscript and a cassette recording of basic Pokanoket expressions. They learn such phrases as "Pooneam, netomp" ("Greetings, my friend"), "Yeauappish" ("Here, sit"), and, of course, "Englishantoowash" ("Speak English"). These expressions prove to be useful during improvised dialogue with the Native American interpreter.

In my experience, the historical Wampanoag most commonly depicted in this scene has been Hobomok. This Wampanoag was mentioned in the period accounts of both Bradford (1981) and Winslow

*Plate 16.* Anthony Pollard/Nanepashemet (with hand outstretched) in the role of Hobomok (Photo by Alan Duffield)

(Arber [1897] 1969). He is portrayed by Anthony Pollard, a talented and resourceful leader in the Wampanoag Indian Program (plate 16). Pollard, who is part Gay Head Wampanoag, also goes by the name Nanepashemet. (He is presently manager of Native American Interpretation at the living museum.)

On the appointed day, Hobomok suddenly appears in the Pilgrim Village. He is dressed in native costume and carries a load of beaver, otter, and fox pelts. Usually the visitors and sometimes even the Pilgrim interpreters are startled by his sudden arrival. This is partly because of the rarity of any Native American presence in the village but also because of Pollard's presence in this particular role. Historically, Hobomok was known to be a warrior and a councilor of Massasoit, the Wampanoag leader. Pollard plays the part, which he has studied, with fierceness and dignity. When Hobomok so abruptly arrives, many visitors don't know how to relate to him. Sometimes they depersonalize him, talking about him in his presence, as if he weren't even there. When I played Edward Winslow in 1985, people would address questions about Hobomok to me, even though it had been made clear that Hobomok spoke English very well.

"Pooneam, netomp" are the first words Edward Winslow speaks. Hobomok replies, "Koowokumish. Toh Kuttinketeam, netomp?" ("I greet you. How are you, my friend?") After these few Wampanoag phrases are exchanged to establish a friendly atmosphere, Master Winslow and Hobomok enter Winslow House. About fifteen to twenty curious visitors follow them. Once inside, a conversation between the two men ensues; they discuss actual historical incidents that involved the Wampanoags of this period. In actuality, Winslow had spent a good deal of time among the seventeenth-century Wampanoag, so the interpreter playing this role can incorporate many interesting anecdotes into the improvised dialogue. Also, Pollard is one of the most knowledgeable historians at the plantation, so the visitors listening to this conversation are treated to some rare facts about seventeenth-century New England Indian culture. As the dialogue continues, Winslow offers Hobomok some beer, but he declines. Finally, at the conclusion of the necessary formalities (it would have been considered impolite for Winslow to talk of trade right away) the Pilgrim and the Indian get down to the business of the day: fur trading.

Master Winslow is seated behind his table, with Hobomok on the opposite side. Goodwife Mary Winslow prepares a dinner on the open hearth, furtively glancing toward Hobomok every now and then with a mixture of fear and curiosity. Although the notes for this reenactment ask the interpreters *not* to make too much of Hobomok's visit, as, historically, he lived close to Plimoth and may have visited quite regularly, the interpreter playing Goodwife Winslow (Barbara Austin) has chosen to appear intrigued by his presence. As she told me afterwards, it was her belief that there would still be some feelings of fear about the Indians, especially among the Pilgrim women, even at this time.

After looking over some of the furs that Hobomok has laid out on a table, Master Winslow asks his brother, John, to go down to the Common Store House and bring back some trade goods. In 1627, the English knew that the Wampanoag were extremely desirous of metal objects such as spades, axes, hoes, and knives. The research staff at the plantation has investigated this subject. For example, in 1627, "five broad howes" [hoes] cost ten shillings. Each of these hoes would have had a trade value of at least one whole beaver pelt. The pelts usually weighed more than a pound. The going rate for beaver pelts in England was close to sixteen shillings per pound (Kemp 1985). This meant that for ten shillings worth of hoes a Pilgrim trader could get as much as eighty shillings worth of beaver. Obviously, the profits to be made in such trading were astronomical; thus had the French and the Dutch come to the New World. For the Pilgrims, the opportunity arose to get out from under the burden of their gigantic debt. To play this scene properly, the actor/historians need to be aware of this information, which will create a certain tension in the air as Hobomok and the Pilgrim trader try to outsmart each other over the bargaining table.

After the bartering is completed, Hobomok usually stays for dinner. In the June 1985 reenactment, about a dozen visitors remained in Winslow House as Edward Winslow, John Winslow, and Hobomok dined and conversed with each other. Pollard has a delightful knack for imitating the kind of naivete that a seventeenth-century Wampanoag might have had regarding the English language. He had both the visitors and the Pilgrim interpreters in stitches with his mock distress about such sound-alike English words as "bare" and "bear." "The same word cannot mean two things. How can this be?" he would say. The perplexity felt by a member of an oral culture when confronting the literate, Bible-reading English Separatists was epitomized in Hobomok's question: "How can you keep your God in a book? The Great Spirit is everywhere. How can you trap him in this book?" The value of this kind of scene at Plimoth Plantation is in its lucid demonstration of profound cultural differences between the Pilgrims and the seventeenth-century Wampanoags.

THE BIG WEDDING SCENE

The most spectacular and colorful event of the summer in the Pilgrim Village is the reenactment called the "English Country Wedding." Actually the term "reenactment" is not really appropriate, for in this scene poetic license is stretched to the limits. As mentioned, this wedding is very unlike the kind that the Pilgrims would most likely have celebrated. Clearly this special event aims to entertain, not to duplicate history. A big draw for the summer vacation crowd, it usually takes place around the second week in July and sometimes accommodates as many as three to four thousand spectators. As the notes on the "Rationale for a Festive Wedding" report:

Weddings done in past years at the Plantation have been far more representative of country weddings in England (complete with all the tradition and superstitious folklore common to the period), than of anything observed here in this colony of Saints. *However*—so that the day will be an enjoyable experience to visitor and villager alike, we have decided on a compromise between historical consistency and good public relations. The wedding celebration this year will include such festive elements as music, song and some dancing, as well as much sporting and feasting. (DeFabio, 1984b)

In fact, few visitors know enough about the period to be aware of the inauthentic aspects of this wedding and, as far as the interpreters are concerned, this special event affords a midsummer opportunity to let their hair down.

Preparations for this particular event begin weeks in advance. A new cast list is posted that includes nearly every interpreter in the village, plus a few from the *Mayflower II* who will be jobbed in for the day. The major recasting is for the family of the bride, Master and Mistress Warren and their daughters; the bride and groom, Mary Warren and Robert Bartlett; the bridesmaids and groomsmen; and the officiating magistrate. The roles of the historical couple (this wedding actually did take place in Plimoth in 1627) are usually played by two of the younger interpreters, since Mary Warren is supposed to be only seventeen years old.

Two weeks or so before this special day, interpreters are given rehearsal time. As is also the case in the preparation of scenes with dialogue for the "Governor's Council" an the "Court Days," the interpreters' lounge becomes a rehearsal studio (the rehearsal process for these events will be described and analyzed in the next chapter). For the "Festive Wedding," many period songs are learned—songs that were popular in England during Elizabethan and Jacobean times but that probably were not commonly sung by the Pilgrims. Psalms in four-part harmony fill the air. Gay rounds, such as "Go to Joan Glover," "The Old Dog," and "The Bells of Oesney," are the order of the day. Even a seventeenth-century version of "Three Blind Mice" is rehearsed. Music will be the major component in the merrymaking of this wedding day, and a little English folk dancing may also be included in the nuptial revels.

Early in the morning on the day of the wedding, the Warren House is strewn with garlands of wildflowers. The bridal bed, also in Warren House, is bedecked with multi-colored flowers and ribbons. This is certainly the most picturesque day of the whole season in the Pilgrim Village. Both bride and groom are dressed in a kind of quasi-public display. Robert Bartlett is prepared for the ceremony in Standish House, at the top of the hill. The bride is dressed by her bridesmaids in Warren House, at the bottom of the hill. At one o'clock that afternoon, Master Warren and his wife come out onto their front step, a trumpet is sounded, and Master Warren calls out: "Let's to the wedding!" By this time, the main street may be lined with thousands of visitors. People scramble out of the way as the groom's party marches in a formal procession down the hill. The bridal party proceeds up the hill. The couple meet in the center of the village, before Governor Bradford's house. One of the magistrates is waiting for them. In 1984, Master Edward Winslow (played by Michael Merritt) performed the ceremony. At this point, the bride and groom stand up on a little raised platform in the midst of a sea of spectators. Magistrate Winslow makes a little speech on the meaning of marriage, the vows are read, and the couple is pronounced man and wife. The audience applauds as the newlyweds kiss (plate 17).

After the ceremony, both interpreters and visitors participate in various sports such as "pillow bash," "nine pins," and "jousting." "Pillow bash" explains itself. "Nine pins" is a seventeenth-century form of bowling. In the "jousting," children (mostly) ride on the backs of adults and try to hit a stuffed bag that hangs from a pole, charging at it on the backs of their "horses," with their "lances" outstretched in front of them. These games and sports give the female (and some male) interpreters time to prepare the wedding feast.

In the early afternoon, the bridale is held, usually in two sittings. The English of this period were famous for their enjoyment of feasting, so this is perhaps one of the most authentic parts of the day's performance. Half of the Pilgrims in the village come to a great table for the first sitting. Due to Massachusetts health regulations, visitors are not allowed to eat the dishes that the Pilgrim wives have cooked over the open hearth (although there is usually a little something to nibble on). When all are seated, Master Warren commences with a solemn prayer. Then the fun begins. Songs are sung, dances performed, riddles told, and a great deal of good "English beer" (actually, German dark

*Plate 17.* The bride and groom in a sea of spectators
(Photo courtesy of Plimoth Plantation)

beer) consumed. Governor William Bradford oversees everything with a stern expression on his face, making sure things do not get too far out of hand. However, for those interpreters who do not play Saints, this day can be a ball. Pranks, ribald jokes, and even a little drunkenness (after all, it is real beer that is consumed on a hot summer day) become part of the Pilgrim merrymaking.

As the afternoon wears on, the bride and groom quietly wander about the village, stopping to visit with their friends and neighbors. Naturally, visitors repeatedly request that the newlyweds pose for a photograph. Late in the afternoon, two traditional seventeenth-century English wedding customs are reenacted in a scene called "The Bedding." First of all, sweet herbs are strewn all about Warren House in order to "expel pensiveness and melancholy" (De Fabio 1985e). Then the bride and groom are put into bed (with their shin-length shirts on) and given a "sack-posset" to drink. After the couple have consumed this sweet delicate beverage, their stockings are thrown at them by a bridesmaid and a groomsman. The old English custom has it that if a bridesmaid hits the groom with his own stocking, then she herself will soon be a bride; if the groomsman hits the bride with her stocking, then he also can expect to be married in the near future. Of course, they must throw these stockings with their backs to the newlyweds. Finally, everyone is kicked out of the bridal chamber and the door is shut; at this point everyone, including the visitors, is instructed to make a racket. The walls of Warren House are beaten with sticks and bare hands; people shout, scream, hoot, and whistle. A little laughter is heard inside. Then, it becomes still. Visitors disperse, and interpreters head away from Warren House, some going off to sing quietly in small groups, others to feed the animals or to finish up other chores. If there is a real relationship between the two interpreters playing these roles, they might stay in bed after five o'clock. Again, "imaginary gardens with real toads in them. . . ."

THE BIG MILITARY SPECTACLE

The final special event of the summer is a re-creation of the colony's annual "general muster." Usually taking place on or about Labor Day, it provides the plantation with an opportunity to present a big military display. This scene is loosely based on the yearly gathering and drills of the whole Plimoth militia, which, in the year 1627, was composed of some sixty men. Because this number of male interpreters is never employed at one time, the plantation has to bring in some "ringers" for "Musket Day." Former interpreters are called back on active duty. For example, Daniel Lombardo, now a library curator in Amherst, Massachusetts, returns each year to become the militia's drummer. Other plantation alumni, along with employees from other departments of the museum, help to fill out the ranks for the day. In 1984, the plantation also invited some seventeenth-century military history buffs from three different places: The Theatre of History of Philadelphia, the Fort Orange Guard of Albany, and the Cavalier Association of Columbus. With the addition of these reenactors, the Plimoth militia was represented with something approaching its proper numbers.

However, the 1984 inclusion of outsiders did cause several interesting problems for interpretation in the village on that particular "Musket Day." Many of the costumes were slightly out-of-period: cavalier costumes, circa 1640, have no place in 1627 Plimoth. Another anachronism was that one of these cavaliers was a woman (with a crepe hair mustache). The fact of her presence (plate 18) was leaked to the press and caused no small embarrassment to the military-minded on the plantation staff. Also, the volunteer interpreters did not really know Pilgrim history very well, so they were easily stumped by visitors' questions. But these extra recruits did help to create the main event of the day—the show of military arts—and the spectacle turned out to be a great crowd-pleaser.

The general muster has become so popular that a "mini-muster" was added to the midsummer schedule in 1985. There has been some negative reaction to this emerging fascination with Pilgrim martial arts. A few of the female interpreters refer to the muster as "Little Boys' Day." On the June 8, 1985, mini-muster day, early in the morning before any visitors were allowed in the village, the women interpreters staged a mock drill that was enormously funny. Regina Porter (the flamboyant redhead mentioned in chapter 3) put on a fake red beard in imitation of Captain Standish and ordered all the women to line up in the street. As she barked out "Unshoulder your piece!" the women, who sported cotton mustachios under their noses, lifted their birch brooms into the air. Porter gave a marvelous burlesque of the captain's harangue. When she made the order to "fire," the women all took off their coifs and put matches under them. The unsuspecting men were flabbergasted by this early morning satire. Such a backstage special event is a pure example of ritual inversion within the play space of the Theatre of the Pilgrims.

As we have seen, the main event of the big muster on Labor Day is the "exercise of arms." Twice during the day, all of the men, fully armed and armor-clad, gather in the center of the village. They are inspected by Captain Standish and his lieutenant. Then they sing a psalm, a prayer is spoken, and they are ordered to march. Two great columns of musketeers and pikeman proceed to march out the northern flanker gate into the newly harvested field just beyond the palisade walls, as hundreds of visitors follow alongside. Once in the field, Captain Standish takes his men through various seventeenth-century military maneuvers. To the beat of the drum, they perform wheels, pike orders, charges, and finally, two or three thunderous volleys. The Labor Day audience responds to this climactic moment with rousing applause.

*Plate 18.* A young woman (in striped shirt at far left) disguised as a "militiaman"
(Photo courtesy of Plimoth Plantation)

### THE MOST FAMOUS SCENE OF ALL

As autumn settles in and the leaves change color all around the palisade wall, the twentieth-century Pilgrims go through the paces that a
seventeenth-century farming community would. Crops are harvested,
foodstuffs preserved, pigs slaughtered (an exhibit that is the delight of
elementary schoolboys). Thousands of schoolchildren, who have recently returned to school after their summer vacations, come to Plimoth Plantation on field trips. Also, senior citizens—known as "white
heads" among the interpretation staff—make stopovers at the Pilgrim
Village on their fall foliage tours. This special time of year provides
visitors with opportunities to chat with a Pilgrim by the fireside, on a
cool afternoon, as the days grow shorter and shorter.

With the coming fall, people begin to think about Thanksgiving and
the Pilgrims, a fusion in the American mind since World War I. Ironically, the Pilgrims did not really celebrate Thanksgiving—the most

famous "scene" of all—in any way that we would recognize today. Two points need to be clarified so that we can understand this. First of all, to the Pilgrims, a "thanksgiving" was a day of prayer and meditation, not necessarily connected with a harvest or a feast. It was a special day of religious observance to acknowledge an act of God's benevolence. For example, in 1623, there was a terrible drought, so Governor Bradford called for a day of "humiliation and prayer." When rain soon followed their prayers, the Pilgrims "set apart a day of thanksgiving" (Bradford [1952] 1982, 130), probably in late July. This notion of "giving thanks to God" ("thanksgiving" was also the name of the prayer that immediately followed a Pilgrim meal) later became identified with the famous 1621 harvest feast described by Edward Winslow.[6] This feast was certainly *not* called a "thanksgiving" by the Pilgrims. Most likely taking place in mid-October, it was a traditional English "Harvest Home," with sporting and feasting, but not a religious holiday. As America evolved from its early Pilgrim heritage, the notions of a religious thanksgiving and of an ancient agrarian harvest festival became intertwined. George Washington proclaimed the last Thursday in November to be the first "National Thanksgiving" and, after a long interval in which many different days were so designated, Lincoln followed suit. When Franklin D. Roosevelt had that date established by "act of Congress as a National day of Thanksgiving," the day was fixed as an American holiday (Stoddard 1973, 12–14).

Actually, the secular way in which Thanksgiving is celebrated today, with its focus on feasting and the accompanying football games, resembles the way the Pilgrims celebrated their harvest feast in 1621. According to James Deetz and Jay Anderson: "Many of the features of the modern version—feasting, the menu in part, and athletic contests—are in the spirit of America's first Harvest Home. The religious component of Thanksgiving, and even the act of giving thanks, are later additions" (Deetz and Anderson 1972, 8).

Of course, other scholars have different views as to how and exactly when this first Harvest Home was celebrated. Since the Pilgrims were deeply religious people and religion influenced everything they did, that may have been a component of the 1621 harvest feast. Today, this special event at Plimoth Plantation—the most famous scene of all—is presented as a frolicking, mid-October "Harvest Home." Because the year represented is actually 1627, the festivities include a reenactment of the recorded historical visit of the Dutch to New Plimoth.

Like the "Festive Wedding," the "Harvest Home" is re-created so that it will be "an enjoyable experience to visitor and villager alike." This three-day feast is scheduled to coincide with Columbus Day weekend. It is the biggest special event of the entire season (three to four thousand visitors per day). These three days of feasting, sporting, and merrymaking are affectionately known amongst the interpreters as "D-days" or "D-daze," the "D" standing for de Rasieres, the leader of the Dutch expedition to New Plimoth. It is a wild time, a kind of Pilgrim blowout. As the notes for the 1984 scenario state: "We want to impress upon the public that this is an *extraordinary* occasion in Plimoth, and that the festive air and goings-on are a *glaring* exception to daily life here" (Travers 1984b).

It is on record that, in October 1627, Isaack de Rasieres, secretary of the new Dutch settlement at New Amsterdam (modern-day Manhattan), sailed up the coast in order to visit and investigate the English settlement at New Plimoth. He and his entourage brought several gifts, along with a quantity of "wampumpeag," a kind of shell money used by the Indians who traded with the Dutch. De Rasieres wanted to encourage the use of this medium of exchange among the New England Indians (James, Jr. 1963, 63). At this time, both the English and the Dutch were interested in acquiring furs from the native peoples. It was a highly lucrative business. The biggest problem affecting negotiations in October 1627 was the English claim that the Dutch were seated on lands belonging to the king of England. This is the background of the scene that is reenacted concomitantly with the 1627 Harvest Home.

During the 1980s, professional actor Toby Tomkins came up from New York City to play the role of de Rasieres. A magnificent costume, based on Dutch designs of this period, was designed for him. Tomkins would be joined by two of three of the regular interpreters who would portray members of his entourage. Usually, there had been a previous reenactment of an earlier Dutch visit, in August 1627, and the same interpreters would re-create their Dutch roles for D-days. However, in 1984, Jeremy D. Bangs, formerly curator of the Leiden Pilgrim Documents Center in the Netherlands (and, at that time, chief curator at Plimoth Plantation) was jobbed in as one of the Dutchmen. This resulted in an interesting scene, which will be described shortly.

At about 12:30 P.M. on this day, the feast is announced. The governor and his wife lead their guests to the bountiful harvest banquet. Usually, it is held either in the Fort-Meeting House or in the field beside the governor's house. The table is elaborately furnished with all kinds of wonderful period dishes: duck, goose, "venison" (often actually goat meat), roasted pig, stewed pumpkin, beet sallet, "frumenty," sweet breads, and a delicious pudding called "fool." This is the most thoroughly realized of all the reenactments of Pilgrim feasting. Once everyone is seated, the governor offers up a prayer. Then the first course is served. Indentured servants and children scurry about, making certain that everyone's cup is filled with good "English" beer (as at the wedding feast, contemporary imported German dark beer is used), and that all present get enough to eat. Recorder music may be played during the meal, and the governor will give his permission for the singing of "country songs." It is a joyous time, with much sporting and merrymaking, usually forbidden in the streets of New Plimoth. However, at the end of the feast, a solemn prayer of thanksgiving is spoken and a psalm is sung.

After the feast, the governor takes the Dutch visitors on a tour of the village. Since actual descriptions written by de Rasieres have been used to re-create Plimoth Plantation, the Dutchmen reenact a careful scrutiny of the settlement. The interpreters improvise dialogue that is intended to approximate the historical negotiations; over the next three days, the English and the Dutch must come to terms on several matters concerning their respective colonies. As the afternoon wears on, the games and sports continue in the open meadows inside the palisade walls. Customarily, there is a military display and, often, a competition of marksmanship is staged. The Dutch and English fire their (unloaded) muskets at a target set up near the bottom flanker. Usually, the English win. It is actually all a deception: a young boy hiding behind the target pulls out small pieces of it, after a musket has been fired, giving the illusion that a ball has hit the mark. A proper stage trick for the Theatre of the Pilgrims!

The three D-days are much alike: the sporting and feasting continues; visitors eavesdrop on the negotiations; military drills are conducted. However, at times, some interesting scenarios spontaneously evolve. In 1984, some real Dutch tourists got rather rambunctious and started to make fun of the interpreters who were portraying the seventeenth-century Dutchmen. One man was particularly derisive and kept shouting, "You are not Dutch! You are impostors!" He began to interrogate the interpreters/Dutchmen about Leiden, not realizing that one of them was, in reality, a museum curator from Leiden. Jeremy Bangs answered his questions, rapid-fire, in fluent Dutch. The poor man's mouth fell wide open, and a blank stare came over his face; Bangs had convinced him of the reality of the Dutch presence in New Plimoth.

In 1985, another curious scene developed when some of the Dutch entourage began playing cards in one of the Pilgrim houses. It was a rainy day, and the interpreters may have been acting out of boredom. Certainly there is nothing in the history books about the Dutch playing cards with the Pilgrims in 1627. As dicing and card-playing were strictly forbidden, this improvised action created a difficult political situation for the governor, once he got wind of it. He could not reprimand the Dutchmen, for such an accusation might insult Secretary de Rasieres and upset their talks. Instead, the actor/historian playing Governor Bradford decided to send his assistant, Master Winslow, to investigate this untoward behavior. By the time Magistrate Winslow arrived on the scene, visitors had already told the Dutchmen that he was coming; the incriminating evidence was quickly hidden away. All Winslow could do was issue a mild warning and leave the Dutchmen to their business.

In 1986, when I played Governor Bradford, I also became engaged in a peculiar, extemporaneous scene with some other interpreters. I was tired from talking with many visitors about the meaning of the Dutch visitation and decided to sneak down one of the back pathways, just to get away for a few minutes. As I approached the bottom of the hill, near the cow barn, I discovered a score of Pilgrim men and women, dancing together in the streets. As the governor, something in me reacted vehemently to this sight—mixed dancing was absolutely not permitted in New Plimoth. I erupted into a scolding tirade on the evils of such untoward behavior and on what a poor showing our village would make to our Dutch guests. The villagers ashamedly apologized. I overheard one spectator say, "Boy, is he pissed!" Actually, I was surprised myself, but my reaction felt right. In truth, many of the scenes in the Pilgrim Village during D-days look more like something out of Breughel than like a settlement of Saints.

At the end of the third day, the Dutch make ready to return to New

Amsterdam. Again, a trumpet is sounded; all assemble in the center of town. Secretary de Rasieres delivers a farewell oration (at noon on this day, the governor had made a speech to the villagers on the outcome of the Dutch visit). Toby Tomkins, in a fine baritone voice, proclaims:

> We must leave you now, with much regret and thanks. Again, I remind you, whereas our two countries have long been allies, so do we affirm our support for you, should the need be, against the French who are your enemies.
>
> (applause)
>
> So let not our nearness be anything of concern, but of comfort, as you do have comfort in this wilderness from the nearness of each man's house to another's. If God favours me, I will come again, or others may; but if I do not, God's blessing upon you all.
>
> (applause; huzzahs. Bradford and de Rasieres descend, entourage and welcoming committee form procession behind drummer, who leads them down the street.) (Travers 1984c)

Governor Bradford escorts the Dutch Party to the bottom flanker. A large group of visitors and villagers, all mixed together, usually follows after them. As the dignitaries embrace and say their farewells, the villagers often sing a parting psalm. The Dutchmen exit out the flanker gate and begin their return voyage to the isle of Manhattos (actually, they are picked up by the truck and driven back to the interpreters' lounge).

After these three days of vigorous feasting and sporting, the interpreters are spent. With all the good beer consumed and all the good fellowship expressed, an air of euphoria permeates the interpreters' lounge at the end of the last day. Hardly anyone gets out of costume right away. Sometimes, more beer is brought out and people start singing the many different songs that they have learned over the course of the season: ditties, ballads, rounds. Thus the reenactment seventeenth-century feast continues into the twentieth-century green-room. I remember that at one of these post-D-days cooldowns, someone suggested Psalm 100 and people spontaneously joined in a gorgeous four-part harmony they had learned that summer. Most of the people in the room have spent a good part of the last seven months living together in the Pilgrim Village. New friendships have been formed, lovers discovered, and, after the reenactment of this archaic harvest ritual, a sense of what Turner (1969) has called spontaneous *communitas* pervades the atmosphere. Someone starts up a Broadway show tune and the interpreters, half in and half out of their Pilgrim costumes, join in. This may go on for an hour or more: songs, jokes, burlesques, more beer. Many people have their arms around each other, relaxing and enjoying the good feelings as the season begins to wind down to its end.

After the "Harvest Home," the real twentieth-century Thanksgiving seems anticlimactic. The most famous scene of all at modern Plimoth Plantation is more of a non-event than a special event. Contemporary Americans who come expecting to find a great feast with turkeys and pumpkin pies and Indians will be disappointed; instead they will meet interpreters who see themselves as "myth-busters."[7] The interpreters will explain how they had a thanksgiving after the 1623 drought, but their harvest feast has never been called Thanksgiving. Visitors who come on Thanksgiving weekend will find the Pilgrims going about the normal day-to-day activities of an agrarian community, preparing for the fast-approaching winter. To them, the fourth Thursday in November was just another working day. Of course, at present-day Plimoth Plantation, these holidays can be some of the busiest times at the box office. All interpreters are required to work at least half of Thanksgiving Day. Usually, an impromptu Thanksgiving dinner is served in the interpreters' lounge, with staff bringing in assorted dishes and the plantation supplying the turkey. Interpreters on break partake of this feast. It is a strange situation: interpreters may have to go back to work, having just gorged themselves on an enormous meal, and, in their Pilgrim roles, tell the visitors that a thanksgiving is really just a day of prayer.

The last day of Thanksgiving weekend is the final day of the season. After this, the "playhouse of the Pilgrims" (both the village and *Mayflower II*) will be shut down for the winter. There is a mixture of sadness and excitement in the air, as there is with the closing of any show. Some of the actor/historians will continue working for the plantation, in the Winter Education Program or in the shop (where reproduction seventeenth-century artifacts are constructed and repaired); others will leave for good; a few will go on the unemployment line.

In the final hour, in the Pilgrim Village, many fond farewells are made to "brothers," "sisters," "husbands," "wives," "fathers," "mothers,"

*Plate 19.* Plimoth Plantation in the off-season
(Photo courtesy of Plimoth Plantation)

"friends," and "neighbors." Hugs and kisses are exchanged in the shadows of the re-created Pilgrim houses. As the visitors gradually leave, interpreters sit in front of their fires, sipping a little contraband tea or wine or whiskey. These will be the last fires to be extinguished in Pilgrim fireplaces for at least four months. Soon, with the coming of the snow, the Pilgrim Village will once again take on the appearance of a ghost town (plate 19).

### THE SHADOW SIDE: HIDDEN AND FORBIDDEN SCENES

Let us turn for a moment to the kinds of scenes that are *not* included in the Theatre of the Pilgrims and examine the reasons for these omissions.

First of all, no scene is represented that would offend general public morality or, more specifically, that morality as it is interpreted by the officers and the board of trustees at the plantation. The governors and the management—the "producers"—of Plimoth Plantation are wary of anything that might create public censure or bad press for their institution. There have been incidents in the past, such as the scandal about the black Pilgrim (see chapter 2, note 6) that have made Plimoth sensitive to the possibility of a negative public image. Today, with its annual general operating budget at $3,911,082 (Plimoth Plantation 1985) the plantation is dependent on the ticket-purchasing public for 90 percent of its revenue. As a tourist production, it must maintain a "G" rating. The museum cannot afford to alienate its customers by presenting interpretations of historical data that would be found offensive.

For example, it is a well-known historical fact that the Pilgrims used the "muck heaps" (compost piles) behind their houses for outdoor toilets. Yet the visitors will never see an interpreter performing such an act. Historical truth, in this case, would upset the sensibility of the present-day museum-going public (and probably that of fellow interpreters as well). This fact of Pilgrim life must be hidden from view (interpreters use a twentieth-century flush toilet that is concealed in one of the re-created seventeenth-century buildings). However, I know of several instances when, since there were no visitors about, interpreters have tried out a reproduction chamber pot or urinated on the muck heap. This kind of experimenting might be compared to actions taken by a Method actor who is trying to prepare for his or her part by asking such questions as "What would it be like to live without flush toilets?", or, to return to the concept of performing ethnography— what are the limits?

In their important article on this subject, Victor and Edith Turner suggest that "culture, social experience and individual psychology combine in complex ways in any 'bit' or 'strip' of human social behavior" (Turner and Turner 1982, 33). As a performance, the living history re-creation at Plimoth perfectly exemplifies Schechner's concept of "restored behavior." But where does the editing of these restored "strips" of behavior begin and end? As Schechner writes, "Restored behavior is living behavior treated as a film director treats a strip of film" (1981, 2). This is a useful analogy in relation to the living museum's reconstruction of history. In order to keep up a "G" rating, certain aspects of the ethnohistorical record must be edited out.

Doesn't this approach conflict with the museum's educational mission—to re-create as truthfully as possible the total material and symbolic culture of the Pilgrims? In its ideal form, set in motion in the late 1960s by James Deetz, the living history method employed at Plimoth

Plantation is a paradigm of performing ethnography. As a model of performance based on the restoration of ethnohistorical behavior, it demonstrates the Turners' conception of "the high reflexive potential of ethnographic performance as a teaching tool, essentially as a means of raising questions about the anthropological research on which they are based" (Turner and Turner 1982, 42). The producers of the living museum, however, apparently want to avoid raising certain questions, especially regarding such difficult subjects as sexuality and perversion.

The prevailing attitude of the producers of contemporary Plimoth Plantation concerning sexual matters seems to reflect the squeamishness of William Bradford himself. In discussing the famous case of John Lyford, a licentious Church of England minister who lived in New Plimoth in 1625 and had, a few years previously in Ireland, "satisfied his lust on" a young female parishioner but "endeavored to hinder conception," Bradford wrote: "The circumstances I forbear, for they would offend chaste ears to hear them related" (1981, 187). This fastidious omission provokes the historical imagination: exactly how did the Reverend Lyford try to "hinder conception"? Isn't this as legitimate an area for historical research as, for instance, how the Pilgrims planted their corn?

The truth is that the more one looks at the historical records, the more one realizes that, even today, the general portrayal of the Pilgrims at Plimoth Plantation, is a kind of cover-up. A seamy side of life in New Plimoth is revealed in *The Records of the Colony of New Plymouth, 1633–1651:* from Master Stephen Hopkins, who "suffers men to drink in his house upon the Lords day," to the "act of adultery and uncleanesse" to "lude & sodomiticall practices" (Shurtleff [1855] 1968). A cursory review of these documents exposes an "X-rated" version of the Pilgrim story. Bradford himself relates in "A Horrible Case of Bestiality" a historical episode that does not match up with the mythologized Pilgrims of the *Mayflower* and the first Thanksgiving. In 1642, a seventeen-year-old boy named Thomas Granger was tried, found guilty, and hanged for committing several acts of bestiality. Before his execution, the animals that he had sodomized were paraded before him and destroyed. Bradford writes: "A very sad spectacle it was. For the mare and then the cow and the rest of the lesser cattle were killed before his face, according to the law, Leviticus XX.15; and then he was executed. The cattle were all cast into a great and large pit that was digged of purpose for them, and no use was made of any part of them" (1981, 356). Although this event took place only fifteen years after the period that is re-created at today's Plimoth Plantation, it is very unlikely that the producers of The Living Museum of 17th Century Plymouth would ever allow such a scene to be reenacted.

Beside bodily functions, eroticism, and sexual perversity, there are many other aspects of Pilgrim history that are not represented in the contemporary living history performance at Plimoth Plantation. I refer to these rejected and repressed facts of history as the "shadow side" of the Pilgrim story. For instance, real human suffering is hardly ever portrayed by the actors/historians. We may hear of Mary Brewster's death and even observe her funeral and the grief of her relatives, but we are never allowed to see Mary herself agonizing in the final stages of her sickness. Such realities of Pilgrim existence as the hardships of working fourteen hours a day at farming or living through the harsh New England winter are not depicted.[8]

The less the shadow side is included in a performance, the less reality it has in general. For "'the living form needs deep shadow if it is to appear plastic. Without shadow it remains a two-dimensional phantom.'" (Carl Jung in Jacobi [1942] 1973, 109) The shadow aspect of the Pilgrim story adds depth and body to the living history performance. In fact, if the performative representations of Pilgrim history are viewed diachronically, it is apparent that more and more of the shadow side has been allowed to penetrate the performance frame. There is certainly more reality in the representation of the Pilgrims today in the Pilgrim Village than there was during the Tercentenary pageant. By the mid-twentieth-century, the sainted ancestors were beginning to slip from their pedestals—but only a little. In the early 1960s, the plantation management could still demand that the hostesses starch and bleach their costumes: "Starched kerchiefs and starched caps and don't let any of your hair show! Bleach! They had to be white! Oh, heavens yes, no yellow in that white!" (Hale et al. 1986). The idea seemed to be that a "pure" people—as the Pilgrims were supposed to be—would have perfectly clean garments. Deetz changed all of that by transforming the Pilgrim Village into a living community where the interpreters labored at authentic seventeenth-century tasks. In Carolyn Travers's words, the Pilgrims had become "real people" (1985).

Real dirt, dust, smoke, animal smells and noises, human cries and laughter entered the picture after 1969. With the development of living history, even more of the shadow side has been allowed into the performance frame. Of course, there is a long way to go. History is still being romanticized in events like the "Festive Wedding." The Pilgrims would probably not recognize most of this reenactment as part of their reality. It is a pretty falsification of history, designed to attract as many tourists as possible. However, compared with the earlier representations of the Pilgrims in performance, the mythicizing, fictionalizing, and sanitizing of Pilgrim history has been considerably decreased.

Finally, I want to mention a few scenes in the Theatre of the Pilgrims that are performed but never witnessed by the audience of visitors. These occur in what MacCannell, using Goffman's terminology, referred to as the "Back region" of a tourist production. In his essay "Staged Authenticity," MacCannell writes: "A back region, closed to audience and outsiders, allows concealment of props and activities that might discredit the performance out front" (1976, 93). In a sense, all the material discussed in this section is related to this notion of back region. As MacCannell explains, the back region is as much a psychological experience as a physical place. The historical information that is kept from public perusal is as much a back region as the actual backstage and offstage areas where interpreters engage in "activities that might discredit the performance out front" (plate 20).

There are many such hidden scenes. Unbeknownst to the visitors, the interpreters, while in costume and, technically, still on the set, engage in outrageously anachronistic behavior. Sometimes satirical skits are performed that stand Pilgrim history on its head. For example, on "Muster Day," 1986, before the gates of the Pilgrim Village were open to the general public, the female interpreters staged a mock trial of two male interpreters. These men were charged and found guilty of "lude & sodomiticall practices." Not only was this a scene that would never be performed for the contemporary ticket-buying public, it also represented a comic reversal of the role of women in seventeenth-century Plimoth, where women were never allowed to be magistrates. In this vignette, which also represents a ritual inversion, a little postmodern feminism penetrated the patriarchal reality of the Pilgrim Fathers.

Perhaps what is most important about the hidden, backstage life of the performers is that the real relationships among the actor/historians

*Plate 20.* Actor/historians backstage in the "goathouse" (Photo by Stephen Snow)

usually create the subtext of the performance that attempts to re-create seventeenth-century reality and that is witnessed by the visitors. "Subtext" is Stanislavski's theatrical terminology for the "inner essence," the deep emotional tone, the psychological nuances of an actor's portrayal of a given scene or character (1963, 136). It is what lies behind the words. The words that the interpreter uses to convey historical information constitute the text of the living history performance, while the real twentieth-century affinities or animosities among interpreters help to create the subtext of the scenes they enact as Pilgrim personalities. On the other hand, the actor/historians sometimes use their role-playing skills to establish and direct authentic relationships with each other. Many a tryst between twentieth-century interpreters has been planned in the guise of a Pilgrim lad chatting with a Pilgrim lass, and real twentieth-century passion has, from time to time, been consummated in the replica of a seventeenth-century bed.

Who these performers are, how they relate to each other and this performance, and how they perceive themselves will be explored in the following chapter.

*Five*

# Actor/Historians

## *The Performers' Background, Training, and Self-Conception*

> Who performers are, how they achieve their temporary or permanent transformations, what role the audience plays—these are the key questions not about dramatic literature but about the living performance event when looked at from the viewpoint of the human beings involved in the performance.
>
> Richard Schechner,
> *Between Theater & Anthropology*, 1985

 few months before the season begins, Plimoth Plantation places an ad in the "Help Wanted" section of local newspapers. This casting call reads as follows:

WANTED: TIME TRAVELERS
Plimoth Plantation is now casting costumed roles for the Pilgrim Village and Mayflower II. Looking for mature, talented people who can study and assume a 17th century dialect and characterization in order to relate the experiences and attitudes of the English colonists to visitors from around the world. Full time (April 1 through November 30) positions open now for persons seeking unique and challenging work. Being capable and flexible isn't a help here—it's a necessity.
(Plimoth Plantation 1986a)

Of the two hundred or so people who apply for this job each year, fifteen are hired (Plimoth Plantation 1986). Most of the individuals who get the job have at least some kind of background in dealing directly with the public, in fields such as sales, teaching, bartending, human services, or, as will be described shortly, the performing arts.

WHO ARE THESE "CULTURAL SPECIALISTS"?

Like the singers, dancers, dramatic performers, storytellers and reenactors of other societies, the actor/historians of Plimoth Plantation are what Milton Singer calls "cultural specialists" (1972). They must become steeped in a cultural tradition—in this case, the ethnohistory of seventeenth-century Plimoth. They must also become skilled at communicating this cultural tradition via *performance*. Singer writes in his study of cultural specialists in India: "One wants to know more about a cultural specialist than can be learned from watching him perform: his recruitment, training, remuneration, motivation, attitude toward this career, his relation to his audience, patron, other performers, and his community—all matters that can best be discovered by interviewing the specialist himself" (1972, 73). Many questions must be asked to uncover the identity of those individuals who become actor/historians. Where do they come from? Why do they want to become Pilgrims? What do they have to say about themselves?

The individuals who become interpreters at Plimoth Plantation come mostly from southeastern Massachusetts, the area from just below Boston to Fall River and from the south shore to the tip of Cape Cod. Many live in towns near Plymouth or in Plymouth itself. A small percentage travel from far away to take the job. In 1984, three new interpreters came from Arizona, Ohio, and New York City; in 1985, three arrived from California, Alabama, and London, England. A small number of English interpreters in the Pilgrim Village is not unusual: in 1984, there were three, and in 1985, four. From 1983 to 1985, an average of forty-one interpreters were employed on a seasonal basis in the Pilgrim Village and eighteen aboard the *Mayflower II*. During the same period, the interpretation staff was divided almost equally between the sexes: 51 percent female, 49 percent male.

The average age of the interpreter is mid- to late twenties. Some say that this is correct for the Pilgrims, since most of the *Mayflower* passengers were young adults themselves. On the other hand, it is difficult to cast such major roles as that of Elder Brewster. Excluding children (usually of the staff) who come in during the summer and play the parts of Pilgrim children, the youngest interpreter would be about six-teen. In 1984, there was such a boy (from a special program in his school) who came at the beginning of the season, but he only lasted a couple of months. The oldest actor/historians are in their sixties. There are commonly two or three retired schoolteachers working in the village or on the ship. However, the majority of interpreters are only recently out of college. The youthfulness of the staff may be explained, in part, by the low salaries: in 1983, starting pay was four dollars per hour and in 1985, five dollars. This economic reality reflects the questionable, if not downright lowly, professional status of the interpreter.

There are many different motivations that bring people to this job. Individuals may come because of their interests in archaeology, his-tory, folklore, crafts, food ways, religion, fantasy, or education. Some come because it's a "fun job"; for others it's "just another job." As one native Plymouthean told me, "That's sort of the industry here, you either pick cranberries or you be a Pilgrim."

It is difficult to draw a distinct personality profile of a typical Pil-grim interpreter, since the staff is usually composed of many different types of individuals. In 1984, there were two interpreters working on novels and two writing doctoral dissertations, an ex-Hollywood actor, a Congregational minister, a nighttime barmaid, a retired high school principal, a college English professor, two trained photographers, a former 4-H instructor, and a self-professed lesbian feminist who fre-quently brought her one-year-old baby boy to work with her. It is the anomalousness of this group that makes their professional identity suspect to many outsiders. Many people look upon the interpreter's job as childish or fly-by-night or see the actor/historians as misfits. Their own jokes and comments indicate that some interpreters intro-ject this negative identity. One interpreter's wife insisted that an adult should be ashamed to do such "silly" work. Some individuals struggle with this sense of illegitimacy about their jobs, and a few work hard toward defining themselves professionally. As seasoned interpreter Kathleen Wall states:

> We're dealing with other peoples' fears and, in order to deal with them effectively, we have to dissipate it completely. That means calling ourselves something else . . . we still haven't decided on what our name is. Are we "cultural interpreters"? Are we "historical infor-

mants"? The whole definition of what we are hasn't been made clear yet, and I don't think it can be, because we're still inventing what we do. (1986)

The interpreters who work at Plimoth Plantation in many ways exemplify what Victor Turner calls "liminal *personae*" (1969, 95). Because Turner's theory of liminality is vital to the subsequent analysis of the overall cultural performance and to this question of the interpreter's identity, I will take a moment to explicate this concept. In developing his ideas about ritual process, Turner borrowed Arnold Van Gennep's (1908) term for the transitional stage of a rite of passage, when an initiand is no longer in his or her old identity but is not yet initiated into a new one. "Liminality" is derived from the Latin word *limen,* meaning "threshold"; it implies a stage of being betwixt and between. To Turner's mind, this is a period of enormous significance, since the individual is freed from the normal constraints of social structure and opened up to new potentials. As Turner wrote: "The liminal in sociocultural process is similar to the subjunctive mood in verbs. . . . Liminality is full of potency and potentiality. It may also be full of experiment and play" (in Benamou and Caramello 1977, 35). The liminal phase in ritual is a time of cultural invention and the transformation of identity.

The interpreters typify liminal personae for two major reasons. First, they are in a profession that is in the process of being invented; in Wall's words, "We're still inventing what we do." The vulnerability of their professional identity is reflected in the fact that many of these young adults are betwixt and between in their own lives. They are between education and a "real job" or just in between jobs. Many are between marriages. Of the forty-three interpreters in the village in 1985, nine were either about to be married or were getting a divorce. Only a small percentage of the interpreters look upon their jobs as real careers; they are aware that they are in a transitional phase of their lives. They are "threshold people" who "elude or slip through the network of classifications that normally locate stages and positions in cultural space" (Turner 1969, 95).

Secondly, like performers all over the world, they take on liminal qualities because their work immerses them in fantasy and play. In fact, one of the main common denominators of personality types who become interpreters is their capacity for play.[1] The job requires that, for eight hours a day, they engage in playacting and live in a fantasy world. They conform to Schechner's model of the "transported performer" (1985, 125–31). Unlike a trance, this is a voluntary transportation; yet as do other cultural specialists who enact a transportation, the interpreters move through a daily performative cycle. Each morning, they (1) *warmup* by getting into their Pilgrim costumes and starting to speak in dialect; they then enter the (2) *performance* by enacting the roles of their Pilgrim characters in a re-created seventeenth-century environment; and, at the end of the day, they (3) *cool down* by taking off their costumes and going to a local bar for a beer.

The main attribute of this type of performance is that the performer returns to ordinary reality basically unchanged. As Schechner points out, "transported performance" is the essence of Euro-American theatre. He contrasts this category with "transformation performance," which is the basis of rites of passage. In that situation, after the experience of an initiation ritual the individual undergoes a real and permanent change in social status and/or identity. Schechner also makes it clear that there are ways in which these two categories of performance combine to affect the life of the performer. A series of transportations, for example, can lead to a transformation, a phenomenon that will be discussed after we explore how the interpreter prepares to enter the role of his or her Pilgrim character. As will be seen, this training process also reflects the interpreter's liminal identity, for, as Schechner writes: "Performer training focuses its techniques not on making one person into another but on permitting the performer to act in between identities: in this sense performing is a paradigm of liminality" (1985, 123).

### ENTERING THE ETHNOHISTORICAL ROLE

The process of entering the Pilgrim role begins with a two-week training session that starts in the middle of March. Each year there is a large turnover of staff, so during the winter months new interpreters must be hired to fill out the ranks. Usually, they come in response to the "Help Wanted" ad depicted at the beginning of this chapter. Around the first of March, each member of the interpretation staff receives "Ye Cast List" in the mail. This consists of a hand-drawn map of the Pilgrim Village, with all the re-created houses represented within the diamond shape of the palisade walls (figure 2). On each house is printed the name of the Pilgrim family who originally inhabited it and

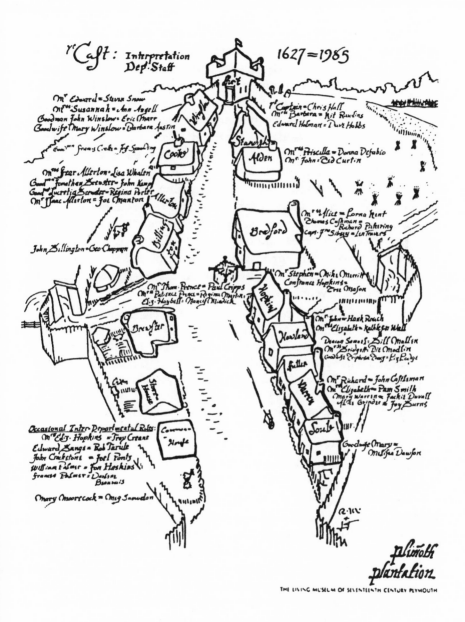

*Figure 2.* "Ye Cast List" for the 1985 season

to the side are written the names of the actor/historians who will portray these roles.

During January, February, and the first two weeks of March, prospective interpreters stop by the interpretation office and pick up their two-volume training manuals, dialect tapes, historical texts, and other research materials. Most important is the biograph, the document that begins to define who the interpreter will be in the village for the next eight months. Before 1985, each interpreter received both a documentary biograph and a personation biograph. The former gave the character's basic demographics: age, religious persuasion, place of origin, former address in the Netherlands (if applicable), occupation, parents' names, children's names, marriage record, ship arrived on. The latter provided basic directions for characterization that resembled Shavian descriptions of dramatis personae. These elaborate delineations of Pilgrim personalities were based on the interpretations of the staff members who devised them. For instance, when I played Richard Warren in 1984, my personation biograph gave me suggestions concerning Master Warren's psychological state:

> He feels he is being overlooked, and he *is, not* because of anything undeserving on his part, or anything he has *done* but because of things he may *not* have done; ruthlessly aspiring men like Standish, Alden & Prence have overshadowed quiet competence. So Richard now adopts their lead, hoping to regain the prominence he feels he has lost. All this is not to say that he is depressed; he is extremely proud of his large family and large (comparatively) house, and looks forward to the weddings (and connections) his daughters will provide—in fact, one may not be too far off.

Indications such as these start the interpreter on his or her central task of building a character.

In 1985, a new approach was attempted. Each interpreter was asked to create a written biographical sketch that would integrate all the study material and "supply your characterization with a personal focus" (DeFabio 1985f). This procedure was designed to make the interpreters think for themselves. It also suggested more sophisticated techniques for helping the interpreter identify with his or her character. For instance, regarding a famous episode from Pilgrim history (before 1627), the Guide to Developing Characterizations advises the interpreter to "*Visualize* the scene, using what knowledge you have of 17th-century life. *You* are the one that must examine the data and eventually draw some conclusions so you can discuss your character's past accurately and sincerely with visitors" (DeFabio 1985f).

Sometime after the second week in March, formal training begins. Prospective and returning interpreters are given a series of lectures with titles such as "17th-century World View," "Social Order in New Plimoth," "Foodways in Plimoth Colony," and "The Military System of Plimoth Colony." Most of these subjects are also discussed at length in the training manual, so interpreters are expected to be very knowledgeable about all this material. In addition to specific information that will aid the interpreter in becoming a Pilgrim, the new staff is introduced to the total living museum organization: management team, marketing, media service, visitor services, curatorial services, and educational department. The introductory program is a joint effort of the interpretation and research departments. Research staff are constantly available to assist the interpreter with anything relating to the intellectual culture of the Pilgrims. Interpreters also have access to the Plimoth Plantation library, which contains some three thousand volumes.

Along with all this historical and intellectual preparation comes some very traditional theatrical training. Each interpreter must learn a specific seventeenth-century English dialect; at present, four regional dialects are used in the Pilgrim Village. Just as in the theatre, well-executed dialect contributes to a good characterization. Interpreters spend hours listening to the tape of their particular dialect specimen and learning the phonic symbol key. In the last few years, study of these dialects has become more sophisticated. In 1984, the plantation received a $45,000 grant from the National Endowment for the Humanities, part of which was used to research dialects in the Pilgrim district of East Anglia (this was reported in Robert MacNeil's television documentary special, "The History of the English Language," in 1985). Also, Martyn Wakelin, a medieval English dialect specialist, has been called in as a consultant. Today, just as an actor preparing for a Shakespearean play would do, the interpreter must master a specific seventeenth-century English vernacular, with all its strange and sometimes difficult vowel sounds and diphthongs.

Here is where the interpreter begins to become the actor/historian. She has been assigned a character and thousands of pages of research materials. She has practiced her dialect with her colleagues, especially newcomers with veterans. Now, she must transform herself into her Pilgrim character. She is advised thus: "As you immerse yourself in reading your training materials, remember that you will be portraying a person that did once actually live and breathe upon this earth, a person that *thought* and *felt*. Trying to discover what thoughts and feelings your character might appropriately express is a delicate process" (DeFabio 1985f). Of course, this "delicate process" is part and parcel of the art of acting. For the new interpreter, there are lectures such as "Informant Method and Characterization" to aid her in creating her role. Also, the neophyte is surrounded by experienced actor/historians, known simply as the deacon, the captain, or Goody Brewster. These old hands have been in the village for six, seven, eight seasons. They feel perfectly at home in their characters, which have become like alter egos to them. Many of these seasoned veterans have enacted their roles for thousands of days—a much longer period than most Broadway shows!

However, the actor/historians must transform themselves into their characters without the benefit of much group rehearsal. As Schechner states: "This is not a play the performers are preparing for but a more improvisational world of interaction not only among themselves but with the tourists who visit the Plantation daily" (1985, 84). In the Goffmanian sense, the two-week training in March is simply the time in which the interpreter formulates his or her "front" (Goffman 1959, 22). As April first approaches, the veteran interpreters, who have been through the "interaction ritual" with the public myriad times and have their "act together," are calm. Many of the new interpreters, though, who are trying out their dialects and characterizations in public for the first time, are as nervous as novice actors on an opening night. Therefore, the day before the season opens, a dress rehearsal is held. As the 1984 Informant Training Schedule reports:

3/29 Thurs. 1:00–5:00 PM
Dress Rehearsal: an In-Costume, In-Dialect, In-Character, In-Village, In-itiation to the joys of Role-playing Interpretation, sans Visitors!

During the regular season, rehearsals are held infrequently. For some special events, such as the "Governor's Council" or "Court Days," the participating interpreters will gather in the interpreters' lounge to read through a script (if there is one, which is seldom the case) or to discuss the basic actions of a scenario. Usually one of the supervisors is present to guide the exchange of ideas and make sure that everyone is aware of the overall game plan; this would probably be either Len Travers or Donna DeFabio, who most commonly design these scenarios. They serve as directors, explaining where and when specific actions are to take place and pointing out how particular characters are to be presented for the occasion; such actions, however, are rarely carried out. These rehearsals are very informal, since for the most part speech and action are improvised during the event itself.

Rehearsals for the songs and, sometimes, the dances that are performed at the "Festive Wedding" and the "Harvest Feast" are stricter. Since complicated harmonies or special period choreography must be learned, interpreters are expected to come prepared to these rehearsals. Breaks are scheduled during the regular working day, so that interpreters can come up from the village and spend time practicing the songs and dances they will perform for these special events. Interpreters also have a model for traditional theatrical rehearsal in the preparation of the plays that are now produced as a regular part of the Winter Education Program. Many interpreters, having already had some kind of theatrical experience, are familiar with terms such as "learning lines," "blocking," and "projection."

However, the real training for the actor/historians at Plimoth Plantation is of the on-the-job variety. This is really a sink or swim situation. A few interpreters usually quit after the first few weeks of work, knowing right away that the job is not for them. Others, either because of disposition or former training, take to the improvisational nature of the performance and eventually become fearless at extemporizing in seventeenth-century dialect, even before a daily audience of three to four thousand (as is the case each August). The skills of the actor/historian are so specialized that it takes a long time to master them. Those few interpreters who stay on for many years form what amounts to a kind of repertory company. Their repertoire consists of the annual special events, which they know inside and out, having become versed in the minute details of Pilgrim history. They can also sometimes play several characters. They will have worked together creatively for so long that they all feel perfectly comfortable in the illusory world of the re-created seventeenth-century village.

It is these few veteran interpreters who truly become cultural specialists. After many years of study and performance they have become steeped in authentic Pilgrim culture and are highly skilled role-players. I would say that of the forty-three interpreters employed in the village in 1985, about a dozen would fit into this category. They are few because of the temporary nature of the job and the low pay scale; however, they do return, season after season, and, I believe, some are truly transformed by their commitment to this performance.

Schechner has presented some excellent models of this kind of transformation. In his essay "Performers and Spectators Transported and Transformed" (1985, 117–50), he writes of an Indian performer, Mahant Baba Omkar Das, who, after years of performing in the *Ramlila* of Ramnagar, has become so identified with his role (Narad-muni) that he is no longer addressed by his birth name but by that of the semidivine sage whom he portrays in the cycle play. There are similar situations with the living history performers at Plimoth. For example, William Mullin, Jr., a retired high school principal, who for many seasons played the role of Deacon Samuel Fuller, was commonly addressed as "Deacon Fuller." Whenever any of his colleagues on the interpretation staff came down with a cold or headache, "Deacon Fuller" would immediately recommend an herbal cure. Mullin's real-life knowledge of herbal medicine came from studying the background for his part. Historically, Samuel Fuller was the Pilgrims' approximation of a physician and pharmacist rolled into one. In both the Ramnagar and Plimoth cases, there is some degree of real transformation taking place in the performer after years of repeating his role. The extent of the change is much greater in the Indian example, in part because of the longevity of the performer's experience. After thirty-five years of performing Narad-muni, Mahant Baba Omkar Das has gained great wealth and prestige from being identified with his role (Schechner 1985, 123). Nothing so astonishing has happened to William Mullin, Jr., but because he has been an amiable and well-informed actor/historian over the course of six or seven seasons, he has gained the respect, admiration, and affection of his fellow interpreters.

Since the interpreters at Plimoth, like actors in Euro-American theatre, are fundamentally transported performers, after a performance they return to ordinary reality, with no changes in personality or social status; they go home at the end of the day essentially the same people they were at the beginning. However, there are instances, as in the case of "Deacon Fuller," when a performer's playing the Pilgrim role over an extended period of time results in some small or partial changes in personal identity. Schechner writes: "If a change occurs within the performer, or in his status, it happens only over a long series of performances, each of which move the performer slightly . . . a series of transportation performances can achieve a transformation" (1985, 126).

Applying Schechner's model to the living history performance at Plimoth, I can see several ways in which the interpreters are "slightly" moved or changed in their personal lives as a consequence of their being in this performance over a period of time. There is, for some, a gradual accruement of Pilgrim characteristics in their real-life behavior. This may begin with casual actions such as those mentioned in chapters 3 and 4: one goes home at night continuing to speak in Pilgrim dialect, or one continues to use seventeenth-century English script in everyday writing. Veteran interpreters often drive to work wearing their Pilgrim costumes or walk around downtown Plymouth on their lunch hours with their costumes still on. Parts of their Pilgrim costumes may even become part of their everyday attire.

Deeper changes can also occur and affect an individual interpreter's emotional and psychological life. In 1985, interpreter Barbara Austin wrote to me, describing how moving she had found being part of the Winslow family, one of the larger re-created extended families in the Pilgrim Village. "I've truly believed in, and loved, our family. . . . I'm proud of our family and what we all created," she wrote (see chapter 4, note 6). This deep experience of *communitas* provided by the role play is not uncommon among interpreters and creates strong bonds that frequently lead to enduring friendships. I too had an intense emotional response to aspects of being a Pilgrim role-player for two seasons. First of all, the thrill of the "roots" experience of re-creating the cultural life of my seventeenth-century ancestors changed my attitude toward the Pilgrims from a snide, negative one to a much more empathetic and accepting one. Secondly, the sense of community that develops in playing out the life of this little village was very moving to me. On my last day as a regular interpreter, a group of "villagers" sneaked up behind my character's (Edward Winslow's) house and serenaded me with a three-part harmony rendition of the Twenty-third psalm. I was so touched that I could not hold back the tears. It made me realize how much I had been affected by living for so many months in the Pilgrim role.

These kinds of experiences undoubtedly leave some lasting marks on the personality of the interpreter. After many seasons of playing the role of a Pilgrim, an interpreter may undergo some partial transformation, coming to a point at which it is not always easy to distinguish the boundaries between the self and the role. Eventually, being transported many times as a Pilgrim impersonator will leave some slight but permanent imprint. The build-up of residues from daily performances will finally result in some small transformations in the real person: a way of walking or talking, a way of wearing one's clothes, a way of being addressed or responding to a name, and even a way of looking at the world.

THE PERFORMERS' OWN CONCEPT OF WHAT THEY DO

The Pilgrim interpreters prepare a role, are trained in a dialect and in how to wear a seventeenth-century costume, play their characters on a daily basis for a ticket-purchasing public, and are "transported," via their performances, to the illusory scene of seventeenth-century Plimoth. Schechner states that the transported performer is "identical to the actor" (1985, 131). James Carroll identifies these living history performers as "actor/historians" (1984, 34). But do the interpreters consider themselves to be actors?

As we have seen, the question of theatrical identity is frequently and heatedly debated among the members of the interpretation staff, some of whom can argue forcefully for either side. Kathleen Wall, a seven-season veteran who has played five different roles in the Pilgrim Village, explains her reluctance to define herself as an actress thus:

> When I came here ["actor"] was a naughty word. So part of that is strictly trained into me. I mean there was no greater way they could belittle what we were doing here than to call us "actors." They looked down their noses. There's still that very puritanical idea and I *am* a New Englander. . . . Opera singers are one thing, but *actors* quite another. And there is, even now, that attitude amongst people like the board of directors and the trustees. . . . That's always been the problem with first person—it was *acting:* it was *fakelore* instead of folklore. And there's a lot of resistance to that. When I came here the program was only four or five years old.

It was a brand new baby. So there was very strong resistance and we really had to fight to define ourselves as something legitimate and as something necessary in the museum world, as separate from something theatrical. (Wall 1986)

We will return to Wall's conception of what it means to be an interpreter in a moment, but it is important to note here that her statement points up two of the main fears concerning the actor identity. Firstly, to be labeled an actor in the museum world is to be considered something illegitimate; this reflects the ancient antitheatrical prejudice that has been so clearly delineated by Jonas Barish (1981). Secondly, to be acting is to be faking, i.e., to be re-creating history based on misinformation. This is the most serious criticism of identifying first-person interpretation with acting.

The pros and cons of the interpreters' actor identity will be elucidated in this section by members of the interpretation staff. During the period 1984 to 1986, I interviewed many interpreters about this central question, and some of their responses follow. To my mind, there is a spectrum between the poles of actor and historian, and most interpreters are probably better suited to one than the other. My position, which I will discuss later, is that the best interpreters integrate the two functions, becoming true actor/historians.

Leonard Travers, Jr., who was the Director of Interpretation at Plimoth Plantation for several years during the 1980s, is from Dartmouth, Massachusetts, and has a Ph.D. in history from Boston University. Travers began working as an interpreter in May 1980. After Robert Marten was fired, in the fall of 1981, Travers assumed that position. He has an extensive background in amateur theatre, having performed in many plays including *Rosencrantz and Guildenstern Are Dead, The Three Musketeers,* and *Room Service,* at his undergraduate college. However, Travers does not view first-person interpretation as acting. He admits that it has "features" of performance, but says that its primary purpose is educational, "to teach people something about the Pilgrims." Although Travers concedes that interpreting a Pilgrim role does require some acting skills, he did not consider himself an actor when he worked as an interpreter in the village. He says:

No. There wasn't a script and there weren't constant stage directions, so I felt a lot more free and easy with my environment. I felt more in control, in command of the situation, and never having to worry about "blowing a line," if you will. There was another kind of pressure, to be sure, but some of the things I found to be pressure in theatre were removed there [in the Pilgrim Village]. I had a chance to speak to the audience, to come down off the stage, if you will, and talk more personally with the visitors, and to share some knowledge, impart some knowledge to them. So, no [I didn't feel like an actor]. Although, I certainly did still think of it often in theatrical terms: whether or not I was "hamming it up"—hamming up my portrayal—whether or not my role was believable, things of that nature. You can never divorce the two [first-person interpretation and acting] I think. (Travers 1986)

James Baker, Vice President of Museum Operations at Plimoth, has a similar perspective. Like many members of the plantation's administrative staff, both men express ambivalence about considering the living museum a theatrical performance. It may be true that "you can never divorce the two," but Travers and Baker both value the educational mission of the living history performance over its theatrical aspect. Travers believes that the interpreters' pedagogical objectives are more important than the portrayal of believable characters (1986). As cited in chapter 2, Baker somewhat reluctantly concedes that there is a theatrical component to this living history representation of the Pilgrims; he says that it "uses a theatrical method just as an orator uses a rhetorical method to get his points across" (1985b). But both these men basically refute the idea that the interpreter is, in fact, an actor.

The opposing position is taken up by veteran interpreter Christopher Robert Hall, who unequivocally views the interpreter as an actor. Hall has spent four seasons in the village and played several roles, including Captain Standish. He is highly respected by both colleagues and visitors. Hall was brought up in Freeport, Maine, and earned a B.A. in history from Gordon College. He is 27 years old. He had worked as museum guide at the Stephen Phillips Memorial Trust House in Salem, Massachusetts, before coming to the plantation at the beginning of the 1983 season. Even though Hall's only experience as an actor was in a high school production of *A Midsummer Night's Dream,* he is confident that, after four years of working as a costumed interpreter in the Pilgrim Village, he could easily become a professional actor. He already considers himself an actor, explaining: "I can say something and believe it. I'm a damned good liar—I believe myself for a while. I can say entire untruths because it's true while I'm saying it . . . when I'm Standish I believe it. For that moment, I believe it" (Hall 1985).

Hall further testifies as to why he deems first-person interpretation to be acting:

> To put forward and feel emotions that you normally wouldn't feel, things that you wouldn't normally have a heavy-duty emotion on. . . . To get really upset about what the Spanish are doing [in 1627]; to get really upset about King James's conduct at a certain point, when he started placating the Spanish instead of sending an army over there. . . . Yes, it's acting, but acting with *good content*—acting with content. And without content, I think we're wasting . . . well, we're not wasting our time—we're putting on a little show that keeps them [the visitors] from going to sleep. (Hall 1985)

Thus Hall honors the educational intention of the performance—the "content"—while at the same time considering himself a professional performer, an actor. His ideas about his performance resemble Schechner's notions of performing in general: "It is behavior that is 'put on.' This is what gives theater its bad name. Theater is the art where the master teacher says, 'Truth is what acting is all about; once you can fake truth you've got it made' " (1985, 121). It is this enjoyment of faking truth, of being able to "say entire untruths because it's true while I'm saying it" that takes Hall's work into the realm of acting. He relishes the act of being in between identities. He delights in the game: being in a role and speaking in the first person as though he really were someone else, while simultaneously maintaining consciousness of himself, Christopher Hall. As he told me in our interview, he gets tremendous pleasure and satisfaction from game-playing. He is, in fact, one of the participants in the regular gathering of male interpreters who play military history games (see note 1 in this chapter). All of these factors would seem to indicate that Hall is one of those ludic personalities that is particularly well-adapted to the interpreter's role-playing function.

"Ludic" is a term that I have borrowed from Johan Huizinga's classic work *Homo Ludens* (1955), a study of the "play element in culture." Ludic derives from the Latin *lūdere*, which means both "to play" and "to mock." As we will see in the final section of this chapter, the interpreters at Plimoth mock Pilgrim history both by imitating it and by making fun of it. Hall's fun-loving sense of playfulness and gamesmanship could be described as a ludic characteristic of his personality. As he says himself, "I'm a damned good liar," or, in the words of journal writer John Engstrom: "The actor, Christopher Hall, is clearly relishing his part as he marches up and down and barks out commands like a 17th-century General Patton" (1985, 40).

Nancy Mindick was one of the most popular interpreters with the general public. She constantly received compliments from visitors for her characterization of the maidservant Edith Pitts. Mindick grew up in Massachusetts and started working at the plantation at the age of twenty-two, immediately after completing her B.A. in English at Bridgewater State College in southeastern Massachusetts. In college, she studied both improvisational acting and playwrighting. She told me that she found this background immensely helpful to her work as an interpreter. Mindick is articulate about why she considers first-person interpretation to be acting (see also the opening quotation in chapter 3):

> It fits into what my definition of acting is, or of improvisational acting. We have to live the lives of these characters, the Pilgrims. We're showing their versions of the world. We're not showing our own. We have to embody the mind-set of these people. You laugh with these people; you live with these people. It's not you. I guess it's part of you. There's a place where you and the character meet. It's a really exciting place. You find that common point between yourself and the character. And that's really exciting. You really live with that character. (Mindick 1985)

Mindick is describing that in-between space of performing in which the life of the performer interfaces with that of the character or role. I have referred to this space as liminal. Schechner interprets such space as being the essence of performance: "This constant movement in the liminal space 'not me . . . not not me' is the matrix of performance. Olivier is not Hamlet, but he's also not not Hamlet; and the reverse is also true: Hamlet is not Olivier but he's also not not Olivier" (1981, 39).

The double negative defines a transitional way of being that is at the very heart of the art of acting. For Mindick, this transitional state is realized in the "common point" where she is not Edith Pitts, but she is also not not Edith Pitts. In this frame of acting in between identities, Mindick is able to actualize her creativity and sense of play.

Nancy Mindick has an exceptionally active imagination and a natural gift for characterization; many interpreters do not have such a strong sense of the reality of their Pilgrim characters. For Nancy Mindick, Edith Pitts was indeed "real." During our interview, she spoke fondly, almost protectively of the maidservant. The actor/historian said of her character: "She was a real person. She has a heart . . . she's a real human being" (Mindick 1985). Many interpreters do not have such a talent for creative dissociation.

Ironically, Mindick's gift for role-playing eventually led to her demise as an interpreter. Her being a crowd-pleaser and a star made other interpreters jealous and resentful. They began to use her lowly identity as a female servant as a way to humiliate her in real life. As Mindick reported in 1985, with some chagrin: "Sometimes I feel as if I'm treated by plantation people as if I'm still in a role . . . sometimes I feel as if I'm treated like a woman—a seventeenth-century woman!" (1985). The success of her characterization undoubtedly created feelings of animosity toward her in some staff members. Unlike the example of William Mullin, Jr., whose identification with his role was treated amicably and positively by other interpreters, Mindick represents an instance in which such identification was exploited in an abusive way. Mindick quit the plantation after her second season, in 1985, because of the low pay, the lack of job security, and, mainly, because of the negative experience of her colleagues' competitiveness and hostility.

To my mind, Mindick reflects both the ludic and liminal characteristics of the quintessential performer. She delighted in the game of role-playing and also possessed that special ability to play in between identities. Perhaps, in the context of a living history museum, she was just a little bit too good at it. She was definitely located toward the actor end of the actor↔historian spectrum. However, she was always serious about her play and, in Hall's sense, always brought good "content" to her performance. One old hand, who had over a decade of experience in the Pilgrim Village, called her "one of the best interpreters" that he had ever witnessed.

Kathleen Wall, who has described herself as a "career Pilgrim," is one of the most responsible and respected of the interpreters. As already cited, she is situated more toward the historian end of the actor↔historian spectrum. Wall is 29 years old, grew up in the Plymouth area and has a B.A. in English and history, also from Bridgewater State. She began working as an interpreter in September 1980. She does not consider herself to be a performer: "Not in any way I would define [performing]. I'm not performing. I'm explaining. I'm talking. I'm doing things, but I'm not performing as such" (1986). Wall sees herself more in the capacity of educator than of actress. She has been employed full-time as a first-person interpreter since the 1981 season, when she began doing the Winter Education Program (see chapter 4, note 8). Along with a core group of other interpreters, Wall maintains year-round employment as a Pilgrim by going out in the off-season and giving first-person educational workshops on Pilgrim culture. As she explains:

> I saw a whole new aspect of how to be a Pilgrim. How not to be a Pilgrim in the confines of a particular setting, but how to be a Pilgrim anywhere. How to go into a classroom—that particular setting—and, for one hour, take over the class and say, "I'm talking about the seventeenth-century. You listen and you listen good." And just having these kids absolutely screaming and yelling by the time you leave, because they're so excited they want to travel back in time with you. They want to leave behind TVs and Pac-Mans. (Wall 1986)

Here is the voice of a teacher interested in stimulating young minds. (These "winter ed" workshops are offered to students ranging from first grade through high school.)

However, when Wall discusses how she transforms herself into a Pilgrim character, she begins to sound more like an actress than teacher:

> It's hard because you never prepare for it. You sort of set yourself up and, then, you keep going with it. It's not a static thing. It's very kinetic and it changes. Elizabeth Howland [one of the Pilgrims that Wall has portrayed] was "June Allyson." I didn't start off saying, "Oh, yeah, let's play her like 'June.' Lets make her perky and bright and short. . . ." It's a sort of thing you build. . . . I'm someone else now. Susannah Winslow is "Audrey Hepburn." I looked at all she [the character] went through and, I thought, "only a tourist would

put up with this!" The only tourist I could think with a faintly Dutch accent [Susanah Winslow had lived in Holland] was Audrey Hepburn—and she's Belgian! There are a lot of parallels between Audrey Hepburn's life and Susannah Winslow's. . . . I think of her [Hepburn] because I was making a switch from one character to another and needed something to hold onto. (Wall 1986)

Wall has played five different characters in the Pilgrim Village. It is interesting that she says she never prepares for her role, because, in the course of our interview, I discovered that she bases her decision on how she will play a given character—what her interpretation will be— on extensive knowledge of her biograph and other historical evidence available to her. The content of her first-person role-playing performance is always substantial. The historian in her attempts to know as much as possible about her character's familial, social, political, and religious background, even to the point of being able to interpret the kind of vocabulary this character might have possessed (Wall 1986).

On the other hand, Wall's method of identifying with her role by means of relating it to a famous personality would be familiar to many actors. I remember once observing a director at the New York Shakespeare Festival, who, confronted with an actor who was completely baffled as to how to interpret a character in one of Shakespeare's chronicle plays, instructed the actor to think of his character as Robert Kennedy. The rationale for this suggestion is the same as for Wall's using the image of June Allyson or Audrey Hepburn to help her get into her Pilgrim part: the need for "something to hold onto." As Wall mentioned in the interview, seventeenth-century people can be highly enigmatic to twentieth-century interpreters, so some bridge is needed, something to help the interpreter identify with his or her role. By utilizing such a strategy for psychological identification with the character, Kathleen Wall presents a synthesis of the two functions of the actor/historian. She is, here, seeming very much like an actor.

Finally, I want to include the perspective of two professional actors who have worked at Plimoth Plantation. I think their ideas and attitudes will throw more light on how the interpreter functions as a performer.

Joffrey David Spaulding, a forty-six-year-old actor/writer originally from Boston, has traveled extensively and lived for many years in Los Angeles. He was trained as a performer at the Boston Conservatory, the Long Island Institute of Music, and Los Angeles City College. He was a member of the Screen Actors Guild and has taught acting classes for film directors at the American Film Institute. In twenty-five years as an actor, he has appeared in over eighty plays. In 1983, shortly before coming to the plantation, he appeared in *River Trip* at Lincoln Center in New York City. During the 1984 season, he portrayed the character Stephen Hopkins in the Pilgrim Village. In our interview, he told me that he prepared for his Pilgrim role in basically the same way he would for a theatrical role. He believes that all the interpreters should be trained in acting skills and thinks that the present-day plantation is most successful as a form of entertainment:

> I think it has more value as theatre than it does as historical information. I think it makes a wonderful tourist attraction because of its entertainment value, and it's a wonderful gig for the people who work there—as an experience in theatre. Historically, I don't think it has one half the value it does theatrically. . . . It aims at being 50 percent education and 50 percent entertainment, whether that's admitted or not, that's what it *aims* at. What it succeeds in doing is giving maybe 75 percent entertainment and 25 percent historical education. And I think of the 25 percent historical education as much as maybe 15 percent is not a correct interpretation of the times. (Spaulding 1986)

Ironically, it is Spaulding the actor who calls for a more authentic embodiment of history. Perhaps because he is a more sophisticated performer than many interpreters, his view of the interaction between the public and the interpreter is more critical. He says that "the only true communication I had with a visitor to the plantation was on a truly modern sense of humor, sense of retrospective . . . the person asking the question and myself answering had an unspoken agreement that 'Yes, this little parody's going on, but the fact is *what* in modern terms?' So, really, you were always talking in modern terms" (Spaulding 1986). Many interpreters admired Joffrey Spaulding's characterization of Stephen Hopkins, but I think Spaulding became disillusioned with the artistic level of the performance in the village. He wanted to see a more profound and subtle re-creation of the characters and the times. He left at the end of the 1985 season.

Another point of view belongs to forty-four-year-old actor Toby

Tomkins, a graduate of Yale University who has been working in professional theatre for over twenty years. He has appeared at the American Shakespeare Festival, the Actors' Theatre of Louisville, and the Charles Street Playhouse, among many others. As explained in chapter 4, in 1982 Tomkins began coming up from New York City each season to play the role of Isaack de Rasieres in the three-day "Harvest Feast." During 1984–85, he rewrote the play *The Evidence Before Us* (originally written by Len Travers), which was performed by the male interpretation staff for the "winter ed" program. In 1986, Tomkins wrote a play especially for Plimoth Plantation, also to be performed as part of the educational outreach programs.[2]

Although Tomkins believes that the essential purpose of the Pilgrim Village is educational, he also feels that the interpreters are fundamentally the same as actors. This is how he explains living history performance to other New York theatre people:

> A lot of people in New York, especially those sort of pseudo-sophisticates in the theatre—I'll say I'm doing a living history thing and [they will respond]: "Oh yeah, see the two-headed snakes or Disney World or something like that?!" I'll say, "No, it's a total environment, everything is very authentic and all the people who work there have characters, which they've carefully built up with research" and so forth. Many of them will say, "I'm not an actor. I'm a museum professional . . ." but they're working exactly the same way actors do . . . they blur their background, they get a character, they get comfortable in the clothes, they get their activity, they know what they're doing. . . . And basically, this is (technically considered) "improvisation from a character"—only it's eight hours a day! (Tomkins 1985)

Tomkins emphasizes that interpreters work "exactly the same way actors do." Like actors, interpreters must develop a skill for becoming a character. They must learn to adapt their psychological instrument to the shape of their character; find ways to empathize with their role; duplicate the emotions of their character in a given situation. If their character is angry at King James's conduct, then they must find a way to feel that emotion. More than anything, they must identify with the actions of their character. They must feel "as if" they were carrying out these actions for the first time, and that they only arrived on the

*Mayflower* seven years ago. Of course, the great difference is that the actor usually performs for two hours on the stage; the interpreter improvises for a whole workday.

During our interview, Tomkins expressed his great enjoyment of first-person role-playing as a seventeenth-century Dutchman. He says:

> It's been a real tonic to my own work as an actor. To have been able to come up here once a year and gone inside that palisado and been somebody else for *that* length of time. It's a stretch to continually, more or less, well, not jump in and out of character, but jump in and out of time; jump in and out of conventions. . . . It's unlike anything I've ever done before, but I still think it does partake of the same sort of techniques that I've always used as an actor. (Tomkins 1985)

I agree with Tomkins. I think that creating roles in the Pilgrim Village does require acting skills. Travers has expressed his concern about the "believability" of the Pilgrim character. Hall speaks of the importance of empathizing with the emotions of the Pilgrim he is portraying. Mindick recounts her discovery of that "place where you and the character meet." And Wall relates her own method of getting into role by identifying with the personality of a famous movie star. Without a doubt, the goals of the first-person interpreter are very much like those of an actor preparing a part for a play. Both want to conjoin themselves with their assigned character. However, at Plimoth, this is being done largely without the benefit of consciously employed techniques. Of the forty-three interpreters working in the Pilgrim Village in 1985, only about five or six had substantial acting training. About 50 percent of the total staff had some kind of acting experience, and the rest were working from instinct, aided by an especially complete naturalistic set and the relaxed atmosphere of a repetitive daily routine.

I came to the job with a fairly extensive background in both amateur and professional theatre.[3] I considered myself to be a competent character actor, by which I mean I enjoy playing parts that are different from my own personality. I take a particular delight in what some actors call "stretching." Plimoth Plantation afforded me the opportunity to play several different roles: in 1984, I portrayed Richard Warren; in 1985, I played the part of Edward Winslow; and I appeared as Governor William Bradford in the 1986 "Harvest Feast."

Working as a costumed interpreter in the Pilgrim Village, I found myself utilizing many of the same techniques that I have used when acting. As I was, early on, trained in the Stanislavski approach, I found myself almost automatically reconnecting with his basic procedural concepts regarding characterization:

> As for inner characterization, it can be shaped only from an actor's own inner elements. These must be felt and chosen to fit the image of the character to be portrayed. . . . If this is effectively prepared, the outer characterization should naturally follow. . . . Let every actor achieve this outer characterization by using material from his own life, from that of others, real and imaginary, by using his intuition, self-observation . . . by studying paintings or books . . . or by noting accidental occurrences—in short from every possible source. (Stanislavski 1963, 33)

Let me give a few specific examples of how I used Stanislavskian techniques, both inner and outer, to prepare for my Pilgrim roles.

When I began creating the role of Richard Warren, I wrote out a brief imaginary biography of the major events in his life *before* 1627, in order to clarify my image of the given circumstances of his life and to help me identify with them. I tried to see myself in his situation and to intuit what it would feel like to live in his life and times. I have often used this method to create a memory for my characters. On the external level, I carefully studied a period portrait of Sir Francis Bacon in order to find the right physical stance (*gestus*) for my characterization. Although it was an imperfect analogy (Bacon was of a much higher class than Warren), I imitated the basic pose, especially the way he wore his hair, beard, and clothes. I used this same procedure when I was developing my characterization of Edward Winslow.

When I portrayed Master Warren as a magistrate during "Court Days" in September 1984, I used Stanislavki's system of "units and objectives" (Stanislavski [1936] 1963, 105–19) to help engage myself in the action of that special scene. As a judge in the court of New Plimoth, I had to try several cases. Using the method of units and objectives, I broke the whole script down into several well-defined actions. Stanislavski developed this technique to help actors focus on the basic actions or "stage task," and to make it easier for them to memorize a script. In this approach, actors are required to analyze and name the "units" or "beats" of a given scene. For example, in the courtroom episode, I entitled my concluding unit "The Denial." The aim of this labelling is to locate the essential quality of the action. Following Stanislavski's prescription, I used a verb to identify my objective in this unit: "I want to explain clearly to Master Hopkins why we have denied his petition so that he will understand and relinquish this course of folly." My stage task was really to convince my fellow actor/historian to give up the error of his ways—to make him really feel that he should finally terminate his petitioning of the court for the right to set up an Ale-House in New Plimoth.

Most non-actors do not realize that when an actor plays a scene he or she is, in fact, earnestly trying to accomplish an action—that the basis of dramatic acting is not pretending but doing. This intentional doing causes genuine responses between the partners in a scene as the actions are carried out. Defining and focusing on the units and objectives of a given scene enables actors to engage themselves more truthfully in their stage tasks.

Another Stanislavskian technique I used in preparing for a Pilgrim role was "emotion memory" (Stanislavski [1936] 1963, 154–81), which I employed in building the character of Edward Winslow. I wanted to capture the intense feeling that Master Winslow must have had for the beautiful country estate he had left behind in England. In order to create this strong sense of nostalgic longing, I would focus my memory specifically on a place where I had lived and that I had loved. I did this both through visual recollection of that place and through the sense of smell. I would recall the scent of apple blossoms at springtime in my special place, and this would fill me with a great yearning to be there. In this way, I could feel the kind of homesickness that Master Winslow must have felt for Worcestershire.

Another technique that I found particularly valuable in preparing to play Governor William Bradford in 1986 was the use of a "super-objective" (Stanislavski [1936] 1963, 256–65). Stanislavski stressed that actors should choose bold, resonate, truthful, energizing super-objectives as they develop their roles in the context of the whole play. Here, of course, the play consisted of all the events of the year 1627 at Plimoth Plantation. On the other hand, this was only one year in Bradford's long life, so I needed to answer the question of what had motivated William Bradford throughout his entire life. In a sense, the super-objective is the character's life's purpose. Everything he or she does leads towards the accomplishment of this central goal. For William Bradford, I defined my super-objective thus: "I wish to walk in God's Holy Way as prescribed in His Holy Word." Since Bradford's life was totally governed by his faith, this seemed like a powerful and organic objective to me, and, as I would have done with a playscript, I located it within Bradford's own writing.

In building the character of William Bradford, I also utilized a technique from Michael Chekhov's acting method known as "psychological gesture" (1953, 63–84). In this approach, the actor attempts to locate a physical gesture or pose that expresses the very essence of the character; performing this single gesture will put the actor in the role. This psychophysical process is highly intuitive. The psychological gesture, that I discovered for the Bradford character helped me to feel his devoutness and dignity. It was an expansive gesture, with my arms lifted straight up toward the heavens, my feet spread out beneath, and my head bowed in humility. It had a kind of "crucifixion" feeling to it but was at the same time prayerful. The inner thoughts that accompanied this gesture were: "I pray to thee, O Lord, give me strength to help this Plantation grow and prosper. Let me be guided by Thy Holy Will."

The psychological gesture is a crystallization of the character's core. It can be repeated innumerable times and used as part of the actor's offstage preparation. For instance, when performing William Bradford for the three-day "Harvest Feast," I would, each morning before the village was opened to the public, find a private place (usually the first floor of the Fort-Meeting House) and practice a series of preparatory psychophysical exercises. I would frequently begin with Spolin's ([1963] 1985, 81) "space substance exploration," moving through space as though it were made up of different kinds of matter: water, snow, mud, molasses. I would allow my body to move in as many planes and at as many angles as possible. The aim of this exercise is to release tension and to bring about a feeling of freedom of movement that maximizes one's sense of creativity. Next, I would enact some of Chekhov's fundamental psychophysical warm-ups, such as "flying," "floating," and "radiating." In this last exercise, I would, following Chekhov's instructions (1953, 11–12), send out imaginary "rays" from my solar plexus and then move to the space where these rays had been directed. Like yoga and t'ai chi, these exercises produce a sense of well-being and a deep relaxation that is helpful to the performer. At the right moment, I would practice my psychological gesture once or twice, in preparation for going onstage, relaxed and ready to perform the role of Governor William Bradford.

I also concur with Tomkin's opinion that the interpreter's performance is "improvisation from a character." Once the character is constructed, the actor/historian at Plimoth improvises from that base, following the thoughts, feelings, and perspective of the seventeenth-century person whom he or she has endeavored to become. James Carroll has also recognized this essential aspect of the performance in the Pilgrim Village. As he told me in an interview: "What it reminded me of was the work an actor does before preparing a role explicitly. . . . As if these people were going to play in *The Crucible* and, before they took on the characters, they went back to create the 'world.' You know, the way an actor works in Stanislavski—how an actor prepares" (1985). Carroll is referring to the kind of Stanislavskian exploratory improvisation with which actors sometimes work in order to discover deeper levels of the "world" of the drama. At Plimoth, the ethno-historical microcosm is the central frame of the performance, and the interpreters are constantly improvising from within it.

However, there are three major differences between this kind of improvisation and what commonly takes place in theatrical rehearsal and performance. First, as Tomkins points out, this improvisation is not for a one- or two-hour show, but for a full eight-hour day. Secondly, the repetition of behavior is much more extensive in this living history performance. In fact, the daily routine makes the job of acting a lot easier. The interpreters don't have to pretend so much that the stage set is their natural environment—at least, on a daily basis, it actually is! The constant replication of daily tasks makes the actor/historians fit seamlessly into their surroundings. Many visitors ask: "Do you really live here?" The redundance makes it all seem very natural. Thirdly, and most significantly, the actor/historians are not only interacting with their fellow players, as would be the case in most stage productions; they are continuously interacting with the audience as well. The naturalistic illusion of the setting and the interpreters' re-creation of seventeenth-century village life is, in actuality, constantly being broken by the intrusion of twentieth-century audience members.

As Schechner has shown, there is a Brechtian aspect to the performance at Plimoth; it is not all "naturalism" (1981, 27). The great German theatre theorist and playwright Bertolt Brecht (1898–1956) developed a technique of acting based on his interpretation of certain Asian styles of acting and known as the "alienation effect," in which he demanded that the performer, at times, disidentify with his or her character. Using this approach, the actor never completely transforms into the character but frequently lets the audience know that he or she is *not* the character and that the performance is, indeed, not real life, but a play. Brecht's purpose was to disallow the audience's suspension of disbelief, so they would not empathetically engage in the performance but instead, consciously think about it. Brecht was the advocate of a politically instructive theatre that would awaken his audience to the evils of certain sociopolitical structures.

Schechner has demonstrated how the Brechtian alienation in the performance at Plimoth is the direct consequence of a naturalistic re-creation being set in the context of a twentieth-century tourist business comprising gift shops, slide shows, and fast food service. Here, the actor/historians are automatically alienated from their seventeenth-century characters because of the constant presence of twentieth-century realities, including the penetration of the tourist audience into their performance space. Brecht, himself, indicated that the portrayal of historical roles contained a built-in alienation effect:

> Historical incidents are unique, transitory incidents associated with particular periods. The conduct of the persons involved in them is not fixed and 'universally human'; it includes elements that have been or may be overtaken by the course of history, and is subject to criticism from the immediately following period's point of view. The conduct of those born before us is *alienated* (italics mine) from us by an incessant evolution. (in Willet 1978, 140)

The contrast of the historical role with the contemporary reality of the performer in itself creates an alienation effect. Schechner calls this paradoxical experience that the audience has—witnessing a twentieth-century individual's attempt to embody a seventeenth-century persona—the basic "kick" of Plimoth's type of performance (1981, 27). It is the awareness of the double identity of the interpreters that gives the audience a unique and pleasurable aesthetic experience.

What kind of acting is this, then? I would say that it is an amateur form of improvisational, naturalistic acting in which the actors are never fully able to identify with their characters because of the alienating influence of the audience and because of their own awareness of educational objectives. The word "amateur" applies because only about 14 percent of the interpretation staff have any professional training in acting. Should only professional actors be hired? I don't think so. This unusual job, which integrates many different abilities in people, is still evolving and defining itself. I do believe that it does, without a doubt, make use of and require acting skills, and that the best interpretations are done by those individuals who have realized both functions of the actor/historian. Those interpreters who can fully enter their roles and invest themselves in their characters' inner worlds—thoughts, feelings, motivations, visions, world view—while simultaneously retaining a substantial knowledge of valid ethnohistorical data will be most able genuinely to educate the public about the Pilgrims. An interpreter's ability to play the role earnestly and skillfully enhances this performance of ethnography. Thus I believe that all interpreters should be trained in *both* historical research and acting techniques, so that they can actualize their ethnohistorical roles, thereby fulfilling the living museum's educational mission.

### THE LUDIC FUNCTION AND THE IRONIES OF DOUBLE IDENTITY

A number of ironies result from these actor/historians having their feet in two different worlds. On many levels, it is their playing in-between identities that makes this performance so fascinating. The playful and serious collision of two worlds (figure 3) gives this historical re-creation its special dynamic.

The living history performance at contemporary Plimoth Plantation beautifully illustrates the operation of the ludic function in postmodern culture. As already described, it is this lively, playful, creative aspect of culture that catalyzes the development of new forms of social experience. Huizinga points out that the word "illusion" literally means "in-play" and is derived from the root Latin word, *lūdere* (*inlusio, illudere* or *inludere*), which he uses to connote the "play element in culture" (1955, 11). In the "play frame," making and destroying illusion becomes an experience of delight and wonder. But this is a two-sided sword. For *lūdere* also has the meaning "to mock," which can be

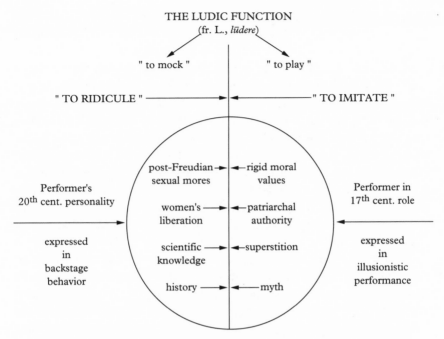

*Figure 3.* A model of how the ludic function operates ambivalently for the actor/historians at Plimoth Plantation, who both imitate and ridicule Pilgrim history. This tension of opposites is one of the most dynamic factors of the performance.

construed both in the sense of imitating (a mockingbird) and ridiculing ("You mock me!"). As figure 3 shows, the tension between these two opposite actions creates the ironical and often humorous quality of the performance at Plimoth. It is the play element in culture that creates the context for this strange, paradoxical situation in which the interpreters simultaneously imitate and ridicule Pilgrim culture.

The interpreters' central task is to imitate, meaning to reproduce authentically, seventeenth-century Pilgrim culture. Their job is to create the illusion of another time and place. However, every interpreter brings to this endeavor his or her own authentic twentieth-century values, which conflict in many ways with the ideals and mores of the seventeenth-century roles. This fundamental alienation from their characters is often expressed in ironic witticisms. The Ivy League-educated interpreter who used to punch out at the time clock announcing, "God is dead after five o'clock!" was confronting the profound religious faith of his daily enactment with his own existentialist point of view.

Many of the ironies resulting from the double identity are expressed in the form of symbolic inversion. Performance, as a ludic phenomenon, perennially provides examples of this cultural process. Simply put, symbolic inversion is "turning the world on its head." Cole Porter's song "Anything Goes" supplies a verbal gem of symbolic inversion related to the Pilgrims: "Instead of landing on Plymouth Rock, the Rock would land on them." The tone of this lyric illustrates an attitude that one wily old-timer at the plantation stated very succinctly: "There's just something comical about the Pilgrims." I believe it is the tension between vastly different cultural attitudes that results in this sort of humor.

The release from the tension between conflicting values is also represented in acts of symbolic inversion, which Barbara A. Babcock describes as "any act of expressive behavior which inverts, contradicts, abrogates, or in some fashion presents an alternative to the commonly held cultural codes, values, and norms" (1978, 14). Some of these parodistic alternatives to stereotypical Pilgrim cultural patterns have already been described. The mock drill invented by the female interpreters, in which Regina Porter burlesqued the role of Captain Standish and the women all put a match to their coifs, clearly demonstrates a reversal of seventeenth-century English values. This improvised scene exemplifies a collision of twentieth-century feminist perspective with the staunch patriarchal code of the Pilgrims' society. The burning of the coif reflects that modern gesture of defiance to patriarchal attitudes—the burning of the bra. Also, this vignette presents a quintessential aspect of symbolic inversion found in performative contexts all over the world—transvestitism—in this case, a woman dressed up to look like a man. I know of another instance when the opposite occurred and a male interpreter entered the village dressed as a Pilgrim maidservant.[4]

Another type of behavior that mocks the Pilgrims' alleged sexual mores is reference to and representative of homosexuality (inversion). I have previously mentioned the female interpreters' staging of a back region mock trial, in which two male interpreters were accused of "lude & sodomiticall practices." This episode took place on "Muster Day," the apogee of patriarchal and militaristic reenactments. I can also recall a male interpreter at a party giving a satirical rendition of a gay Pilgrim man meeting a "gorgeous" Indian brave when the Pilgrims first landed at Provincetown. This stand-up comic act reflected a double irony: the notion of a "gay" Pilgrim, as well as the historical fact that the Pilgrims made their initial landing at the site of Provincetown, which, today, is a mecca of gay culture in America. There is certainly a major collision of values between the social significance of contemporary "P-town" and the prototypical puritan morals of the Pilgrim Fathers.

Huizinga asserts that "a play-community generally tends to become permanent even after the game is over" (1955, 12). This is surely true of the interpretation staff at Plimoth Plantation. Just as their working days are defined by playful illusion, an intense, sometimes sardonic, playfulness frames their after-hours social activities. Some parties that take place in the Pilgrim Village itself give telling glimpses into how the tension of the opposites is released in various kinds of acting out. "Sleep overs" in the village (once known as "copulation parties") usually involve a real twentieth-century letting of the hair down. Undoubtedly, the unrepressed, Dionysian behavior at these "blasts" would horrify the real Pilgrims.[5] But, as Turner has said about such rites of reversal, "Emotionally, nothing satisfies as much as extravagant or temporarily permitted illicit behavior" (1969, 176). Perhaps the inversion of Pilgrim culture is exemplified nowhere better than at the end-of-the-season cast party known as "the crappies," at which interpreters engage in performances of all kinds with roaring and raucous satirical humor, turning the world of the Pilgrims on its head. Babcock writes: "Such 'creative negations' remind us of the need to reinvest the clean with the filthy, the rational with the animalistic, the ceremonial with the carnivalesque in order to maintain cultural vitality" (1978, 32). In this case, it is also a function of the cool-down process, in which the interpreters are relinquishing their Pilgrim roles on the last night of the season and doing so with much laughter and good cheer.

The tension of opposites represented in figure 3 is always at play in the double identity of the actor/historians and is continuously released in the many types of offstage humor and satire in which the interpreters involve themselves. All of it reflects the process of the ludic function within the play-community at contemporary Plimoth Plantation, and I include the visitors in this communal play frame, as well.

The many ironical and parodistic scenes that the interpreters invent are a testament to one of their most positive qualities—their creativity. But the audience also discovers a unique pleasure in observing the coincidence of opposites. Schechner has written that "spectators enjoy what can best be described as a postmodern thrill at the mix or coincidence of contradictory categories" (1981, 26). It is the ludic function of culture operating in the liminal space of the re-created village that most defines the essential quality of this cultural performance. In the final chapters, how this ludic function has evolved and how it operates in a postmodern cultural context will be discussed in detail.

# Six

# Pilgrims and Tourists

## *The Performer-Audience Interaction*

This is a great way to learn history!
Yes, but how do we know it's authentic?

Two visitors at Plimoth Plantation,
15 August 1985

*O*ne of the most fascinating features of the living history performance at Plimoth Plantation is the audience. Known as "visitors," they come from all over the world. During the course of a
busy summer day, an actor/historian may perform for and interact
with an African foreign exchange student, an expatriated Russian, a
Cambodian Buddhist monk, a family from India, a bevy of Japanese
tourists with their sophisticated photographic equipment, a *Mayflower*
descendent from Salt Lake City, and an Englishman who just happens
to come from the same shire, town, and neighborhood as the Pilgrim
character whom the interpreter portrays. These are among the thousands who tour the plantation on the busiest days of the season. They
exemplify Dean MacCannell's notion of modern mass leisure time, as
it is reflected in international tourism and sightseeing (1976).

In his thought-provoking study on the "sociology of leisure," Mac-

Cannell explains how tourism demonstrates what it means to be a modern person in the late twentieth century and how sightseeing reveals the deep structures of modern society. He states: "After considerable deductive labor, I discovered that *sightseeing is a ritual performed to the differentiations of society*" (1976, 13). In a non-Marxist style, he elevates the phenomenon of international tourism to a place of enormous symbolic, sociological and political importance. For Mac-Cannell, tourism and sightseeing produce and mirror the kinds of differentiations from which the consciousness of modernity is constructed. Ways in which our society differs from those of the past are evident in tourist attractions. MacCannell points out how the post-industrial restructuring of work relations is reflected in tourist sites where tourists observe others going about their labors. Plimoth is a case in point, and it also demonstrates other kinds of differences between pre- and post-industrial society that help to define modernity. MacCannell writes that such tourism experiences are largely the domain of a growing international middle class: "Modern international mass tourism produces in the minds of the tourists juxtapositions of elements from historically separated cultures and thereby speeds up the differentiation and modernization of middle-class consciousness." (1976, 27). It is certainly the contrast between past and present that creates the greatest part of Plimoth's attraction and entices over 700,000 people to visit the Pilgrim Village and the *Mayflower II* each year.[1]

Why do they come? There are many different motivations. Some come simply because they are attracted to the Pilgrim myth. For instance, Ed Kolleski, a recreation therapist of Polish descent from Highland Park, New Jersey, came because the Pilgrim story has great "romantic appeal" for him (Kolleski 1985). Mishi Kawa, a Tokyo businessman working for two years in the United States, wanted to see the myth's great symbols. He explains: "The other day, my English teacher in my town talked about Thanksgiving Day and also about Plymouth, Plymouth Rock. . . . So, I was interested in seeing the Plymouth Rock and *Mayflower*, of course" (Kawa 1985).

There are some visitors who make the journey because they feel deeply connected to the religious aspect of Pilgrim culture. They perceive the Pilgrims to be their spiritual ancestors. Of the sixty-six people that I interviewed, five came specifically for religious reasons.[2] Valerie Almagatta, a thirty-one-year-old Hawaiian woman, felt Christian fellowship with the interpreters as she interrelated with them because of "our belief in the same God." She says: "Part of the reason why I came was to ask questions about how they believed, why they broke away, and how they were persecuted." (Almagatta 1986). Oon June Kim, a twenty-seven-year-old Korean visitor, was advised by a friend to make the journey to Plimoth Plantation, where "the nations of Americans lived and inherited their precious things like religion." Kim states: "I'm a Christian and so I suggested to a friend of mine that we will visit this area where the older generations of Americans really cared for their religion and religion is their way of living, at the time" (Kim 1986).

Sometimes, those individuals who come to the plantation expecting to experience an immediate spiritual kinship with the Pilgrims are rudely awakened. For instance, "born-again" Christians often enter the Pilgrim Village wanting to discuss their theological interests with the inhabitants. They are shocked to discover that the idea at the core of their belief—that a person can be saved by faith alone—was considered a heresy by the Pilgrims. In fact, the spiritual teacher of the Pilgrims' Leyden (Holland) community, John Robinson, wrote a well-known defense of the Calvinist doctrines of predestination and election. According to these theological positions, everything is already established by the law of predestination and only the elect are saved. Thus there is no such thing as salvation through the choice to believe. As Robert M. Bartlett wrote: "He [Robinson] believed that the doctrine of free will would lead to religious and political chaos while the concept of the sovereignty of God and his rule over man would preserve the dignity of the individual and a harmonious body politic" (1971, 155–56). These differing religious beliefs frequently lead to heated debates between this type of visitor and the actor/historians who are trying accurately to portray the Pilgrims' theological perspective. The ethnohistorical data forces a showdown with individuals who are absolutely certain that the Pilgrims maintained beliefs exactly the same as their own. An interpreter who is earnestly attempting to embody the mind-set of a seventeenth-century Saint will feel very uncomfortable with a twentieth-century fundamentalist who is trying to proselytize from a contemporary born-again Christian point of view, precisely because of the misunderstanding of the differentiation of ideology.

Another visitor group that often feels an immediate religious and cultural affinity with the Pilgrims is the American Mennonite community. They come mainly from Pennsylvania and Virginia, as well as other parts of the United States, to visit Plimoth Plantation. These people have a strong sense of cultural identity and continuity. Their manner of dress and demeanor evoke the aura of a pre-industrial society: the men wear wide-brimmed black hats similar to those worn by Pilgrim interpreters, and the women wear little lace or linen bonnets very much like seventeenth-century coifs. Confusion often results when Mennonites and Pilgrim interpreters are in the same vicinity. Mennonite visitors are sometimes mistaken for Pilgrims, even though many of the younger Mennonite women sport Adidas on their feet. On the other hand, some visitors do not realize that the plantation is a historical re-creation and believe that the Pilgrim interpreters are a group, like the Mennonites or Pennsylvania Dutch, who have maintained the continuity of their cultural traditions since the seventeenth century.

In actuality, there are some theological parallels between the Mennonite religion and the Church of the Saints. Both Protestant sects influenced by a Dutch experience, they are predicated on congregational autonomy and are offspring of reformation movements in the mid-sixteenth century. Many of their fundamental tenets would be similar. As Phillip Schrock, a twenty-seven-year-old Mennonite who visited the plantation in September 1986, explains: "I think basically they [the Saints] understood the Scriptures almost like our forefathers would have, except for maybe a few areas like non-resistance and possibly a few others" (Schrock 1986). The non-resistance mentioned refers to the fact that Mennonites are required to reject military service, a pacifist attitude not embraced by the Pilgrims. The other major difference is that these visitors do not espouse Calvinist views.

A fairly large segment of visitors come to the plantation because they believe they are blood relations of the Pilgrims. Most of these belong to the General Society of Mayflower Descendants, which has chapters in every state and holds triennial congresses in Plymouth. Many of these individuals are motivated by ancestor worship. (Remember that the Pilgrim houses in the village were funded by descendants of the original tenants.) On certain days, such visitors inundate the village. It can be a formidable task for an interpreter to portray Edward Winslow with his decendants looking on.

Others, who have a less formal genealogical connection, are still spurred on by a sense of some hereditary link to the Pilgrims. They may have recently discovered a family tree that shows a tie to the early Plimoth settlers, or they may have just heard that "somewhere along the line" they are related to this one or that one. Debbie Bordeaux, a twenty-nine-year-old mother from California, brought her children to Plymouth in order to show them "the historical side where I come from—my side of the family." She says: "My family goes way, way, way back. I don't know exactly how far back. I haven't really gotten back there, yet. But I'm thinking so [that they are Pilgrim descendants]. It would be nice to know that we were" (Bordeaux 1986). Two of the visitors interviewed felt they were Pilgrim descendants. One was certain of a connection to the Winslows; with Mrs. Bordeaux, it seemed to be a case of wishful thinking.

Individuals from totally different cultural backgrounds, with no possible blood lines to the Pilgrims, may still identify with this ancestral past, feeling that the Pilgrims are part of their personal heritage. This viewpoint is expressed by Bruce Jendreas, a young Polish-Catholic man from Manchester, New Hampshire, whose own great-grandparents came to America by sea in the early 1900s and built up a little farm just outside Chicago:

> Looking back at what my great-grandparents were—I can identify [with the Pilgrims] to that extent—drawing ties between what my great-grandparents did, coming over on a boat and starting up this small farm. They built a house and, then, when their first son was old enough to get married, they built him a house. . . . I've always liked this type of atmosphere: very rugged country, self-sustaining, think-for-yourself type of life. (Jendreas 1985)

Americans of many different ethnic backgrounds can relate to the Pilgrim image of hard-working, immigrant farmers. Many make return trips to the plantation, again and again, because of a powerful nostalgia for the agrarian past. As one visitor put it: "You get off the highway, you come here, and you walk in, and it's quiet . . . it's an oasis from modern life" (Laniere 1985).

Sometimes this homesickness is for a past that is not so distant. An African student once told me how much the conical, thatched-roof cow shed in the Pilgrim Village reminded him of his homeland;

Cambodian refugees have pointed out the similarities between the Pilgrim houses and their own recently relinquished homesteads; a Yugoslavian man once took a flail right out of my hands while I was thrashing wheat in my role as a Pilgrim farmer and showed me how they did it in the "old country." Most peoples have experienced an agrarian stage of development. Today, in this jet-age, computerized world, the brief escape into a pastoral past is one of the most attractive features of Plimoth Plantation.

Many visitors come because they want their children to see the "first scene of American history." In general, the plantation is a great place for a family outing. As Jerry Haber of Weston, Massachusetts, explains: "Bringing children here is a lot of fun because their eyeballs open wide and it's all new to them. Anytime we either re-learned or learned something through the eyes of the children, it's always been terribly fascinating and a lot of fun" (Haber 1985). For many families, in addition to being a diversion like a trip to Disney World, the experience has patriotic overtones. However, for some minority families the tour through the village may have a different kind of educational purpose. Michael Dunn, a young black man from Fall River, Massachusetts, whose ancestors came to America aboard a slave ship, brought his children in order to teach them "perspective on what did happen." He says: "Being an Afro-American, I have different views about some of the settling and some of the consequences that it had on the indigenous population and my own ancestors" (Dunn 1985). For the Dunn family, the situation is even more complicated because Mrs. Dunn is part Wampanoag. She describes her ambivalent feelings about being in the Pilgrim Village: "It's weird being here. [I'm from] the same tribe that these folks wiped out. It's hard to explain because I don't really feel apart and yet I do. It's very strange being an Indian [here]" (Dunn 1985).

The conflicting emotions that Mrs. Dunn experiences on her visit to the Pilgrim Village are certainly understandable. For some ethnic groups, especially those with Native American or Afro-American backgrounds, the image of the Pilgrims conjures up everything that is wrong with America. There is a sense of negative identification: these are not their ancestors but "villains" in the larger historical frame. Although the Pilgrims did not "wipe out" anybody's tribe, undoubtedly some of their progeny contributed to the genocide of Native American peoples. It is not surprising that a Native American visitor would feel bitterness, resentment, and even outrage when faced with this re-creation of one of the first English settlements in America.

These feelings are demonstrated in public at least once a year, at the annual Day of Mourning held every Thanksgiving Day. Hundreds of Native Americans gather on the hill overlooking Plymouth Harbor to express their anger and grief. They have designated the landing of the *Mayflower* as the symbolic beginning of the demise of their people. They want to discredit the sentimental portrait of the Pilgrims and Indians sharing the "first Thanksgiving feast" by focusing on the historical and political realities of America. Yet, with all of this, the process of acculturation has had an enormous impact. It is not so surprising that Mrs. Dunn also feels part of this re-creation of the Pilgrim story. The need to present American culture in a way that helps to create integration and harmony among America's diverse ethnic populations is a challenge to all museums and, as a living museum, Plimoth has a special responsibility in such a matter.

From its inception in 1947, Plimoth Plantation's primary objective has been to educate the public. As the Articles of Incorporation state, the main goal is "the historical education of the public with respect to the struggles of the early Settlers in the Town of Plymouth" (Plimoth Plantation 1948, 8). Many of the visitors are motivated principally by the desire to learn something more about Pilgrim history. Some, like Helen Haskell from Holbrook, Massachusetts, are simply enamored of the subject. Of her experience in the village, she says: "I just like the whole thing. I just like seeing history before you. You know, not just like reading books, but *before you*: going into how they do things, what they say, and how they make things, and seeing what the things look like. . . . I like the whole thing. I love it" (Haskell 1985). Others are formal students, ranging from kindergartners to graduate researchers. They come by the tens of thousands. The children and teenagers are mostly on that traditional "lark," the field trip. Whereas most American schoolchildren are introduced to Pilgrim history through their history textbooks, many pupils from the New England and Atlantic states first meet up with the Pilgrims in this living history performance. The majority of these public school students are local. In 1984–85, the Massachusetts Council on the Arts and Humanities funded an Open Door Program, which provided free admission to over 8,400 students from thirty-four communities in Plymouth County (Plimoth Plantation 1985).

Many different types of educational experiences take place at the plantation. Serious high school and college students, amateur historians, folklorists, and archaeologists, among others, come to investigate such topics as seventeenth-century New England architecture, animal husbandry, horticulture, Pilgrim culinary techniques, and Separatist theology. Some come to study the plantation as an illustration of museology, or as a tourist phenomenon, or, as I have, as a cultural performance. Many of the younger students, especially at the junior high and early high school level, would rather "Pilgrim-bait" (see chapter 3, note 7) than ask earnest historical questions. If they become so wild that even a skilled interpreter cannot calm them down, they sometimes have to be asked to leave the village.[3] I have seen adolescents destroy reconstructed artifacts in the Pilgrim houses and run amok in the streets. On the other hand, there are many genuinely inquisitive teenagers who become fascinated with this re-creation of Pilgrim culture. Al Lum, a Chinese-American student from a high school in Pearl River, New York, where the senior class regularly takes its trip to the plantation, particularly enjoyed the illusion of time travel: "You get to go back and experience—actually like almost live—the way people did before we had all this technology, before we had like lightbulbs and cars" (Lum 1985).

Because of its naturalistic acting style and the convincing scenic illusion, this living history performance can be a wonderful pedagogical tool. Interpreter Regina Porter recounts how a black girl from an inner-city elementary school watched her, with true amazement, as she (in her character as Goodwife Lucretia Brewster) bent over the hearth and scoured a filthy, charred cooking pot. After about twenty minutes, the child blurted out: "I thought you were an actress, but now I *know* you're for real!"

THE TOURIST AS AUDIENCE

Of the more than seven hundred thousand annual visitors, the largest portion is undoubtedly tourists. Of my sample of sixty-six visitors, if the eight students and the one person with a special research project are excluded, fifty-seven, or 86 percent, fit into the tourist category. Even those with motives other than recreation or diversion can loosely be defined as tourists. Bikini-clad vacationers who buzz through the village on a whirlwind tour as a break from sunbathing on the beach, students from a Southern Baptist Bible college making a bus tour of

New England, Chinese physicists accompanied by their M.I.T. translator, senior citizens on a fall foliage tour, an Oregon family of *Mayflower* descendants, black children from the inner-city ghetto—all are touring this re-created historical setting, in some fashion. Some go about it deliberately, like Margo Meyerbachtal of San Francisco, who says: "I research every place that I go and I just gather as much information as I can about it, and I wrote the [Plymouth] Chamber of Commerce, ahead of time" (Meyerbachtal 1985). Others, vacationing in Massachusetts, make a spontaneous stopover. Patty and David Jacobi found brochures directing them to Plimoth Plantation in the Boston-area Holiday Inn where they were staying (Jacobi 1986). Joyce Cullingford of Inkbearer, England, came on "a touring holiday" (Cullingford 1986). Her American contemporary, eighty-year-old Leo P. Holland, came on a "bus trip from Philadelphia, touring all around" (Holland 1985). The DiDinado family, recently arrived from Italy, brought along a translator so that they could appreciate their experience in the village.

Since the largest number of visitors are tourists, the whole living history performance must, in many ways, be viewed as what Bruner and Kirshenblatt-Gimblett have called a "tourist production" (Bruner and Kirshenblatt-Gimblett 1985, 1988, 1989, and Kirshenblatt-Gimblett 1988). As we saw in chapter 4, Plimoth Plantation is a "tourist setting" placed in the larger context of a "recreational geography" based upon the Pilgrim story. For several years, Bruner and Kirshenblatt-Gimblett have devoted their attention to the study of the "organization and semiotics" of performances that are specifically produced for tourist audiences. They write: "Tourist Productions—the settings, events, and artifacts created for tourists—and their marketing constitute the most elaborated and expressive mode of communication in the entire tourism system." (1989, 250). Following MacCannell's lead, these two authors have explored the cultural significance of "tourist productions," especially focusing on the issues pertaining to the invention of culture and the construction of meaning. In their work, they have made a strong case for accepting tourism as a kind of "ethnographic discourse." Regarding Plimoth Plantation, Kirshenblatt-Gimblett notes: "In this case, a 'living history museum' has taken as its model the touristic experience, thus signalling a reciprocity between tourism and historical and ethnographic representations." (1988, 61).

The evolution of the performative style of representation at Plimoth has been highly influenced by the emergence of international tourism and the proliferation of tourist productions all over the world. As MacCannell suggests, tourists today expect a high degree of "staged authenticity" in the performances that they pay for; they look forward to a heightened level of spectacle or "show" (1976, 105). Plimoth provides this experience in staging such special events as the "Festive Wedding," which is precisely timed to occur at the height of the tourist season in Massachusetts, or "The Dutch Visit to New Plimoth," which takes place on a three-day, holiday weekend, affording many people time for a brief tour of the plantation.

The massive tourist audience that attends the daily performances at Plimoth Plantation can be analyzed with the aid of a typology of tourist experiences developed by Eric Cohen. Cohen has predicated his classifications on the concept of a quest for the "centre which for the individual symbolizes ultimate meanings" (Cohen 1979, 181). He has made use of Turner's notion of pilgrimage as a journey to a sacred "centre," no matter where that centre is in geographical relation to one's home. As Turner states:

> A pilgrimage center, from the standpoint of the believing actor, also represents a "threshold," a place and moment "in and out of time," and such an actor—as the evidence of many pilgrims of many religions attest—hopes to have there direct experience of the sacred, invisible, or supernatural order, either in the material aspect of miraculous healing or in the immaterial aspect of inward transformation of spirit or personality. (Turner 1973, 214)

In many ways, the pilgrim of older cultural models is the prototype for the modern tourist. Both leave home in order to seek a special experience. What Cohen has done is to categorize this experience by relating it to a cultural and/or sacred centre; each type of tourist relates in a different way to this centre. At the farthest end of the spectrum are those tourists who can be classified as "modern pilgrims" (figure 4).

Cohen defines five modes of touristic experience, beginning with the "recreational." This first type is the easiest to recognize. Such people are simply out for a good time, a little fun, a break from the boredom or anxiety of daily living. Their centre is their own culture and the tourist experience "restitutes the individual to his society and its values, which, despite the pressures they generate, constitute the

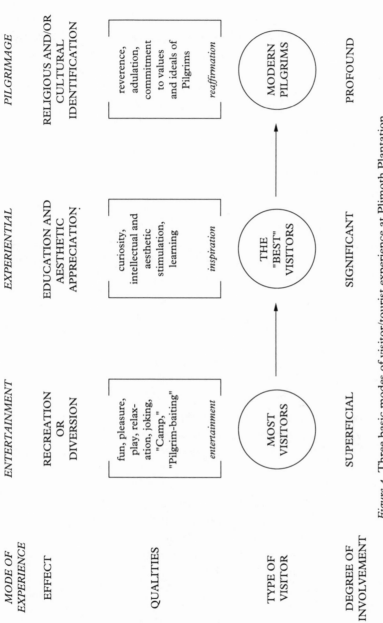

*Figure 4.* Three basic modes of visitor/tourist experience at Plimoth Plantation

centre of his world" (Cohen 1979, 185). The vast majority of the audience at Plimoth Plantation is made up of this kind of tourist: vacationers, families on day trips, holiday travelers, and some motivated by other reasons, who all basically see the plantation as a form of entertainment. Many of these recreational tourists perceive the living history performance to be a form of theatre and view the interpreters as actors.[4] As Ed Sachs, a high school history teacher from Pearl River, New York, explains: "Their quality, to me, is that of outstanding, professionally trained actors. But I think once you are ready to suspend your disbelief—once you get into it—that they are accepted as transporting you back in time. I think that can happen very quickly" (Sachs 1985). Exactly why Pilgrim history has become theatricalized today will be analyzed in the last chapter. However, it is my own opinion that this willingness to suspend one's disbelief in order to be entertained is the most common mode of experiencing Plimoth Plantation. I agree with Cohen's statement that:

> Such recreation-oriented tourists should be looked upon less as shallow, easily gullible simpletons who believe any contraption to be 'real', or as stooges of a prevaricating tourist establishment, but rather as persons who attend a performance or participate in a game; the enjoyability of the occasion is contingent on their willingness to accept the make-believe or half-seriously to delude themselves. (Cohen 1979, 184)

Cohen's second mode of tourist experience is the "diversionary." A person in this category is poorly adapted to his or her society and is profoundly alienated from his or her own cultural centre. As Cohen writes, this kind of experience is "a mere escape from the boredom and meaninglessness of routine . . . but does not 'recreate'—i.e., it does not reestablish adherence to a meaningful centre, but only makes alienation endurable" (1979, 186). Some people do, undoubtedly, enter the gates of the Pilgrim Village for the same reason that they walk into a bar or a movie theatre or, for that matter, take drugs. They want to escape the pain of a centreless existence. For this type of tourist, the plantation is a kind of amusement park and conforms to this individual's regular pattern of amusements and diversions. I remember one Sunday morning when two transvestites, who were obviously either drunk or on drugs, made their way down the main street of the Pilgrim Village. The incongruity of their presence was both funny and sad. What could the experience of the 1627 village possibly mean to them, as they giggled and wriggled their way from house to house? In truth, they were putting themselves on display as much as they were touring the re-created Plimoth.

A few other visitors, like these, come to "camp" on the Pilgrims, to make a big joke out of it all, in order to provide themselves with another titillating, anesthetizing divertissement. These visitors particularly enjoy a very caustic kind of "Pilgrim-baiting." On the other hand, the diversionary mode of experience can be viewed in a positive fashion. There are some people who, sickened by the quality of post-industrial, technological society, look upon the plantation as a form of pastoral oasis. As Angela Monihan of Norwell, Massachusetts, says: "I'd love to live in a little village like that, working outside. . . . It's a completely different way of life than what we live. I think it would be fun to live the way *they* do, rather than the way we do. . . . No television! No McDonalds! You know, all the garbage!" (Monihan 1985) For those individuals deeply alienated from postmodern culture, the experience of the village or the ship represents a brief, but soothing, respite from their daily angst.

Cohen's first two tourist types, the recreational and the diversionary, constitute the bulk of the visitor audience. In figure 4, I have listed them both under the heading "Entertainment," because both experience the plantation essentially as a form of entertainment—as a tourist production, akin to Disney World, the World's Fair, and Silver Dollar City. For different reasons, both groups are seeking out a way to amuse themselves; for the majority of the seven hundred thousand visitors (plate 21), Plimoth Plantation represents one such way.

The last three categories of Cohen's model, the "experiential," the "experimental," and the "existential," each represent a mode of touristic experience in which the individual is alienated from his or her own cultural centre, but, to a lesser or greater degree, becomes absorbed in a cultural "other." In this case, the cultural "other" is the Pilgrim culture, as it is reflected and re-created by the actor/historians in their daily performance. These three modes are in alignment with MacCannell's concept of the tourist as a seeker of authentic experiences (1976, 91–107).

Daniel Boorstin, in his classic work, *The Image: A Guide to Pseudo-Events in America* ([1961] 1987), condemns all tourists as persons who

*Plate 21.* Tourists fill the streets of the Pilgrim Village.
(Photo courtesy of Plimoth Plantation)

are desirous only of superficial and phony experiences. In fact, he seems to blame the tourists themselves for the proliferation of "pseudo-events." Again and again in his own work, MacCannell defends the tourist against this derisive and denigrating attack. He states: "None of the accounts in my collection support Boorstin's contention that tourists want superficial, contrived experiences. Rather, tourists demand authenticity just as Boorstin does." (1976, 104). MacCannell's notion is that tourists provide, in fact, one of the best paradigms for modern humanity in general. Lost in an alienating social environment, they are constantly in search of genuine and authentic experiences. In a statement that illuminates the kind of experience provided by Plimoth to Cohen's final categories of tourists, MacCannell writes: "For moderns, reality and authenticity are thought to be elsewhere: in other historical periods and other cultures, in purer, simpler life-styles" (1976, 3). The tourists in these last three categories reflect just such yearning. They want something deeper than recreation or diversion. Often in search of inspiration for their own lives, they want to incorporate some essence of this re-created past, something purer and simpler that they can take home with them.

At this point, the audience member moves beyond a superficial encounter toward a deeper intellectual, aesthetic, or spiritual involvement with the living history performance. In figure 4, I have subsumed Cohen's experiential and experimental classifications under the single heading "Experiential," by which I mean to infer a type of meaningful experience that may include, but goes beyond, mere entertainment.

Like Cohen's third type, the experiential tourist, some visitors do come to the plantation in order to "look for meaning in the life of others" (Cohen 1979, 86). These are the "seekers," both cultural and religious, who really want to be touched by the life of the Pilgrims. This group composes the best audience for the actor/historians. Both parties are engaged in an effort to realize an authentic experience: the interpreters are doing their best truly to *re*-present genuine Pilgrim culture, and the visitor is genuinely appreciating the act of interpretation. Often, such visitors have a special interest in Pilgrim culture. They are amateur (or professional) historians or folklorists, religiously motivated visitors, *Mayflower* descendants, or just people who are fascinated by the Pilgrims. Frequently, they have a longing to "live the Pilgrim life" themselves. They are fed up with all the alienating aspects of contemporary culture and long for the simplicity and communality that appear to be present in the Pilgrim Village. However, as Cohen explains, the experiential tourist always stops short of actually entering the cultural life of the "other":

> The actual experience is primarily aesthetic, owing to its vicarious nature. The aesthesis provoked by direct contact with the authenticity of others may reassure and uplift the tourist, but does not provide a new meaning and guidance to his life. This can best be seen where 'experiential' tourists observe pilgrims at a pilgrimage centre: the pilgrims experience the sacredness of the centre; the tourists may experience aesthetically the authenticity of the pilgrims' experience. (Cohen 1979, 188)

In the present case, the actor/historians experience a simulated Pilgrim life, and the tourists, aesthetically or intellectually, appreciate their role-playing. But no matter how much the experiential tourists say they want to play the Pilgrim role, in the end, they do not.

There are few opportunities for tourists at Plimoth Plantation to enter Cohen's fourth mode, the experimental. For the truly interested, workshops are sometimes given in the village on how to cook over an open hearth or how to rive a piece of oak. A few individuals are enthusiastic enough to study the historical texts and re-create tools, weapons, or clothing on their own. But this is really not the same thing as experimenting "with alternative lifeways" (Cohen 1979, 189).

In Cohen's final mode, the existential, the tourist becomes "fully committed to an 'elective' spiritual centre, i.e., one external to the mainstream of his native society and culture" (Cohen 1979, 190). Cohen presents such examples as persons who find true fulfillment at an Israeli kibbutz or an Indian ashram and return on a regular basis. In one case, a woman named Vicky became absolutely enthralled with Pilgrim life in the village. She flew in from California several times a year in order to attend special events at the plantation such as "Opening Day," the "Festive Wedding," and the "Harvest Celebration." Some interpreters joked that she was a "Pilgrim groupie." I don't know exactly what Vicky's motivations were, but she told me on several occasions that she felt most at home in the Pilgrim Village. She was very committed to the Pilgrim story; in California, she made herself a Pilgrim costume and gave workshops on Pilgrim history. As far as I know, she continues to return regularly to the plantation. For Vicky, the Pilgrim Village has become a real pilgrimage centre; she has discovered something in this re-creation of another cultural world that profoundly nourishes her.

As Cohen explains, "The visit to his centre of the tourist travelling in the existentialist mode is phenomenologically analogous to a pilgrimage" (1979, 190). A small percentage of visitors, like Vicky, have a strong psychological or spiritual connection to Pilgrim culture and so make regular trips to Plimoth Plantation, which has come to "symbolize ultimate meanings" for them. These include some *Mayflower* descendants, some religious persons, some plantation members, and other individuals who deeply identify with some aspect of the Pilgrim story. I would place these visitors in my final category, "Pilgrimage" (to the far right in figure 4), because these tourists, like pilgrims all over the world, receive genuine spiritual revitalization from their periodic journeys to Plimoth.

The modes of experiencing the living history performance at Plimoth move from the enjoyment of an *entertainment* to the inspirational *experience* of learning and/or aesthetic appreciation to the realization of a modern *pilgrimage*. This is diagrammed in figure 4. Looking from left to right, we see that the experience of the performance becomes more and more central to the life of the tourist/spectator. Although these three categories have been segregated here for the purpose of classifying the tourist audience, in actuality a visitor may experience more than one mode simultaneously. For instance, a tourist/spectator might be deeply involved in the experiential mode, listening to an interpreter expound on some knotty points on Separatist theology; in the same moment, this visitor might be highly entertained by the characterization of this particular actor/historian. In my third category, "Pilgrimage," the visitor who tours Plimoth Plantation is, in fact, a modern pilgrim. In most cases, this individual already reveres and idolizes Pilgrim culture, and the visit to the plantation takes the form of a pilgrimage to a "pilgrimage center" (to use Turner's term). It is a reaffirmation of his or her faith. This sacralization of the re-created historic site will be discussed in the last chapter.

INTERACTION RITUALS

On a hot day in August, 1985, I was performing as Edward Winslow in the reenactment of a Dutch visit to New Plimoth. A group of tourists were listening to a "Dutchman" and me converse about farming in the New World. Suddenly, one visitor turned to another and blurted out, "This is a great way to learn history!" The friend instantly retorted, "Yes, but how do we know it's authentic?"

Occasionally an audience member will question the authenticity of the living history performance. They become suspicious, in Goffman's sense of that word, as "a person feels who begins, rightly or not, to think that the strip of activity he is involved in has been constructed beyond his ken, and that he has not been allowed a sustainable view of what frames him" (Goffman 1974, 122). As MacCannell has pointed out, the tourist yearns for authentic experiences. The tourist industry responds by creating productions of "staged authenticity." On many levels, Plimoth Plantation is such a production.

From a critical perspective, such tourist productions represent Boorstin's "pseudo-events." In the early sixties, Boorstin analyzed and criticized what he perceived to be an expanding category of artificial and titillating popular entertainments and "media events" in American culture. They are labeled "pseudo" because they are "intended to deceive" ([1961] 1987, 9). They are not genuine, spontaneous, or "God-created" happenings but fabricated, highly manipulated, invented occasions, designed to draw attention to themselves and engineered for mass appeal—such as Pilgrims in television ads, enticing the tourist audience to come to a special event at Plimoth Plantation. As Boorstin writes: "In order to satisfy the exaggerated expectations of tour agents and tourists, people everywhere obligingly become dishonest mimics of themselves. To provide a full schedule of events at the best seasons and at convenient hours, they travesty their most solemn rituals, holidays, and folk celebrations—all for the benefit of tourists" ([1961] 1987, 103). We have seen that the "Festive Wedding" is set up so as to meet the expectations of the summer tourist crowd.

However, the first-person role-playing performance at Plimoth—what Robert Marten called "character imposture"—need not be looked upon as a sham, a fake, a fraud. It can just as well be viewed as a game, a play of illusion, an artistic means of presenting bona fide historical facts. How it is perceived depends upon how the individual performers and spectators approach what Erving Goffman identifies as the "interaction ritual."

In his perceptive essay on the "sociology of occasions" (1967), Goffman generalizes that all human social interaction is ritualized behavior structured with a strict set of rules and is usually connected with the psychological reaction called "losing face" or the avoidance of such experience, "saving face." The staged interchange between actor/historians and audience at Plimoth fits Goffman's conceptual specifications for an "interaction ritual." There is a well-defined code of etiquette for the encounter between interpreters and visitors that is essentially based on the polite and willing suspension of disbelief. In this "play frame," both parties have explicit expectations of the behavior and characteristics of the other. The most fundamental rule is that *the role-players will not be unmasked and thereby forced to lose face.* For the sake of the game, everybody will pretend that these are indeed the real Pilgrims. Goffman states that "the human nature of a particular set of persons may be specially designed for the special kind of undertakings in which they participate, but still each of these persons must have within him something of the balance of characteristics required of a usable participant in any ritually organized system of social activity"

(1967, 45). In other words, there are requisite manners and expected modes of behavior for both performers and spectators if the game of living history is to be successfully played. Guidelines of decorum must be met if interaction is to run smoothly. However, at times (not infrequently), both parties, either seeking a different kind of pleasure or out of sheer perversity, break the rules or attempt to interfere with the established code of good form. On these occasions, when the delicate membrane of the illusion created by the willing suspension of disbelief is damaged, very different kinds of relationships develop between the ethnohistorical role-player and the audience.

There can be cynical perfomers as well as cynical spectators. I know of a few instances in which interpreters made up historical information, just "to have some fun" with the tourists. Here, the performers view the visitors, perjoratively, as being "just tourists." There have also been cases of what Goffman refers to as "fabrications," in which the audience is "induced to have a false belief about what it is that is going on" (1974, 83). I was told about two interpreters, during the 1970s, who used to form what Goffman calls a "collusive net" (1974, 84). One, dressed as an Indian, would row out in a canoe on the little pond, far below the Fort-Meeting House. The other, who gave musket demonstrations on the top of the Fort-Meeting House, would say to the visitors gathered about him: "You see that Injun on the water there? Watch this!" And with the thunderous report from the musket, the "Indian" would fall into the water. For a moment, the visitors would be aghast, not realizing that the musket was only loaded with a blank. Such pranks can be the result of boredom with routine as much as a disdainful attitude on the part of the interpreter. There are also, as we have seen, audience members who try in a belligerent manner to make the actor/historians break out of character. These visitors, feeling that they are being "conned," get in a huff and want to expose the interpreter's "act." Thus the actor-audience relationship is based on what each party brings to it. The best relationship occurs when both parties are sincere and want to play the game together: the actor/historians want to do their best to embody and communicate historical information, and the visitor/audience wants to allow them, even encourage them, to do just that. The situation breaks down if either or both groups behave cynically.

To use Goffman's terminology (1959) again, most of the audience is aware that there is a "back" to the "front" that the performers present to them. A small percentage of visitors are credulous, believing the performers actually live in the Pilgrim Village; these spectators often look upon the interpreters as a backward sect who refuse to enter the modern world. Most visitors, however, are aware that the actor/historians resume their twentieth-century lives after five o'clock. Yet it is surprising how many of these visitors *don't* want to think about it. For those who are truly charmed by the performance, contemplating the "back" is not a pleasing idea. As Marsha Sewell says: "I'm sad to know that they return to twentieth-century lives" (Sewell 1985). There are also visitors who want to break into the back regions. They are enticed by the feeling that there is something they are not being shown. As MacCannell describes: "A back region, closed to audience and outsiders, allows for concealment of props and activities that might discredit the performance out front. In other words, sustaining a firm sense of social reality requires some *mystification*" (1976, 93). Sometimes visitors have to be kicked out of back regions like the "goathouse," the main backstage area inside the village (plate 20). They may accidentally wander into this domain where the performers temporarily let down their front and are shocked to discover electric lights and Pilgrims smoking cigarettes. Overly curious or cynical visitors may consciously attempt to penetrate such back regions. If they are relentlessly aggressive in this pursuit, they may be asked to leave the village or the ship, but this rarely happens, since most people want to enjoy the atmosphere of playful deceit that is created in the front.

Most of the audience is willing to suspend disbelief and accept the symbolic time—1627—even though their digital wristwatches measure the minutes of their participation in the performance. As they move through the living history environment, there are three basic temporal/spatial contexts that define their interaction with the actor/historians.

Firstly, the most fundamental relationship between performer and spectator at Plimoth Plantation is "the conversation." The visitors come up to the interpreters, who are in their roles as Pilgrims, and begin asking them questions. The actor/historians answer "as if" they were the seventeenth-century persons whose names they carry. The first-person interpreter may also ask questions of the visitor, thereby creating a dialogue. The first situation, in which the interpreters merely answer questions, is a remnant of the old museum guide func-

*Plate 22.* An interpreter performing a task while talking to visitors
(Photo courtesy of Plimoth Plantation)

tion. They perform a seventeenth-century task and explain to the
inquiring visitor what it is that they are doing (plate 22). On the other
hand, the kinds of dialogues that take place between the visitors and
interpreters at the plantation today are indicative of the emergence of
the theatrical function. As a 1986 Plimoth Plantation press release
states: "Conversing with these folks from the past is the most engaging
aspect of a visit to Plimoth Plantation. All are quick to explain why
they came to this country, compare life here with life in England,
describe their hopes for prosperity, or repeat some village gossip. But
be warned—the conveyer of gossip could land in the stocks!" (1986b)
Through their conversations with the actor/historians, the visitors are
seduced into participating in the illusory drama of everyday life in
New Plimoth. That is why I say that, once the visitors have come
through the gates of the palisado, they have entered a Pilgrim playhouse.

In his unpublished M.A. thesis, "Living Museums: Coney Islands of the Mind," Maurice J. Moran, Jr., offers two helpful insights concerning the spatial organization of the performer-spectator interaction at Plimoth. Quoting an article on theme parks in *Theatre Crafts* (September 1977), he points out how such a park that focuses on providing its audience intellectual stimulation through the fantasy of time travel is, in many ways, similar to an environmental theatre production: "The total concept of the parks—to create illusion—is a theatrical claim as well. Nothing is to shatter the illusion—'the spectator is totally enveloped and the only escape is through a peripheral exit'" (Moran, Jr. 1978, 26). He cites Plimoth as a paradigm of this kind of environmental theatre/theme park. Inside the palisade walls, the audience moves about on its own, autonomously discovering or choosing the moments of the performance it wishes to observe. The attention of the audience is directed by several types of environmental staging (figure 5), but the audience can always decide not to witness or participate in any given scene.

The audience-participation format employed in the living museum at Plimoth is also a reminder of the countercultural theatre of the 1960s in which many of the staging concepts of environmental theatre were developed. (The influence of this kind of theatre on the living history movement will be discussed in the final chapter.) It is important to note that audience-participation is *the* fundamental mode of actor-audience interaction at Plimoth. The audience rarely just stands or sits, watching what goes on. There are constant opportunities for them to join in the action. Most commonly, the performers and spectators interact and converse in the same space. Thus they are "on stage" together. But the big difference between this and a theatrical event, as Moran suggests, is that the audience in the living museum largely organizes its own time and space.

Regarding the spatial arrangement of the performance, Moran also directs our attention to a much older model of the shared performer-spectator space: the ancient fairground design. As he says, "The layout of the theme parks, if nothing else, links them to their cousins the fair and carnival" (Moran, Jr. 1978, 27). In fact, when it is looked at from the bird's-eye view, the Pilgrim Village resembles nothing so much as Bartholomew Fair (compare plate 11 with figure 5a). Like a fairway, the main street of the village is lined on either side with "booths," i.e., houses, into which the spectator may enter. The Pilgrim house is the main stage of the basic interaction—the conversa-

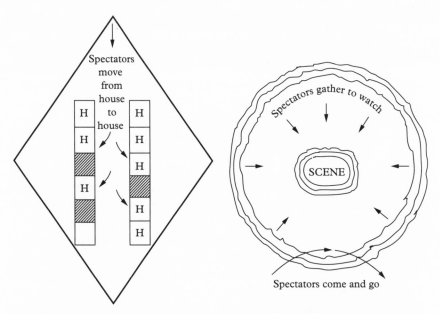

a) "The Conversation" takes place in the Pilgrim Houses (H) set up like booths at a fair.

b) "The Improvised Scene" may erupt anywhere. The spectators spontaneously gather to watch it.

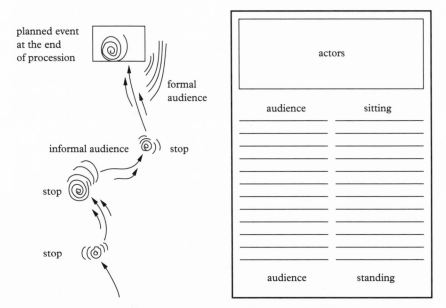

c) Processions can be either "improvised" or "planned." Usually, they move to a fixed goal.

d) "The Planned Scene" is often set up exactly like traditional theatre.

*Figure 5.* Four types of environmental staging used in the Theatre of the Pilgrims (b and c are adapted from Schechner 1977, 113–14)

tion—between the performer and spectator. In theatrical terms, the house is really the essential unit.

However, as the visitor wanders about the village or the ship, the opportunity for conversing with an actor/historian may arise spontaneously in different places. The interpreter may be thatching a roof or working in the saw pit or cooking the noonday meal in the galley of *Mayflower II*. The visitors address the interpreters wherever they find them. As we have seen, these verbal exchanges may take different forms, being informative, humorous, or antagonistic, depending on what emotional/psychological attitude each party brings to this face-to-face encounter.

The second major organizing principle of the actor-audience relationship is "the improvised scene." This type of interaction is mobile and can take place anywhere in the village or on the ship. Whereas the conversational setting is essentially stationary, with the visitors standing or sitting as they talk with the actor/historians, in an Improvised Scene (Figure 5b) the audience may have to move from one place to another in order to observe the scene unfold in its entirety. Often, the action develops out of a fictional conflict between two or more Pilgrims, In this case, the visitors listen to, really "overhear," what may be an intense dialogue *between* the Pilgrims. Such an event, not always planned, is very much like an eruption in everyday life and naturally captures people's attention. Heads turn and people quickly gather. Schechner has called this sort of eruption "one kind of 'natural' theatre" (1977, 113). These improvisational scenes evolve from the routine interaction of the interpreters as they portray the daily life of the Pilgrims. Schechner's model is followed in the depiction of this kind of spontaneous outbreak in figure 5b. Loud voices are heard; a crowd gathers around the action; a plot unfolds. The actors suddenly move somewhere else to engage another Pilgrim in the drama, the crowd following after them. Perhaps they go into the governor's house, where the scene develops further and then moves on to another location. The audience follows, as it would at an environmental theatre performance, although at Plimoth Plantation the events are unscripted.

An example of the improvised scene was cited in chapter 3: the incident of the ribbon-giving in which Master Winslow was obliged to discipline the wayward maidservant Bess Haybell. Just as in a social drama in real life, once a "breach" is made, the moment has to move toward its "crisis." It is gossip that frequently sets these improvised scenes in motion. Gossip can be used by both the performer and the spectator to instigate dramatic action. Visitors may say they heard one Pilgrim say such and such about another Pilgrim, thereby starting a scene. Or one Pilgrim may tell a visitor a rumor that will quickly spread throughout the village and eventually erupt into a scene. As the press release said: "Be warned—the conveyor of gossip could land in the stocks!"

Although the interpreters do not usually collude about the premise of these improvised scenes, neither are the scenes always entirely spontaneous. Sometimes two or more interpreters will get together and prearrange actions that will take place in the village at a specific time. This "playwriting" is often done in the style of a prank. For instance, in the summer of 1985, when I played Edward Winslow, a gaggle of visitors rushed into my house to tell me that my servant, John Beavun, had been discovered "playing at dice." I was also informed that his partner in crime was Edward Hollman, the young man boarding with Captain Standish. As playing at dice was a serious crime in New Plimoth and I was a magistrate, this event was cause for weighty rumination. The audience, understanding the historical context of the situation, was eager to see what I would do next. I was put on the spot. I later found out that the two interpreters, Jay Hansen (John Beavun) and David Hobbs (Edward Hollman), had designed this little scenario early that morning, in order to liven up the village that day. Once such a premise is initiated and gossip starts spreading through the village among the interpreters and the visitors, no one knows how the scene will unfold. The actor/historians must be on their toes. On that day, the crowd followed me to the Standish House and listened as I interrogated the captain concerning Goodman Hollman. Then the captain and I went to search out the rascals, with one of the visitors who had witnessed the wrongdoing leading the way. About twenty-five people followed us as we marched down the hill to the scene of the crime—the deserted hovel at the far eastern end of the village. Discovering my servant with the dice, I was obliged to improvise a speech severely reprimanding him for his immorality. Some of the crowd followed us back to the house, as I continued to instruct John Beavun on the proper comportment for a manservant in New Plimoth.

The improvised scene can also take place in one area and last some time, during which the audience basically remains stationary. A good example of this was discussed in chapter 3: the encounter between Captain Standish and the Winslows concerning the rampant sheep. Such extemporaneous scenes resemble short one-act plays, except that the audience can ask questions and make comments, and the actors improvise all of their dialogue.

The last principal method of organizing time and space in this living history performance is "the planned scene." In this type, the visitors sit or stand just as if they were at a play. They are, in these instances, truly "spectators": "ones who look or watch." Many of the special events described in chapter 4 belong to this category. At the "Festive Wedding," visitors stand and watch the spectacle of the ceremony and the feast (plate 17). At "Court Days," they stand or sit and observe the courtroom dramas reenacted by the actor/historians. Rarely do visitors ask questions when the framing of the performance is reminiscent of traditional theatre; they seem to know that they are supposed to behave like an audience.

Many of the planned scenes begin as processions. Although there is an aspect of procession in many of the improvised scenes (as in Master Winslow's march down the hill to the scene of the crime, described above), in the planned scenes, the processions are formal and choreographed, moving toward a fixed goal. They concur with Schechner's specifications for a procession, having "a fixed route and a known goal. At several points along the way the procession stops and performances are played. Spectators watch the procession pass by, some may join and go on to the goal" (Schechner 1977, 114). For example, during "D-days," the event always begins, after the official greeting of the Dutch at the bottom flanker, with a stately procession led by Governor Bradford and Secretary de Rasieres. People fall in along the way. Part way up the hill, the procession comes to a halt, and a brief military drill is performed for the benefit of the visiting dignitaries. Then the procession moves to the center of the village, where a large crowd gathers and de Rasieres delivers a dramatic oration. After a brief rest in the governor's house, the actors and the audience all gather one more time for a final procession to the main event of the day—the feast in the Fort-Meeting House. Formal processions also initiate the action of the "Funeral of Mary Brewster," the "Governor's Council Meeting," the "Festive Wedding," and "Court Days." The pattern for

*Plate 23.* The audience walking alongside the actor/historians in an informal procession (Photo by Alan Duffield)

this kind of staging is diagrammed in Figure 5c. Usually, the procession moves from the bottom of the hill and proceeds to a destination at the top of the hill. Sometimes spectators stand on the sidelines and watch the performers pass by; at other times, the audience immediately joins in, tramping alongside the actor/historians to the fixed goal (plate 23).

A preplanned scenario and rehearsal time are the major defining characteristics of this final category of performance organization, along with the fact that the interpreters do not expect on these occasions to interact with the visitors. Although the segregation of visitors and interpreters is never absolute at Plimoth, it is these enactments that are most like traditional theatre. Whereas in the conversation and the improvised scenes the interpreter is often partly or completely surrounded by the audience, in the planned scenes the space is frequently (except in the processions) organized like a conventional theatrical performance, with the audience seated in front of a platform upon which the actors perform (figure 5d). These planned scenes in the

Fort-Meeting House—the "Governor's Council" and "Court Days"—
lead right into the formal production of such plays as *The Evidence
Before Us* by the interpretation staff. These plays (see chapter 5, note 2)
are taken outside the confines of Plimoth Plantation to other institutions such as museums and schools. At this point, the re-creation of
Pilgrim culture leaves the realm of living history and enters the
domain of traditional theatre. The actor/historians, here, join their fellow thespians on the road.

In this chapter, the complex interaction of actor/historians and visitors at contemporary Plimoth Plantation has been analyzed. However,
because this interaction constitutes a postmodern performance that
operates on several levels simultaneously, its totality is difficult to represent. What seems like a simple naturalistic presentation is, in fact,
filled with signals that contradict each other. Schechner has also recognized this:

> The contradictions and anachronisms—framed and carefully kept
> separate (all gifts and books, restaurants and toilets, slide projectors
> and brochures, are outside the Village proper)—are what gives Pli-
> moth and its sister restored villages their special kick. The contra-
> dictions are hidden, almost, and revealed at special times and
> places: like the magician who shows a little bit of his magic. It keeps
> the appetite whetted. So inside the Village it is all naturalism; but
> taken as a whole the Plantation is, after all, somewhat like Brecht
> and Foreman. (1981, 27)

The contradictions, of course, are constantly present. The illusion
of the seventeenth-century setting is broken the moment the visitors
enter, looking like inhabitants of the twentieth century and carrying
equipment such as Instamatics, video packs, and Walkmans. Yet the
interpreters must keep up their "front." What are actor/historians to
do, for instance, when a twelve-year-old boy presents them with a
Polaroid snapshot he has just taken? The performers must learn to
maintain a kind of split consciousness akin to Brecht's *Verfremdungsef-
fekt* ("alienation effect"). It would be absurd for the actor/historians to
attempt complete transformation, for they are constantly confronted
with alienating anachronisms. Here is Brecht's advice:

> The actor does not allow himself to become completely trans-
> formed on the stage into the character he is portraying. He is not

[Bradford, Winslow, Standish]; he shows them. He reproduces their remarks as authentically as he can; he puts forward their way of behaving to the best of his abilities and knowledge of men; but he never tries to persuade himself (and thereby others) that this amounts to a complete transformation. (Willet 1964, 137)

Interpreters using the alienation effect would never allow themselves to identify fully with their characters but would show or demonstrate various important aspects of their historical roles. As with Brechtian actors, their primary function is pedagogical—"to make the spectator adopt an attitude of inquiry" (Willet 1964, 136). The actor/historians must maintain a relaxed, neutral attitude, so that they can make points about the historical period and the significant behavior of the historical characters. In this, they retain some of the stance of the museum guide who points out the historical meaning of certain artifacts. However, the actor/historians do this *in role*; furthermore, they are unlike Brechtian actors in that the alienation effect is mostly superimposed on them by the contextual incongruity of twentieth-century people and things. In the game of living history, the performers do give indications to the audience that they, too, are aware of the play frame, and they also make alienating gestures, while simultaneously pursing the serious purpose of ethnohistorical education.

The optimal situation occurs when both performers and spectators recognize the contradictions but agree to maintain the play frame anyway. The audience member signals the actor/historian: "I know you're not really a Pilgrim, but I'm going to play along with you, regardless." The interpreter signals back: "I know you know I'm not really a Pilgrim, but I'm going to perform *as if* I were, for your education and enjoyment." This kind of interaction ritual can be extremely entertaining; the frequent laughter in the village and aboard the ship is proof of this. As Cohen put it: "The enjoyability of the occasion is contingent on their willingness to accept the make believe." (Cohen, 1979, 184) The majority of visitors, who are recreational tourists and simply want to enjoy this amusing interplay, are quite satisfied to remain at the surface of the front. The experiential visitors want to go deeper. They also agree to maintain the playful illusion, but they are more inquisitive; they want to deepen their appreciation of Pilgrim culture. The cynical spectator wants to puncture the front and burst through to the back in order to "expose the fraud." Other visitors want to penetrate the front

out of irritation with the pretense; they refuse to accept the interpreters as seventeenth-century characters at all. There was even one
case in which a female visitor became so infatuated with a male interpreter that she tried to penetrate right into his twentieth-century life.[5]

In the end, the experience of Plimoth Plantation generally represents a time when Huizinga's "play-factor" comes most alive in our
own culture. As Schechner has said, it provides a "postmodern thrill
at the mix or close coincidence of contradictory categories" (1981,
26). It is a wonderful example of Turner's liminality operating in a
contemporary, postindustrial setting. For Turner, the very essence of
liminality is "the analysis of culture into factors and their free or
'ludic' recombination in any and every possible pattern, however
weird" (1982, 28). What could be weirder than the re-creation of a
culture that detested the theatre by means of a theatrical re-presenta-
tion? How did this strange recombination of cultural factors come
about? In the liminal time and space of this interaction between the
actor/historians and the visitors at Plimoth Plantation, we discover the
efflorescence of a whole new genre of cultural performance.

*Seven*

# The Emergence of a New Genre
# of Cultural Performance

> One might ask, what causes this pervading need
> to act out art which used to suffice by itself on the
> page or the museum wall? What is this new pres-
> ence, and how has it replaced the presence which
> poems and pictures silently proffered before?
> Has everything from politics to poetics become
> theatrical?
>
> Michel Benamou,
> *Performance in Postmodern Culture,* 1977

any people regard Plimoth Plantation as a museum. It calls
itself a museum—The Living Museum of 17th Century Plymouth. The English word "museum" derives from the Greek
*mouseion,* which means "of the muses." In a literal sense, then, a
museum is a "place of the muses," and one of the nine sisters is Clio,
the muse of history. Pilgrim history has until recent times been portrayed in poetry and paintings. Today, Clio has bounded off the printed
page and down from the museum wall in order to frolic with her sisters in the performing arts. History at Plimoth Plantation is now expressed through performance.

As we saw in chapter 1, the present-day performance at Plimoth is
in perfect alignment with the quintessential meaning of "performance"
that Turner has extracted from the Old French, *parfournir.* It is a
"bringing of completion"; an "accomplishing"; and act of "thoroughly

furnishing" (Turner 1979, 82). Like ritual and aesthetic performances all over the world, it is a cultural performance that embodies specific cultural entities. Most of this study has been devoted to documenting this process of embodiment in the performance at Plimoth; now it will be analyzed and defined.

The emergence of living history performance at Plimoth is a magnificent example of Turner's concept of liminality functioning as cultural creativity. It is well known that Turner based his theory on Van Gennep's work (1908) concerning the rites of passage among tribal peoples. Turner perceived that the middle phase of some rituals is a time of heightened individual and social creativity. He characterized this liminal period as "anti-structural," because when the normative, repressive social structure is temporarily suspended, an awakening of creativity results. Turner appreciated Brian Sutton-Smith's extension of his theory to include the "protostructural." Turner wrote: "What interests me most about Sutton-Smith's formulations is that he sees liminal and liminoid situations as the settings in which new models, symbols, paradigms, etc., arise—as the seedbeds of cultural creativity in fact" (Turner 1982, 28).

The performance at Plimoth represents just such a new model risen from a situation of contemporary cultural creativity. It reflects the pattern of liminal creativity in tribal rituals. Cultural factors have been recombined to shape a new kind of performative representation for a cultural group that, ironically, abhorred the very idea of celebratory ritual and theatre. As Turner suggested in his later writings:

> Just as when tribesmen make masks, disguise themselves as monsters, heap up disparate ritual symbols, invert or parody profane reality in myths and folk-tales, so do the genres of industrial leisure . . . *play* with the factors of culture, sometimes assembling them in random, grotesque, improbable, surprising, shocking, usually experimental combinations. (1982, 40)

It is important to note that this new kind of performance at Plimoth has emerged at a specific time and in a particular cultural context. It has been shaped by various aspects of postmodern American culture. Turner took pains to distinguish between the functioning of liminality in pre- and post-industrial settings. For the latter case, he coined the term "liminoid," referring to a phenomenon that "*resembles* without being identical with 'liminal'" (1982, 32). This distinction is vital to the following analysis.

We saw in chapter 1 that the Pilgrim story is part of the great Puritan social drama that was resolved, in one way, through the settling of New England in the first half of the seventeenth century. Turner contends that such social dramas are the raw stuff from which later aesthetic dramas are constructed. This historical episode is certainly one source of the Theatre of the Pilgrims. However, a more archaic basis for the living history performance can be located in tribal rituals. Turner also pointed out that "full-scale rituals of this sort are the matrix from which later performative genres have sprung" (1977, 35).

If there is one form of ritual process that the contemporary performance at Plimoth profoundly *resembles*, it is what Mircea Eliade describes as a ritual that reactualizes an *illud tempus* (Eliade 1963, 1965, 1973). In rites of this kind, the sacred history of the tribe is made present, again, through performance. Eliade employs the term *illud tempus* (literally, "that time") to signify that moment, according to a tribal people's mythical conception, when the gods, heroes, or ancestors founded the people's culture. Eliade based much of his theory on the practices of Australian aborigines, who refer to the sacred time of origin as "the dream time." The aborigines believe that through their rituals they are able to reinstate this mythic era. Eliade writes:

> For what is involved here is a fundamental conception in archaic religions—the repetition of a ritual founded by Divine Beings implies the re-actualization of the original Time when the rite was first performed. This is why the rite has efficacy—it participates in the completeness of the sacred primordial time. *The rite makes the myth present* [italics mine]. (1965, 6)

I believe this is the underlying pattern we see in the performance at Plimoth. Isn't what happens at Plimoth also a reactualization of a "tribal" history?

The Pilgrim story has some characteristics that Eliade has located in tribal origin myths. Among the Bhils of Central India, for instance, Eliade finds the "myth of the territorial settling of the group—in other words, the history of a *new beginning*, a counterpart to the Creation of the World" (1963, 24). In the eyes of their filiopietistic nineteenth-century descendants, God had led the Pilgrims to found a new nation on Plymouth Rock. What is the Pilgrim story if not the "history of a new beginning"? As early as 1769, celebrations were created to commemorate the legendary landing on Plymouth Rock. In 1820, Daniel Webster could proclaim: "Forever honoured be this, the place of our father's refuge! There is a local feeling, connected to this occasion, too strong to be resisted; a sort of *genius of the place*, which inspired and awes us. We feel that we are on the spot, where the first scene of our history was laid" (Webster 1825, 5–9).

Webster was speaking, in Plymouth, on the occasion of the celebratory ritual that came to be known as Forefather's Day. His words are reminiscent of Eliade's account of an Australian rite of reactualization: "The ceremonies are carried out at spots associated with the mythical history of the tribe: that is, the sites where the totemic Heroes performed the rituals for the first time. Each actor represents a mythical ancestor; as a matter of fact, he reincarnates that Ancestor" (1973, 82). Webster has designated Plymouth as a sacred spot where the heroic deeds of the ancestors were first performed. Felicia Heman's famous late nineteenth-century poem about the Pilgrims, "The Landing of the Pilgrim Fathers," reaffirmed this sacralization of the historical site: "Ay, call it holy ground,/ The soil where first they trod!" However, it was not until the last quarter of the twentieth century that these "mythical ancestors" were "reincarnated" by the actor/historians at Plimoth Plantation.

It is my contention that, even today, the Pilgrim story resonates as a national origin myth. Most Americans celebrate Thanksgiving and are at least vaguely aware of the basic features of the story. For many, it still has powerful symbolic overtones. As Dwight B. Heath has pointed out, parts of the story have "undergone a complex process of transformation and emerge as modern myths in our national folklore" (Heath 1963, vii). For a few people the Pilgrims resemble "totemic heroes." These individuals project religious feelings onto everything connected with the Pilgrims, and for them a visit to Plimoth Plantation amounts to a pilgrimage of their own.

I am not saying that we view the Pilgrims in exactly the same way that the Australian aborigines did their mythical ancestors. But there are some reverberations of a mythological connection between modern Americans and the Pilgrims. Claude Lévi-Strauss has said that "in our own societies, history has replaced mythology and fulfills the same function" (1979, 43). What is important here is the liminoid quality of resembling the primitive pattern. The Pilgrim story resembles an aboriginal "origin myth," and the re-creation of that story at Plimoth Plantation is similar to the way in which the aborigines reactualize, through ritual performance, the *illud tempus* of their sacred tribal history.

How does this help to define living history as a performance? David Cole has developed a theory that theatre is essentially located in the process of making an *illud tempus* present. Cole has studied rituals in which possession states occur. He finds that "the analogy between such rituals and theatrical performance is not far to seek. In each case, an *illud tempus*—in ritual, that of the gods; in theatre, that of the Images—is made present through being incarnated by hungans/actors who seem, for the time, to 'become' their god/Image" (1975, 34–35). Since Cole uses a specialized vocabulary to build his performance theory, I will take a moment to explain his terminology as it relates to theatrical process.

In the evolution of any theatre production, several basic actions must take place. First of all, the actors are given a script. This script usually renders an account of another time and place—what I have previously described as the given circumstances and what Cole, mythopoetically, refers to as the *illud tempus*. The script presents the time of origin of the happenings that have been created by the playwright. For instance, in *Hamlet,* the *illud tempus* would be Shakespeare's imaginary world of Elsinore. The actors, prepare to transform themselves into the characters that dwell in that imaginary domain; it is their task to bring these characters into the present. In Cole's most fundamental definition of theatre, it makes "*imaginative truth* present," or, as he emphasizes, evokes its "presence" (1975, 6). He refers to the characters in a script as "images," relating them to the numinous gods or ancestors of a ritual *illud tempus*. In Cole's conception, the actors must make a psychological, intuitive journey to the realm of these images. Here is where all of the preparatory exercises in imagination, psychophysical work and intense focus of concentration come into play. During the rehearsal period, the actors use all their creative techniques as vehicles to enter their roles.

At this point, Cole brings in his major theoretical construct: an analogy to the processes of two non-Western ritual actors, the shaman and the hungan. He formulates a concept of modern acting that synthesizes the different functions of these two figures. Most simply put, the shaman is a master of the ecstatic journey to the realm of the gods, the *illud tempus*; the hungan is a master at being possessed by the gods, at trance possession. In the combination of the shaman/hungan ritual actions, Cole perceives the essence of theatre: "I call this reversal in which the actor goes from shaman to hungan—from masterful explorer to mastered vehicle—the 'rounding.' The rounding is the defining characteristic of theatrical performance. It is in the moment of the rounding that the theatre, as an event, is born" (1975, 15). In the whole process of the "rounding," the actor journeys to the realm of the images, becomes possessed by the image, and returns to present the image to the audience. This rounding, then, is the primary psychological mythopoetic experience of the performer in theatre.

So far, Cole's model can be usefully applied to the performative experience of the actor/historians at Plimoth. They also delve deeply into the world of another time and place. They also journey to an *illud tempus* based on a "sacred tribal history." Like Cole's actors who allow themselves to become possessed by the images that inhabit the *illud tempus* of a script, the interpreters often identify strongly with their Pilgrim characters, even to the point of partial transformation of their own personalities ("Deacon Fuller"). Actors perform their rounding in the context of a stage set; actor/historians do so within the framed setting of the Pilgrim Village or the *Mayflower II*. Both types of performers are fulfilling the function of bringing an image into the present, of giving it presence.

However, the use of Cole's theory becomes problematic, once the audience enters the picture. All of the performers' preparations, their efforts to make the rounding happen, are aimed, finally, at bringing their images before an audience that will observe and judge. Cole feels strongly that there must be a clearly defined boundary between the actors and their audience. He predicates his view largely on the belief in the numinous quality of the actor who is invested with the archetypal energy of the image. He is really invoking a kind of ritual prohibition based on a concept of the sacralization of the actors and the possibility of their being polluted by spectators who are too close. Cole speaks out adamantly against the experiments in audience participation:

*There is no "area between" spectating and acting.* Where the partici-
pationists have supposed a fascinating middle ground, there is only
a sharp frontier. Actor and spectator are not, like male and female
according to some psychologists, mere opposite directions along a
gradually shading spectrum. To have rounded and to have been
rounded upon are two different levels of reality. Theatre consists in
braving each of these levels by the other; bring everyone onto a
common level, and *theatre has stopped being the case in that gathering*
[italics mine]. (1975, 76)

To Cole, theater is simply not a participatory event; trying to include
the audience in the performance process immediately negates its reality as theatre. He writes: "Audience participation, in seeming to provide a way of drawing nearer to the theatrical event, in fact abolishes
it" (1975, 79).

This is a crucial question regarding the analysis of the living history
performance at Plimoth. It is ironic that Cole, who bases so much of
his theory on the ritual process of tribal peoples, should abandon the
concept of communality that is so central to the rites and ceremonies
of such groups. However, the theoretical slack is taken up by Schechner, who has devoted many years to studying the ritual and performance processes in non-Western cultures. He writes:

> Wherever we turn in the primitive world we find *theatre* [italics
> mine]—the interplay among space, time, performers, action and
> audience. Space is used concretely, as something to be molded,
> changed, dealt with. . . . Our culture is almost alone in demanding
> uniform behavior from audiences and in clearly segregating audi-
> ence from performers and audience from others in the area who are
> neither audience nor performers. (1977, 28)

It is not surprising, then, to find that Schechner is an impassioned advocate of audience participation. In 1973, he wrote: "There is no technique more important to the development of contemporary theatre
than [audience] participation" (1973, 60). Why did he say this? What
were his grounds for making such a strong statement? Schechner was
beginning to develop his own performance theories at a time when
American culture was experiencing a powerful awakening of participatory democracy in the civil rights movement and the emergence of the
counterculture. The use of audience participation during this period
reflected a desire to democratize and humanize the closed system of

orthodox theatre. For Schechner, it also represented a "laboratory for trying out ways of responsivity" (1977, 60). Tremendously influenced by the ideas of John Cage and by Allan Kaprow's concept of "happenings," Schechner, among others, embraced a whole new vision of performer-spectator relationship and the uses of the performance space.

During the 1960s, many theatres, in many different ways, incorporated audience participation into their performances. The Living Theatre, the Bread & Puppet Theatre, the Open Theatre, and Schechner's own Performance Group are some of the most famous American examples. Audience participation was vitally important in each of these theatres. Schechner defined a new kind of theatre that was diametrically opposed to the traditional separation of audience and performers. He called it "environmental theater":

> Environmental theater encourages give-and-take throughout a globally organized space in which the areas occupied by the audience are a kind of sea through which the performers swim; and the performance areas are kinds of islands or continents in the midst of the audience. The audience does not sit in regularly arranged rows; there is one whole space rather than two opposing spaces. The environmental use of space is fundamentally *collaborative*; the action flows in many directions sustained only by the cooperation of performers and spectators. Environmental theater design is a reflection of the communal nature of this kind of theater. The design encourages participation; it is also a reflection of the wish for participation. There are no settled sides automatically dividing the audience off against the performers. (Schechner 1973, 39)

I have quoted Schechner at length because his conception of environmental theater fits so well with the way in which Plimoth Plantation actually functions. In the Pilgrim Village, the performers and the audience share the space, and the "action flows in many directions sustained only by the cooperation of performers and spectators" (figure 5). Although in the 1970s, this kind of theatre was called "new," "experimental," and "avant-garde," it is, in fact, rooted in the ritual processes and performative patterns of traditional and oral cultures. During the 1970s, Schechner did fieldwork in New Guinea, Indonesia, and India, where he saw models of and for performance that validated his own theoretical definition of theatre.

So here, then, is another concept of theatre: one in which the intermingling of performers and spectators during the performance is considered a genuine theatrical activity. Such a theatre is "a middle world where actual group interaction can happen—not only through audience participation but by subtler means of audience inclusion and environmental staging" (Schechner 1977, 94). When one thinks of the variety of environmental staging techniques employed at Plimoth Plantation and the variety of ways in which the audience is integrated into the performance, it is apparent that this living history performance fulfills Schechner's definition of theatre.

It should be clear, by this point, that the living history performance at Plimoth transcends the scope of a tourist production. That is only one frame through which to view it. Combining Cole's definition of theatre with Schechner's, we can see how this performance reflects the ritual roots of the theatre in that it reactualizes the *illud tempus* of a tribal origin myth. The images of the Pilgrims are brought into the present by the actor/historians in the same way that ritual actors all over the world have enacted and made manifest their mythic ancestors. The interpreters undergo the same kind of rounding experience that Cole has described for actors in a play. Highly influenced by the cultural transformations of the 1960s and 1970s, the living museum at Plimoth has taken the shape of a large environmental theater, utilizing several types of environmental staging including traditionally presented dramatic scenes. Produced by the management of the plantation at a cost of $14,247 per day (Ingram 1987), it is mostly directed by the supervisors in the interpretation department (although much of the general action is created by the actor/historians themselves). It has an audience of around seven hundred thousand people a year. And, although highly theatrical, the living museum is also responsible for the dispensing of accurate ethnohistorical information about the culture of the Pilgrims. It is a complex, multileveled performance that appeals to tourists, scholars and ancestor-worshipers alike. In contemporary America, it represents a new liminoid genre of performance that has been shaped by several cultural factors in our postmodern society.

THE POSTMODERN THRUST TOWARD PERFORMANCE AND THE BLURRING
  OF GENRES

Michel Benamou, while director of the Center for Twentieth Century Studies at the University of Wisconsin and one of the organizers of the

1977 International Symposium on Postmodern Performance, posed a question: "Has everything from politics to poetics become theatrical?" His question refers to the proclivity for and fascination with performance that is prevalent in our contemporary culture. In postmodern society, the barriers separating art and life have broken down. As Jerome Rothenberg has pointed out, there has been "an unquestionable and far-reaching breakdown of boundaries and genres" (Benamou 1977, 13). The present-day living history performance at Plimoth has been shaped in several ways by postmodern influences.

First of all, the second half of the twentieth century has been characterized by the pronounced effect of media on human consciousness. Plimoth Plantation came into existence at about the time the first tiny television screens began to appear in American homes. The plantation grew up in the age of television. In the late 1960s, Deetz wrote:

> The second consideration in the presentation of a living 1627 village is based on current thought concerning media. Marshall MacLuhan [sic] tells us that media in modern America are changing from "hot"—very structured and linear, with a high information content—to "cool"—non-linear, with little structure and low information content and requiring the involvement of more than one of the senses to fill in the picture. In MacLuhan's terms, print is hot; television, cool. The Village is also cool in media. (1969, 37–39)

The presentation of history in the Pilgrim Village has been shaped in a society that has been profoundly transformed by the medium of television.

Peoples' expectations have been conditioned by the omnipresence of television in contemporary culture. One of the questions visitors frequently ask upon entering a re-created Pilgrim house is: "Where's your television?" One inventive actor/historian used to respond "Oh, indeed, our elders ofttimes 'tells a vision.' Is that what you mean, sir?" On a less literal level, most visitors today are oriented toward a multi-channeled, cool-media approach to experience. They expect to be able to switch back and forth among channels easily, to experience a rapid transformation of frames, to enjoy an interplay of contradictory categories. Schechner has noted that: "historical restoration is actually a version of the postmodern. It assumes that spectators, and restorers, can shift temporal channels. Moving through a restored environment involves swift adjustments of frame and accurate processing of multiplex signals" (1979, 20). The cultural climate conducive to such experiences has been fostered by television.

This kind of simultaneous cognition of contradictory categories is a mark of the postmodern; it is in essence the pleasure of postmodern consciousness. Schechner has called it the *"maya/lila"* perspective (1979, 11). These Sanskrit words mean "illusion" and "play," respectively. Television has nurtured a cultural attitude of viewing contradictory frames of experience as the "play" of "illusion." Just as one can switch from the news (real events) to soap operas (fictional events) on television, so, in the Pilgrim Village, one can focus on either the illusory historical scene or the twentieth-century contradictions (such as visitors with their video equipment and Polaroids) or both simultaneously. This paradoxical experience, which provides the majority of visitors with a sense of play and fun, is what makes the village so attractive to the postmodern spectator. The ironic interplay of frames is heightened at Thanksgiving when real television crews and media stars like Tom Brokaw enter the illusory Pilgrim Village. At this time of the year, Pilgrim interpreters have even appeared on major network talk shows.

It is my thesis that, regarding Plimoth, people have become more fascinated with the interplay of contradictory categories than with the narrative delineation of Pilgrim history, and that the predominant place of television in popular culture is responsible for this attitude. As Ihab Hassan has written: "Postmodernism derives from the technological extension of consciousness, a kind of twentieth-century gnosis, to which contribute the computer and all our various media (including the mongoloid medium we call television). The result is a paradoxical view of consciousness as information and history as happening" (1981, 35). Television has precipitated the "You Are There" history-as-happening perspective of postmodern culture, conditioning its mass audience to expect a multi-channeled experience. It is no surprise then that in the 1980s history has been transformed into play and performance, and that such an experience has great mass appeal. Surely the representation of the Pilgrims at Plimoth today owes as much to television as to the history textbook.

The second important feature of postmodernism as reflected in the performance at Plimoth has been characterized by Benamou as the contemporary "playfulness of art" (1977, 4). The breakdown of the boundaries between art and life opened up many new approaches to art. One of the most influential new forms was the "happening." In 1966, the originator of the happening, Allan Kaprow, defined its first rule: "The line between art and life should be kept as fluid, and perhaps as indistinct, as possible" (1966, 188). Kaprow's seminal thinking on the art/life relationship was to affect experimentation in many fields of art. His work sparked experiments in dance and theatre. Schechner admits that his term environmental theater derives from Kaprow's writings (Schechner 1973, 68). The 1960s saw the proliferation of all kinds of performances that destroyed the traditional framing devices separating art from life and performer from spectator. (The name of one theatre company during that period was The Fourth Wall Demolition Company.)

It was a time of vital and creative experimentation in the theatre. As Michael Kirby has written: "New theatrical ideas can be seen as having a validity equal to that of new philosophical concepts or new scientific theories. Like philosophy and science, avant-garde theatre changes culture and perception, thereby changing life itself" (1974, ii).

Many of the experimental concepts of the 1960s had become part of the mainstream culture by the 1970s. As Kirby suggests, the practices of the avant-garde inevitably shift the perspective of the general culture. Eventually, Soho loft experiments show up on Broadway. What was once radical and even threatening becomes an acceptable way of organizing and perceiving time and space. The new ideas filter down to even the most conservative cultural institutions and what was once daring experiment is embraced by the bulwarks of tradition. It's all a part of cultural process. Schechner wrote in 1981: "Audience participation, on the decline in theater, is increasing in theme parks and restored villages" (1981, 28). Thus Plimoth illustrates the transposition of cultural invention.

Undoubtedly, the most significant postmodern trend discernible in the Plimoth performance is what Clifford Geertz has identified as the blurring of genres in the humanities and social sciences. In his celebrated 1980 essay in *American Scholar,* "Blurred Genres: The Refiguration of Social Thought," Geertz posited that a whole new synthesizing of disciplines—a "jumbling of varieties of discourse"—was taking place. In his examination of this phenomenon, Geertz pays special attention to the "dramatistic perspective in the social sciences" and the usefulness of the "drama analogy" in explaining sociocultural processes:

> The recourse to the humanities for explanatory analogies in the social sciences is at once evidence of the destabilization of genres and of the rise of the "interpretive turn," and their most visible outcome is a revised style of discourse in social studies. The instruments of reasoning are changing and society is less and less represented as an elaborate machine or a quasi-organism than as a serious game, a *sidewalk drama* [italics mine]. (1980, 168)

Geertz goes on to demonstrate how the drama analogy has substantially influenced the thinking of a number of important social scientists. One noted exponent cited frequently in this study is Erving Goffman, who wrote a series of books that define the significance of role-playing and stage management in everyday life. In the 1960s and 1970s, society was beginning to be interpreted in terms of a theatrical paradigm. With this extensive application of the drama analogy, it is no wonder that Michel Benamou posed the question that he did.

It was not coincidental that role-playing became the operative method of ethnohistorical interpretation at Plimoth Plantation during that time. The interpretive vision of social life as a "sidewalk drama" had also penetrated the domains of history and museum studies. The force of the "dramatistic perspective in the social sciences" was about to create a new way of thinking about the presentation of history. As Cary Carson writes:

> After twenty years in the business of ancestor worship, it [Plimoth Plantation] was born again in 1967 when Jim Deetz, a Harvard anthropologist, became its associate director. He set about investigating the Pilgrim Fathers (and the Pilgrim Mothers and Pilgrim Offspring, too) in the same way that his academic colleagues studied Australian bushmen. . . . Research proceeded along those lines, and soon after, so did interpretation in the replicated Pilgrim village. Interpreters stopped *lecturing* about the early settlers and started *doing* the things they thought the colonists had done. (1981, 27)

"Drama" is derived from the Greek *dran,* meaning "to do." Under Deetz's tutelage, the interpreters at Plimoth began to *do,* to embody historical actions that they had once only talked about. By 1969, Deetz was discussing the Pilgrim Village in terms of Marshall

McLuhan's concepts, and the interpreters were beginning to explore the meaning of various ethnohistorical data through improvisational enactments. The creation of a new "blurred genre" was underway.

The developments at Plimoth—the gradual transformation of an outdoor history museum into a large environmental theatre—have been paralleled by another important area of genre blurring: the synthesis of theatre and anthropology. In the last quarter of the twentieth century, there has been much overlap and exchange between these two fields. In 1985, Schechner published a book on the cross-fertilization of the two disciplines, *Between Theater and Anthropology*. A number of social scientists have also written about this subject, including Kirshenblatt-Gimblett (1991), Turner (1979, 1982, 1986) and Turnbull (1979). One noted collaboration on the artistic level was the work anthropologist Colin Turnbull did with theatre director Peter Brook. At the International Center for Theatre Research in Paris, Turnbull assisted Brook's company in developing a theatre production that was based on his own anthropological study of the Ik, a tribe in northern Uganda. Through their improvisational explorations of Turnbull's ethnographic data, Brook's actors were able to augment areas where Turnbull's interpretation of the culture seemed weak or faulty. Turnbull was impressed with how the company intuitively came to understand the symbolic importance of the mountain to the Ik: "Peter Brook and his company *knew* that the mountain was not only the thing that kept them alive, they knew that it made their seemingly inhuman way of living both worthwhile, and, in a curious way, beautiful. They knew because they improvised, for a year, and then another" (1979, 9).

There are other important examples of the interface of theatre and anthropology at the level of professional theatre, such as Eugenio Barba's International School of Theatre Anthropology.[1] However, what is so significant about the Turnbull/Brook cooperative endeavor is that it represents an approach that is useful not only to professional actors but also to people simply trying to understand a culture very different from their own. It presents a model for role-playing as an investigative tool for understanding the mysteries of human behavior and cultural differences. It appears to be similar to some of Deetz's early experiments in "doing" at Plimoth. Turnbull and others have elaborated upon this model at the academic level.

Victor and Edith Turner have created courses based on the interface of anthropology and theatre at several American universities. Like the Turnbull/Brook exchange, their stated purpose in combining the two disciplines is "to aid students' understanding of how people in other cultures experience the richness of their social existence" (Turner and Turner 1982, 33). They have utilized their performing ethnography method to explore the processes of social and symbolic action of various cultures, including Ndembu, Kwakiutl and Barok. They have developed an excellent model for the *"high reflexive potential of ethnographic performance as a teaching tool"* (Turner and Turner 1982, 42). What is important about this interdisciplinary approach is its focus on providing a deep, specific learning experience regarding another culture.

At George Washington University in the late 1970s, Turnbull co-created an interdisciplinary course entitled "Anthropology, Drama and the Human Experience: Interdisciplinary Approach to the Study of Social Values." Like the Turners, he stressed the value of using improvisational acting to reconstruct ethnographic data in order to reveal some of the hidden meanings of social action. In discussing a hypothetical re-creation of a Mbuti fire ceremony, he points out the pedagogical usefulness of such an experiment, saying that "the ethnographic reality and the inherent logic and structure of an 'invented' drama would coincide" (1979, 8). Turnbull called his method "anthrodrama," expressing his conviction in the validity of this blurred genre: "So long as our focus is on human behavior in its infinity of form, we [theatre and anthropology] belong together and can help each other in the task of communicating ideas and stimulating critical thought through simple human understanding" (1979, 14).

The models of performing ethnography that the Turners and Turnbull present are important to the analysis of the kind of performative re-creation that emerged at Plimoth in the late 1960s and early 1970s. I believe that James Deetz, who sparked the transformation of Plimoth, was influenced by the same "refiguration of social thought" that had enticed his fellow anthropologists into their experiments with drama and role-playing. Once the museum guides began to enact the ethnographic data related to Pilgrim culture rather than just talk about it, the living museum was set on a course of developing performing ethnography as its essential educational and presentational mode.

Turner wrote: "The movement from ethnography to performance is a process of pragmatic reflexivity . . . the attempt of representatives of one generic modality of human existence, the Western historical experience, to understand 'on the pulses,' in Keatsian metaphor, other modes hitherto locked away from it by cognitive chauvinism or cultural snobbery" (1979, 92). Ironically, Turner is speaking here of cultural "others." But in fact, once the Pilgrims were taken down from their familiar pedestals, *they* became cultural "others" and, for the sake of a truthful representation, required the same honest, laborious ethnographic investigation as any enigmatic foreign peoples. With the development of the living history approach, the time had also come to do away with "cognitive chauvinism and cultural snobbery" concerning the Pilgrims.

The influence of media on the way we perceive, the breakdown of the boundaries between art and life, especially in the performing arts, and the efficacious merger of theatre and anthropology in the forms of anthrodrama and performing ethnography all contributed to the sociocultural context from which the living history performance at Plimoth evolved. With the erosion of the barriers between historical education, entertainment, and ritualistic ancestor worship, a new form of cultural expression began to emerge, something never quite seen before. At Plimoth Plantation, the Pilgrim story was becoming both a source of inspiration and a source of amusement; the *illud tempus* of our national origin myth was beginning to be actualized in a new multidimensional fashion, becoming a combination environmental theatre, historical museum, and a*muse*ment park—definitely a blurred genre.

A NEW GENRE OF CULTURAL PERFORMANCE

Thus far I have shown that the living history performance at Plimoth is both a *liminoid* genre and a *blurred* genre; now I want to explain how it is a *new* genre—specifically, a genre of "cultural performance," to apply Singer's term (1972). The contemporary performative representation of the Pilgrims corresponds to the definition of cultural performances established by the leaders of a recent anthropological conference (the seventy-sixth Burg Wartenstein Symposium) on that subject: "They are occasions in which as a culture or society we reflect upon and define ourselves, dramatize our collective myths and history, present ourselves with alternatives, and eventually change in some ways while remaining the same in others" (MacAloon 1984, 1).

We have seen that the performance at Plimoth dramatizes Pilgrim history, reflecting the ancient pattern of tribal rituals that reactualize the *illud tempus* of an origin myth. The Pilgrim story has become a modern myth, and the Pilgrims serve as national symbols. A comparison can be made with Beverly Stoeltje's description and analysis of the cowboy as a national symbol and the rodeo as an "American cultural performance" (Stoeltje 1981, 124). Stoeltje's insightful writing on these subjects is helpful because of the analogous position that Pilgrims and cowboys hold in the American popular imagination: both are icons of our pioneering past, and, in the course of the development of American culture, both have taken on mythic proportions. The cowboy is the figure of that frontier hero who typifies rugged individualism. The Pilgrim Fathers were, at least at one time, apotheosized as the heroic founders of the nation. Both depictions reflect overly masculinized, patriarchal versions of our cultural heritage, but as Stoeltje says about the cowboy: "It should be no surprise that the cowboy image expresses national ideology since, as Paredes has pointed out, the heroic cowboy developed along with the national identity" (1981, 126). The Pilgrims, of course, are at the very root of our national identity. Stoeltje goes on to explicate how the performance of rodeo, as a representative American cultural performance, reveals some of the basic "constituents of the culture," especially the ideological conflict of work and play in our society. She writes that "rodeo replays cowboy history, reflecting the contemporary influences and communicating the opposition between work and play characteristic of American ideology" (1981, 150).

Historically, the cowboy is much closer to us than the Pilgrim. However, as Stoeltje points out, it was the demise of the range cowboy and the coming of the corporate cattle industry that catalyzed the emergence of rodeo as a performative genre that would unify and re-create the image of this frontier hero in his rough, rugged, and humorous form. The performance of rodeo reconstitutes specific values associated with the cowboy. The performance of living history at Plimoth does the same thing for the Pilgrims. Both performances reveal a longing for the pastoral life of the pioneer spirit; both reactualize the presence of mythic American heroes. As rodeo reveals the courage and humor of the cowboy, the living history performance displays the earthiness and fortitude of the Pilgrims.

In the late nineteenth and early twentieth centuries, the Pilgrim story was represented mostly in what Roger Abrahams has identified as "static" genres, such as paintings, etchings, and statues. Abrahams's system for classifying folklore genres is useful in analyzing the performative transformations of Pilgrim representations, because he constructs his scheme on the basis of the performer-audience relationship (Abrahams 1976, 207). For instance, in the static genre of painting, the performer (the artist) is completely removed from the audience once the object (the painting) is completed. What becomes apparent in viewing the evolution of the Pilgrim representations from the perspective of Abrahams's scheme is that there has been a gradual movement in the direction of the "play" genres. In this type of genre, there is much more interaction between the audience and performer; Abrahams measures this in terms of "interpersonal involvement."

After the paintings came the *tableaux vivants,* which were really not much more than extensions of the paintings, basically re-creating the same scenes already depicted on canvas. In Abrahams's terms, this is still a static genre, since the performer and spectator remain in separate spheres and do not interrelate. The picture frame and the proscenium arch are both devices for distancing the performer from the audience. With the pageant, the audience at least surrounded the performers. Abrahams would probably locate the Tercentenary pageant in his third category of play genre, which includes folk drama and festival activities. However, he comments that in forms like folk drama "contact between performers and audience is almost completely severed—this is what is meant by the term, 'psychic distance.' Identification with the conflict occurs vicariously, rather than through participation, as in a game" (Abrahams 1976, 205). In the pageant, or "festival drama," the performer is still largely removed from the audience. It is interesting that there was no further development of the festival drama as a representation of the Pilgrim story. The precedent was there in Baker's 1921 production. The founders of Plimoth Plantation had planned to construct an amphitheatre where pageants could be performed. One thinks of the way in which the history of North Carolina's Rowan Oake Colony had been re-created in Paul Green's famous "symphonic drama" "The Lost Colony," which, in 1937 blending "music, dance, and theatre turned historical drama from pageant to characterization and central storyline" (Sumner 1975, 15). Many other communities adapted Green's model but this was not to happen at Plimoth, and the Pilgrim representations instead moved in the direction of the more interactive play genres.

I view the Pilgrims' Progress as being a transitional form, connecting the pageant drama to the beginnings of the living history performance. In Abrahams's scheme, it would probably be categorized as a religious ritual since it basically functions as a rite of ancestor worship. It is still fairly static, even being described as a form of "tableau." However, the Progress does move through the streets of Plymouth, thus breaking down to some extent the barrier between audience and performer that is present in the formal theatrical productions. Also, the performers in this event have demonstrated some playful tendencies toward role-playing. As reported in chapter 2, there actually was a point of convergence between the Progress and the representation of the Pilgrims during the early days of Plimoth Plantation—the performers wore the same costumes! In fact, I have located one photograph from the late 1950s, and I cannot discern whether it shows an actual Pilgrims' Progress or the guides and hostesses reenacting the painting, *The Pilgrims Going to Church*.

The plantation of the early 1960s was without a doubt an outdoor museum. The costumed staff were essentially museum guides who directed the visitors' attention to various static exhibits (the wax mannequins set up in tableaux) and answered the visitors' questions concerning Pilgrim history. At this time, the representation of the Pilgrims was becoming what Abrahams calls a "conversational" genre. In this most interactive of the genres, the audience comes face to face with the performer. The performer, in turn, "directs his expression in an interpersonal fashion to a limited number of others as part of everyday discourse" (Abrahams 1976, 200). Of course, the museum experience is not really everyday discourse; it is framed in many special ways. Although the guides and hostesses at Plimoth were not role-playing per se, they were dressed in seventeenth-century costumes. The performative representation at this point was a mixture of the play and conversational genres, pregnant with possibilities and ripe for a major transformation.

Dell Hymes has provided us with a term to designate that moment of transition when, in the course of performance, performers switch from one genre to another. He calls this a "metaphrasis," "a technical term for interpretive transformation of genre" (Ben-Amos 1975, 20).

Although Hymes, in his article "Breakthrough into Performance," is discussing the styles of presentation in the oral tradition of Chinookan narrative cycles and basically focuses on the value of philological analysis to the ethnographic study of verbal performance traditions, I think his terminology can be applied to that major transition in the styles of presentation at Plimoth that began taking place in the early 1970s: the switch from third-person narration of the teaching-style interpretation to the first-person role-playing called living history. In Hymes's case study, there is a shift in the traditional styles of presenting the coyote tales, from the indigenous mode of mythic recitation, with its special pedagogical function, to the more colloquial story-telling form, with its good humor and fascination with character. In many ways, this parallels the transition at Plimoth from the narrative presentation of the Pilgrim Fathers (mythic figures) to the first-person impersonation of real historical characters. Hymes, of course, is talking about a breakthrough into a traditional mode of performance, what he defines as "full, authentic or authoritative performance" (Ben-Amos 1975, 18). At Plimoth, the breakthrough is a bursting forth into a *new* style of presentation, the authenticity of which is constantly in question. Nevertheless, I think, from a longitudinal perspective, that what occurred at Plimoth Plantation can also be labeled a metaphrasis in Hymes's general sense of an "interpretive and performative trans-formation of genre" (MacAllon 1984, 10).

What were the conditions that sparked the interpretive and perfor-mative transformation of genre at Plimoth? What made the moment ripe for a "breakthrough into performance"? There were two principal factors that spawned this breakthrough, one ideological and the other ludic. We saw in chapter 2 how the revolutions of the 1960s removed the Pilgrims from their pedestals. Frances Fitzgerald (1979) has given a brilliant account of how the social upheaval of this period affected the interpretation of history in schoolbooks. Michael Wallace (1981) has shown how the popular movements of that era began to alter the presentation of history in the museums. Cary Carson, in an article entitled "Living Museums of Everyman's History," describes the democratizing effect that living history has had on the museum world:

> This "total history" is, therefore, inherently democratic history. It rejects the traditional notion that rules are more important than the ruled, that might confers the right to be remembered, or that money

does all the talking historians need listen to. . . . Total history gives rhyme and reason to everyone in a historical community, the nobodies no less than the somebodies. (1981, 25)

The counterculture's questioning of authority, the grassroots "Greening of America," and the populist movement in history museums were all indicators of the major ideological shift that catalyzed the metaphrasis of Pilgrim representation at Plimoth. In the words of Carolyn Travers, whose father was the museum director at Plimoth during the 1960s, the Pilgrims were interpretively transformed from "sainted ancestors" to "real people" (1985).

In retrospect, it is easy to see that the next step was inevitable. The plantation had completely furnished (as in *parfournir*) the Pilgrim environment. Unlike the guides and hostesses of the early days of the museum village, the interpreters of the early 1970s walked about in replicated historical costumes and spent time in the re-created houses reenacting the daily routines of the historical characters. As Deetz (1987) has suggested, it was becoming almost impossible for them not to speak in the first person in such a complete simulation of the historical daily lives of the Pilgrims.

By 1978, Plimoth existed in a kind of ludic field. The cultural milieu of the late 1970s, the convergence of theatre and anthropology, the *maya/lila* perspective that Schechner has described, all created just the right conditions for a momentous performative transformation of Pilgrim representation. The step into first-person role-playing defined the presentation at Plimoth as a whole new genre of cultural performance.

Plimoth fits into the context of what Jay Anderson has called the "living history movement." This movement attained such popularity that in his most recent work Anderson identifies "a total of about ten thousand outdoor museums, historic sites, events, publications, organizations, suppliers, games and films [that] use historical simulation" (1985, 440). The movement may be described as one in which various methods of simulation to re-create the past are used. More and more museums are taking such an approach. Here is an excerpt from a 1985 article on the collaboration of several museums in Hawaii that created a living history presentation on the "impact of the Protestant missionary on Hawaii's life and culture":

> There has been in recent years a growing interest in *recreating* history through the techniques of role-playing. At Sturbridge Village or

Plymouth Colony of New England, at Colonial Williamsburg or the dozen of other historic sites across the nation developing a "Living History" program, visitors have the opportunity of meeting and interacting with the historic characters who had once lived at those sites. . . . The use of the performing arts to bring alive the human past is, of course, nothing new. Shakespeare, for example, relied heavily upon historic personalities and events in the construction of many of his tragedies and film biographies have been a staple of the Hollywood cinema. However, through historic role-playing the audience is not just entertained or provoked by retelling historic events— the viewer becomes a part of the past and thus can share with the historian the dialectical process. (Cowing and Grant 1985, 1)

I do not see the whole living history movement as constituting a genre; it is too varied and complex. Some role-playing is done in the first person and some in the third person. The simulation of life in the past can take many different forms. However, I do see Plimoth as constituting a new genre because it is exceptionally well integrated. It was one of the first outdoor museums to employ first-person interpretation and, since the emergence of first person, it has evolved under special circumstances that have led to a much greater degree of theatricalization than is found in other living history museums. Firstly, the cast is relatively small (compared to places like Colonial Williamsburg, in Virginia, or Fort Williams, in Ontario). Secondly, the environment is extremely well bounded and contained. Thirdly, the history of the single year that is reenacted, 1627, is filled with many naturally dramatic events. Fourthly, it has built up a tradition of specific reenactments. And, finally, most people are familiar with the fundamental features of the story and the most famous of its characters.

In 1978, Plimoth Plantation underwent a metaphrasis that has led to the development of a whole new performative representation of the Pilgrims. It is because of the intensive theatricalization of this contemporary representation that the performance at Plimoth may be characterized as a new genre. Today, many people consider this performance to be theatre. Schechner says that "the 'first-person interpretation' technique used at Plimoth is very effective theatre" (1985, 88). Anderson states that "walking into the village is akin to stepping into a historical drama" (1985, 37). Deetz came to perceive his living museum as a form of improvisational theatre (1987). As visitor Jacklyn Wilkin put it, entering the Pilgrim Village is "like walking onto a stage" (1986). Finally, I would like to include the comments of two interpreters with backgrounds in theatre. Tony Kelso is a two-year veteran who was trained in acting and directing at Hamilton College and did graduate study in theatre history at Tufts. During the 1985 and 1986 seasons, he played the role of Thomas Cushman in the Pilgrim Village. Kelso thinks of the plantation as theatre: "Yes. It's street theatre. I think it's back to its elemental level in a way. The way you make these people [the Pilgrims] alive, for me, is not only the interaction, but the stories you're telling. . . . You're telling a story and that's what theatre is" (1986).

Noel Arsenault, also a two-year veteran, has a degree in acting from Westfield State Teachers College and worked for two years in regional theatre in Massachusetts. In 1985, she portrayed Constance Snow in the Pilgrim Village and, in 1986, Mistress Fear Allerton. She states: "I think it is educational theatre, but *theatre*. . . . It's based on facts, but it's being portrayed to you by live people and it's not real. It can be as historically accurate as you [the interpreter] can make it. And the more research you do, the more accurate it can be. But it will never *be real*. It will always be fictitious. And I think no matter how much people get out of this, educationally, they also come here to be entertained" (1985).[2]

In the last decade, Plimoth Plantation has drastically altered the way it presents the Pilgrims to the public. In the late 1960s, affected by the enormous changes in the cultural climate, Plimoth allowed the Pilgrims to become "real people." Their representation has become more and more historically authentic ever since. Ironically, it has also become more and more theatrical. This portrayal of the Pilgrims represents a new genre of cultural performance in postmodern America and a kind of theatrical performance that would have been unthinkable to the original settlers of Plimoth Plantation.

CONCLUSION

In "inscribing" the total living history performance at contemporary Plimoth Plantation in all its multiple dimensions, I have attempted what Clifford Geertz calls a "thick description" (1973, 27). Figure 6 is meant to illustrate the various frames in which the audience can experience this cultural performance. On the top line of each frame are

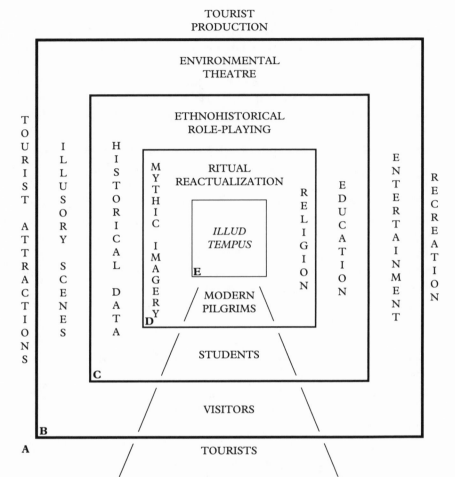

*Figure 6.* The multidimensional Cultural Performance at Plimoth Plantation

labels for the fundamental categories of performance: Tourist Production, Environmental Theatre, Ethnohistorical Role-Playing Performance and Ritual Reactualization. On the left-hand side are listed the types of phenomena that produce the experience: Tourist Attractions, Illusory Scenes, Historical Data, and Mythic Imagery. On the right-hand side are designations that categorize the result of each type of experience: Recreation, Entertainment, Education, and Religion. From the bottom up, in the brackets, are the four fundamental types of audience members: Tourists, General Visitors (who are not necessarily tourists), Students, and Modern Pilgrims, or individuals who are on a genuine pilgrimage to this site.

In the widest frame, dimension A, the performance at Plimoth is experienced as a tourist production that is part of a very large network of such productions. This frame is filled with all kinds of tourist attractions that relate to the Pilgrim image, from the Pilgrim Gift Shop to the wax museum, "Where your Pilgrim heritage comes alive." The plethora of businesses devoted to the tourist trade inspires visitors to tag Plymouth as a "tourist trap."

In their writings on tourist productions, Bruner and Kirshenblatt-Gimblett have suggested that we need not cursorily dismiss such productions as valueless and meaningless. In fact, their work has been devoted to demonstrating how this modality of performance reveals much about the "construction of meaning" in a given society. They advance the notion that tourist productions are particularly worthy of scholarly attention because they unmask the very process of cultural invention (1985). Bruner and Kirshenblatt-Gimblett are following the lead of MacCannell, who typified the tourist as one of the best sociological models for modern humanity in general. MacCannell hypothesized that tourism represents a kind of modern ritual behavior in which tourist sites become sacralized through special framing (1976). The tourist productions in the Plymouth area abound with such sacralized sites: Plymouth Rock, the *Mayflower II*, and Plimoth Plantation itself.

The second major category of experience at Plimoth, dimension B, occurs after the visitor has actually entered the Pilgrim Village; it encompasses the whole theatrical aspect of the Plimoth experience. Schechner (1981), among others, has indicated that Plimoth is effective theatre. Once the visitors are inside the stage setting of the recreated village, they experience something like Stanislavski's naturalistic theatre, because the living museum presents its historical characters in reenactments that take place as if real life were happening in the here and now. The Pilgrim Village resembles naturalistic theatre in providing a delightful illusion for those who are willing to suspend their disbelief. On the other hand, there is a component of Brechtian theatre because the illusion is constantly being broken (a form of alienation) by the presence of contemporary artifacts such as radios, tape recorders, and video cameras, as well as by the audience itself. It is the juxtaposition of the illusory past with a very real present that creates a special kind of postmodern thrill in this environmental theatre where the audience continually interacts with the actor/historians as they perform their daily tasks.

It is also theatrical according to MacCannell's term "staged authenticity." The Pilgrim Village is a front region that simulates a back region. Everything is staged to provide the illusion that the audience is observing people exposed in their daily routine. Of course, it is a well choreographed performance that creates this false back region. The audience is never permitted into the real back region. One of the purposes of this study has been to reveal and explicate the true back region of this cultural production, so as to make the total living history performance more understandable.

This theatricalization is ironic in that the real historical Pilgrims looked upon theatre as an abomination. They were at the forefront of the Puritan movement that mobilized itself against the theatre in England and succeeded in shutting down the theatres in the third decade of the seventeenth century. Thus the emergence of the highly theatrical living history performance at Plimoth exemplifies what the Greek philosopher Heraclitus called *enantiodromia,* meaning that "sooner or later everything runs into its opposite" (Jung [1953] 1966, 72). The real Pilgrims' characteristics of moral rectitude and rigidity make them especially vulnerable to the process of symbolic inversion in this cultural performance. In the theatrical frame, the original Pilgrim culture (or, more frequently, our stereotypical views of it) is subject to what Barbara Babcock describes as the "'aesthetic negative,' whereby any moralistic thou-shalt-not provides material for our entertainment" (1978, 19). Of course, most of the satires of Pilgrim culture occur in the true back region of the performance, where only the staff is entertained.

For me, dimension C is the most significant category of experience because it embodies Plimoth's central educational mission: to render, insofar as possible, an accurate portrayal of the cultural life of the real Pilgrims. This ideal is constantly in jeopardy because of the caesuras in the ethnohistorical data and the sometimes incorrect interpretations of the information that is available. Still, Plimoth has made great strides in the direction of historical accuracy because of the protocols established by James Deetz and the subsequent removal of the Pilgrims from their pedestals to become objects of honest and rigorous ethnographic scrutiny. Deetz was influenced by the same refiguration of social thought that motivated anthropologists like the Turners and Turnbull to develop their methodology for performing ethnography. In fact, like these fellow anthropologists, Deetz utilized improvisational role-playing in requiring his staff of cultural informants actually to *do* what the Pilgrims *did*, as a way of exploring how the people from a distant culture behaved, thought, felt, and looked at the world. In his writing (1969), Deetz pointed out how different seventeenth-century Pilgrim culture was from any form of twentieth-century American culture and how enacting simulated situations based on ethnographic evidence could help to correct those tired cliches that for centuries have accompanied the stereotypical Pilgrim with his buckled shoes and buckled hat.

Schechner has identified the major difficulty with the ethnohistorical role-playing format for representing Pilgrim culture—the same problem that exists for many performances based on the restoration of behavior: "The event restored has been forgotten, never was, or is overlaid with so much secondary stuff that its historicity is lost" (1981, 5). Sometimes the first-person role-playing performance at Plimoth is based on what Schechner labels "nonevents." The problem of authenticity also arises if material is presented as factual when it is only conjectural. In such a case, living history becomes "fakelore" rather than folklore. However, I believe it is becoming rare for cynical fabrications, in the Goffmanian style of impostorship, to be served up to a credulous public. In fact, Plimoth has included a constant critical surveillance as part of the performance process, so that any material that is discovered to be historically incorrect can be quickly removed. With more and more ethnohistorical data available as criteria for what is authentic and what is not, Plimoth continues to grow as a veridical performance of ethnography.

As Cary Carson (1981) has pointed out, for its first twenty years or so, Plimoth was in the business of ancestor worship. Certainly one of the major motivating factors in re-creating the Pilgrim Village was the power of the mythic imagery relating to the "sacred ancestors." The desire to restore "tribal history" goes all the way back to Daniel Webster, who, in 1820, proclaimed that it would be wonderful to behold the Pilgrim Fathers as they actually lived. Amateur archeologist Harry Hornblower, with $20,000 of his own father's money, took up Webster's challenge and, in 1945, the plans to create the Pilgrim Memorial Village were set in motion. From its inception, Plimoth was meant to be a memorial to the Pilgrim Fathers, whose heroic saga has become a "modern myth in our national folklore" (Heath 1963, vii).

Dimension D of figure 6 focuses on the mythological and religious realm of the Plimoth experience. At the core of this is dimension E, what Eliade called an *illud tempus*: a "that time," when the founders of a culture—gods, heroes, or sacred ancestors—were present on the earth. It represents the sacred time of origins, what the Australian aborigines call the dream time (Eliade 1973). Within dimension D, the audience member experiences the performance as a ritual reactualization of the time of origins. The rite is effective because it "participates in the completeness of the sacred primordial time" (Eliade 1965, 6). So, at the heart of this experience is dimension E, which represents mythic time and space. It transcends the frames of historical reality and defines a domain of the deep, archetypal, mythic imagery that produces religious experience.

Cohen, who developed a typology of tourist experiences, designates a special category for those individuals who discover a site that resonates as a spiritually alive, sacred "centre" for them. As he writes: "The visit to his centre of the tourist travelling in the existential mode is phenomenologically analogous to a pilgrimage" (1979, 190). Thus I label those visitors who constantly return to Plimoth because of its profound spiritual meaning to them "modern Pilgrims."

Turner (1982) has provided a term for the kind of ritual-like characteristics of the Plimoth performance. He defines all the qualities that resemble the liminal aspects of tribal ritual process as "liminoid"—"liminal-like." Theoretically this is important, because it is in the frame of liminality that what Huizinga (1955) designated as the "play element in culture" bursts forth in all its glory. The total living history performance is a liminoid phenomenon; it also, as it manifests liminality, unleashes the "play-factor" with all its potential for cultural creativity. As Turner emphasized: "To my mind it is the analysis of culture into factors and their free or 'ludic' recombination in any and every possible pattern, however weird, that is of the essence of liminality, liminality *par excellence*" (1982, 28). In everything that surrounds

Plimoth, the play element in culture has come dynamically alive in a contemporary American sociocultural setting. What could be weirder than Pilgrims re-created through a highly theatricalized role-playing performance, or Pilgrims on television, or Pilgrim images plastered all over the Plymouth area for every conceivable kind of advertisement for the tourist trade? It is gross and, at moments, poetic. What is so wonderful about the whole context of this contemporary cultural performance at Plimoth *is* the strange, experimental, ludic recombination of all of the cultural factors contained in dimensions A through D (figure 6) and the paradoxical way in which the Plimoth performance simultaneously honors and mocks the culture of the Pilgrims. It is a profound expression of cultural freedom and creativity.

Finally, out of this whole evolutionary, creative, transformational process, a new genre of cultural performance has come into being. Just as rodeo emerged from a complex recombination of cultural factors that helped to integrate and re-create the image of that frontier hero, the cowboy, living history evolved, at Plimoth, into a unique and performative re-creation that restores the bucolic past and reactualizes the presence of another American hero, the Pilgrim. Much of this study has been devoted to an examination of the process of development of this performance. My aim has been to elucidate the evolution of a new genre of cultural performance. Hymes's term "metaphrasis" can be applied to what took place at Plimoth during the early 1970s, when the style of presenting the Pilgrims shifted from third-person narration of history to the first-person role-playing of historical characters.

In the liminoid setting of contemporary Plimoth Plantation, the traditional techniques of museum and theatre have been conjoined in a new, experimental, serious, and playful way. Through the influence of the ludic function, a highly theatricalized re-creation has been developed to represent a cultural group that detested the theatre. Plimoth offered special conditions that made this metaphrasis possible. It is a world that is bounded, literally, by the palisado walls. It focuses on one special time frame—the year 1627 at New Plimoth. It has several excellent historical sources on which to base its scenarios. Although Plimoth is akin to the type of historical simulation that goes on elsewhere in the living history movement, it developed uniquely and can be said to constitute a new genre of cultural performance. Its present form is well integrated and consistent and will probably remain the same for many years to come. Perhaps other living museums with equally well-bounded environmental contexts will begin to copy Plimoth's style of presentation and transform themselves into environmental theatres that attempt to reactualize a specific cultural history. For, today, the Theatre of the Pilgrims at Plimoth Plantation is a substantial ethnohistorical re-creation that constantly improves in its historical accuracy. It is a performance that offers its audience a unique multidimensional experience—be they tourists, scholars, or modern pilgrims.

# Notes

PREFACE

1. When the colony was being settled, the spelling most frequently used for its name seems to have been "Plimoth." However, a quick perusal of seventeenth-century English manuscripts will show several different spellings, even in the same paragraph. I have used "Plimoth" to refer to that first settlement where the Pilgrims constructed their village called Plimoth Plantation and "Plymouth" to designate the township that developed there after the century.

2. Several techniques of acting will be discussed in the text of this study. The Method approach to acting, as it was originated by the great Russian actor/director Konstantin Stanislavski (1863–1938), is a naturalistic, non-histrionic, truthful kind of acting. It requires the actor to focus on the "given circumstances" and to identify with them. In a play, the given circumstances are simulated by the stage setting and the actions; however, method actors are known to research their roles by going to environments that more realistically simulate those depicted in the playscript, such as hospitals, prisons, or ghettos. Immersing themselves in these surroundings enables the actors (so the theory goes) to achieve greater empathy with the characters they portray.

CHAPTER I: OF PILGRIMS AND PERFORMANCE

1. Like the preceding, many of the scenes from the living history performance described in this study are composites. They have been reconstructed from my field notes (1984–86); from my memory of work as an "actor/historian" for two seasons (1984–85) in the Pilgrim Village; and from photocopied scenarios that are commonly handed out to the costumed staff before many of the special reenactments, such as "The Funeral

of Mary Brewster." If a scene is presented in the form of the verbatim transcription of a taped recording, it will be cited as such.

2. The Pilgrims did not refer to themselves as "Pilgrims" in their own time. Later generations applied this term to them, probably because Bradford, paraphrasing Heb. 11. 13–16, had once designated the members of the Scrooby-Leyden congregation about to embark for America as such: "They knew they were *pilgrims* [italics mine], and looked not much on those things, but lift up their eyes to the heavens, their dearest country." (Bradford 1981, 50)

3. Ben Jonson's play *The Alchemist*, first acted in 1610, contains several scenes that scathingly satirize the Separatists. Jonson probably based his portrayal of these Separatists on the information available to him in London of the goings-on in the Ancient Exiled English Church at Amsterdam. In one of these notorious scandals, the pastor of that church excommunicated his own brother for publicly criticizing the luxurious way in which the pastor's wife appareled herself. In *The Alchemist*, the two Separatist characters are listed as "Tribulation Wholesome, a Pastor of Amsterdam" and "Aninias, a Deacon there."

4. The early history of "Plimoth" can be read in three period texts: *Of Plimoth Plantation* (Bradford 1981 and [1952] 1982); *Mourt's Relation* (Heath 1963 and Fiore 1985); and "Good News from New England" in Arber ([1897] 1969).

5. I have read original editions of both of these pamphlets at the Harvard Theatre Collection, Harvard University. "Th' Overthrow of Stage-Playes" was first published at Middleburg, in 1599; the "Shorte Treatise" in London, in 1625. As there are few extant original copies of these publications, especially in America, it is quite possible that the ones I read had, in fact, belonged to Elder Brewster.

6. From its inception, the living museum at modern Plimoth Plantation "recognized that the story it proposed to present of the first European settlers in New England was interwoven with that of the native Americans who preceded them. The organization had made several attempts to acquaint the visiting public with the lifeways of the seventeenth century Wampanoag Indian and the significant interrelationships between the two greatly differing groups living in the same land" (Young 1972, 1).

The first plans for Plimoth Plantation, in 1948, showed a sketch of "a small Indian Village consisting of several typical houses" (Plimoth Plantation, Inc. 1948, 18). During the early years of the museum, a non-Native American demonstrated how to make arrowheads at this re-created Indian campsite. Later, non-Native American museum guides, costumed as Pilgrims, lectured on Wampanoag lore and history at this site. It was only after a massive Native American protest in Plymouth on Thanksgiving Day, 1970 (during the 350th anniversary of the coming of the *Mayflower*) that the plantation initiated a special Native American Studies Program. By 1973, costumed Native American personnel staffed the Wampanoag campsite. Since that time, the Wampanoag Indian Program at Plimoth Plantation has undergone many transformations.

Because of the complexity of its evolution and, mainly, because it no longer utilizes the first-person role-playing technique, I will not discuss the Wampanoag Indian Program in this study. Truly, it deserves a book to itself. However, in chapter 4, I will describe a point where the Native American and Pilgrim programs at Plimoth Plantation intersect in a living history performance: the reenactment of fur trading in the 1627 Pilgrim village.

7. There were several minor dramatic works on the subject of the Pilgrims written before 1921. These include: Joseph Croswell's *A New World Planted: The Adventures of the Forefathers of New England*, 1802; Beulah Marie Dix and Evelyn Greenleaf Sutherland's *A Rose O' Plymouth town*, 1908; and Edward W. Stirling and A. Hayes's *The Mayflower: A Play of the Pilgrim Fathers*, 1920. I don't know if any of these plays were ever produced. In any case, compared with the development of living history performance, plays have had little impact on the popular imagination. The great play about the Pilgrims envisioned by Edward Arber (see the quotation at the beginning of this chapter) has yet to be written.

8. George Pierce Baker offered the first drama course ever to be given at an American university when he began to teach playwriting at Radcliffe in 1903. Oscar Brockett writes: "Later opened to Harvard University students, the course was enlarged in 1913 to include a workshop for the production of plays. Baker attracted many of America's most talented young men, including Eugene O'Neill, S. N. Berman, and Robert Edmond Jones. . . . In 1925, Baker moved to Yale University where he established a drama department which was to provide professional training for many later theatre workers. (Brockett 1968, 631)

9. I am indebted to Terry Geesken, a curator at the Film Still Archive, The Museum of Modern Art, New York City, for identifying four old photographs from *The Courtship of Miles Standish*. According to Geesken, this film is no longer in existence.

Since 1923, two other major movies about the Pilgrims have been produced. In 1952, *The Plymouth Adventure*, starring Spencer Tracy, Van Johnson, and Gene Tierney, with direction by Clarence L. Brown, was released by MGM. In 1979, George Schaefer directed a made-for-television movie, *Mayflower: The Pilgrim's Adventure*. It starred Anthony

Hopkins in the role of the famous ship's master, Christopher Jones, and Richard Crenna as Elder William Brewster. To say the least, the script took great liberties with history. A critic for *Variety* (28 November 1979) described the bulk of this film as "soap-operaish romantic twaddle."

CHAPTER 2: THE DEVELOPMENT OF A PERFORMATIVE REPRESENTATION
OF THE PILGRIMS AT MODERN PLIMOTH PLANTATION

1. Isaack de Rasieres described the Pilgrims' procession to the Fort-Meeting House in 1627:

> They assembled by beat of drum each with his musket or firelock, in front of the captain's door; they have their cloaks on; and place themselves in order, three abreast, and are led by a sergeant without beat of drum. Behind them comes the Governor, in a long robe; beside him on the right hand, comes the preacher with his cloak on, and on the left hand, the captain with his side-arms and cloak on, and with a small cane in his hand; and so they march in good order. (James, Jr. 1963, 76–77)

2. Deetz gives a different account of this occasion. He feels that Trask's memory has probably distorted what actually took place that day. Deetz recalls that, although there was resistance from the board of governors to his new approach, David Freeman supported him from the beginning. Deetz says Freeman was simply saddened by the way the village looked that day, saying, "It's right, but it's not as nice as it was" (Deetz 1987).

3. Most of the veteran hostesses, some of whom had been at the plantation since 1959, moved out of the village after Deetz began to implement his new approach. By 1977, when first-person role-playing began to emerge, the former hostesses formed the nucleus of the new visitor services department. They didn't like the new mode of representation. In the beginning, they thought it was "weird" and "far-out," and they didn't want to do it (Hale et al. 1986). Most of these women were housewives working on a part-time basis. Although today they've come to appreciate the way in which the Pilgrim Village is re-created, their leaving it really marks the major transition from the old style to the new style of interpretation.

4. "Interpreter" and "informant" are both used to designate the costumed employees at Plimoth. "Cultural informant" came into vogue during the emergence of first-person interpretation. Today, the terms are used interchangeably, although I would say "interpreter" is the more popular of the two.

5. In the 1990s, the living history performance at Plimoth is generally following the direction set in the 1980s. Perhaps the skills of some individual interpreters have deepened, since there is now a job title called "master interpreter." As the Manager of Colonial Interpretation, John C. Kemp, informed me in a telephone interview (5/14/92), the most important developments in the 1990s have been (1) the implementation of a more integrated approach to interpretation that has resulted from greater collaboration between the curatorial, research and interpretation departments, and a closer relationship with the Native American interpretation program, (2) more Dutch characters in the Pilgrim Village, and (3) the emergence of a true ensemble approach to the enactment of daily life in the Pilgrim Village. Kemp also mentioned that one of the interpretation supervisors had given acting workshops for interpretation staff members. On my most recent visit to Plimoth Plantation (6/12/92), I was privileged to attend the morning meeting for staff before the gates of the living museum were opened to the public. I was delighted to overhear that two of the new interpreters were appearing that week in a community theatre production. To me, this was an indication that the link between first-person role-playing and theatrical performance is still very strong.

6. This was a fascinating episode in the annals of Plimoth Plantation because of the many issues it raised. Robert Marten had originally read a copy of a historic militia listing that said: "Abraham Pierce Blackamoor." Marten took this to mean that Abraham Pierce was a blackamoor. Later investigations by scholars in the field showed that the copy upon which Marten had based his interpretation was inaccurate. The clincher came when Peter Gomes, a black historian and theologian from Harvard, said that Marten's interpretation was impossible. By this time, the press had gotten wind of these goings-on at the plantation, and articles such as "Guess Who's Not Coming to Dinner" appeared in the Boston *Patriot Ledger*. The pernicious racism with which this country still struggles was thus brought into conflict with the heroic myth of the country's founding.

7. There have been several occasions in my experience when the administration at Plimoth Plantation has shown insensitivity to the creative illusion-making labors of the interpreters. For example, once in the summer of 1984, a maintenance crew was sent down to set up floodlights for an evening cooking workshop before the visitors had left and while the interpreters still had to act as if it were 1627. This incident caused great chagrin among the interpretation staff, and a formal complaint was made to the administration. Of course, there is a certain irony in all of this, in that the visitors are constantly alienating the illusion with their cameras and video equipment.

CHAPTER 3: WITHIN THESE PALISADE WALLS: A PILGRIM PLAYHOUSE

1. In the fall of 1987, Plimoth Plantation inaugurated a new ten million dollar Visitor Center where visitors are now oriented by means of a sophisticated "high-tech" slide show. However, the upstairs of the old "movie building" continues to house the changing rooms and lounge area of the interpreters.

2. As Jean Poindexter Colby has pointed out (1970, 104), the difficulty with following this schema was that William Bradford's original layout only shows one side of the street and halfway down the other. According to former museum director David Freeman, the rest of the houses were plotted out based on the best information available and "reasonable conjecture."

3. I have heard from several of the veteran interpreters that this all-day service was reenacted at least once in the last decade. It was so unbearably long for both the interpreters and the visitors that it has never become part of the repertoire of reenactments. Thus the core of the Pilgrims' culture—their religious practice—has proven to be very difficult to re-create at Plimoth Plantation.

4. This discrepancy can create a real problem for the interpreters in Winslow House. When I played Edward Winslow in 1985, I said that my brother, Gilbert, built the left side of the house and I built the right. Many visitors would ask about the divergence of architectural styles in this particular house.

5. This "day" is really a pastiche of many days I experienced in the Pilgrim Village. All of the events described herein actually happened, but not necessarily on a spring day. Some occurred in the summer and fall during the 1984 and 1985 seasons. However, this section does follow the basic patterns of a day in the Pilgrim Village.

6. Once, in the summer of 1985, the supervisors put up a notice on the interpreters' bulletin board stating that many visitors had complained about the "rudeness" and "unfriendliness" of the female interpreters. The women, who spend much of their time in front of the hearth, often have to perform with their backs to the visitors. Some visitors take this as a sign of hostility. The do not understand that seventeenth-century open-hearth cooking requires constant attention and that what they are really confronting in this situation is the "woman's place" in Pilgrim culture.

7. "Pilgrim-baiting" is a favorite sport at Plimoth Plantation. Many visitors, especially teenagers, deliberately endeavor to break the illusion of seventeenth-century life by asking questions about television, video cassettes, or rock stars, or by pointing out the airplanes that occasionally fly

overhead, or by calling attention to the fire extinguisher that is necessarily concealed in every Pilgrim house. This is all part of the play—the game—of the village.

8. As Schechner states in his essay "Performers and Spectators Transported and Transformed": "Getting out of the role is sometimes harder than getting into it. Little work has been done on the cool-down,' at least in the EuroAmerican tradition . . . What the cool-down does is return the performer to an ordinary sphere of existence: to transport him back to where he began" (Schechner 1985, 125). The interpreters are, in this case, coming out of their non-ordinary existence as Pilgrims back into their ordinary twentieth-century lives.

CHAPTER 4: SCENES FROM THE THEATRE OF THE PILGRIMS

1. Actually, what we today consider Thanksgiving is not re-created. What is reenacted is the mid-October Harvest Home. This will be explained in the section "The Most Famous Scene of All" in this chapter.

2. The fact that only this one day is represented aboard the *Mayflower II* can easily confuse visitors who also stop over in the Pilgrim Village. For instance, on the ship, Governor William Carver is very much alive on February 21, 1620; in the 1627 village, he is long since dead. The same is true for Mary Brewster, who is dead in the village after April 17, 1627, but still alive in the ship re-creation. A visitor may tell an interpreter working in the village that "I just saw your wife on the *Mayflower*" and the interpreter will have to answer, "That's impossible! My wife, she's been dead these past seven years!" For the most part, the 1627 villagers have to ignore the presence of the *Mayflower* (which, historically, returned to England in 1621).

3. Maurice J. Moran, Jr., in his M.A. thesis, "Living Museums: Coney Islands of the Mind," draws the analogy between living museums and amusement parks. He quotes Walt Disney's famous edict: "You've got to have a wienie at the end of every street" (Moran, Jr. 1978, 19). Interpreters at contemporary Plimoth Plantation have been known to refer to their living museum as "Disneyland East." During the plantation's season, the special events serve as the "wienies."

4. "Sister-in-love" was the Pilgrims' equivalent of "sister-in-law." When I played Master Winslow, I frequently used this term in reference to my brother's wife.

5. Barbara Austin, who played the role of Mary Winslow during the 1985 season, is not a trained professional actress. However, she told me

that she got so caught up in enacting this particular scene that she felt "as if" it were really happening to her. Later, she wrote to me: "I've truly believed in, and loved, our family. I loved the wedding day—it felt so genuine. I know the Winslows are make-believe. But our family was real and so was the love. I'm proud of our family and what we all created" (letter to the author, 12 October 1985).

6. Here is Edward Winslow's actual description of the 1621 feast that has erroneously come to be known as the "first Thanksgiving":

> Our harvest being gotten, our governor sent four men on fowling, that so we might, after a special manner, rejoice together after we had gathered the fruits of our labors. They four in one day killed as much fowl as, with a little help beside, served the company almost a week. At which time, amongst other recreations, we exercised our arms, many of the Indians coming amongst us, and among the rest their greatest king, Massasoit, with some ninety men, whom for three days were entertained and feasted; and they went out and killed five deer, which they brought to the plantation, and bestowed on our governor, and upon the captain and others. And although it be not always so plentiful as it was this time with us, yet by the goodness of God we are so far from want, that we often wish you partakers of our plenty. (Fiore 1985, 72)

Winslow does not say exactly when "this time" was, but it can be assumed that "our harvest" would have been about the middle of October.

7. When the film *Ghostbusters* came out in the summer of 1984, interpreter Barbara Austin drew a design that parodied the well-known logo of that film. Her drawing comically reflected, to the interpretation staff, their function of debunking the many myths and stereotypes concerning the Pilgrims, that are still held by the visitors. She called it "Myth-busters." It showed two clichéd Pilgrims—a man and a woman—with the stereotypical buckled hat and starched collars, all in black and white, circumscribed and bisected by a diagonal line meaning: "Not Allowed."

8. It is true that, as part of the Winter Education program, schoolchildren are brought into the village for workshop during the winter months and do observe a female interpreter preparing a meal on the open hearth. More commonly, interpreters with slide projectors in hand make first-person presentations in the classroom. The undesirability of portraying Pilgrim life in the harsh New England winter is further exemplified by the plantation's construction of a new year-round, heated Visitor Center. Also, a new Fort-Meeting House was erected in 1986 with a well-concealed heating system.

CHAPTER 5: ACTOR/HISTORIANS: THE PERFORMERS' BACKGROUND,
TRAINING, AND SELF-CONCEPTION

1. I think one of the most significant characteristics of the interpreters is their capacity for play. During my two years at the plantation, I observed several instances of highly involved adult play forms. For example, there was a small group of male interpreters (about half a dozen) who met on a regular basis to play "war games." These were board games upon which famous episodes of military history could be re-created. The men, who were mostly in their late twenties, became obsessed with this fantasy diversion, spending hours to create miniature soldiers and work out complicated, Napoleonic strategies. Other interpreters were seriously involved with the fantasy game known as Dungeons and Dragons. A few acted in plays in local community theatres while also performing as Pilgrim interpreters. All of this "play activity" attests to an extraordinarily well-developed ludic faculty in these individuals. How this ludic function relates to liminal personalities will be analyzed in the last chapter.

2. Since 1984, these plays have become an important component of the plantation's educational outreach program (which administers "winter ed"). They probably were inspired by the "Court Days" performance that is regularly enacted in the Pilgrim Village. Both plays are courtroom dramas based on the *Plymouth Colony Records* (Shurtleff [1855] 1968). Students become the jury and are allowed to debate the final judicial decision. The first play, *The Evidence Before Us,* dramatized the 1675 murder trial of an Indian in New Plimoth. As the 1985 Annual Report states: "The reenactment presented the relationship of the early colonists and the native people, and pointed out how the law and political climate influenced or were influenced by that relationship" (Plimoth Plantation 1985 Annual Report). Tomkins's new play, entitled *Cursed Tennets: The Quaker Troubles at Plimoth, 1656–1661,* is a dramatization of the Plimoth court trial of some zealous Quakers who disrupted the colony with their unorthodox religious practices. As Tomkins told me in a telephone interview (4 January 1987), this play focuses on the issue of tolerance for individual differences in a democratic society.

Leonard Travers has also told me of the possibility that, in the near future, such dramatic productions may be performed in the new Visitor Center, in order to show the public other aspects and eras of Pilgrim history (Travers 1986). This proliferation of dramatic activity further illustrates the expanding theatricalization of the Pilgrim story.

3. I am forty-seven and have been performing in plays since I first appeared in an amateur production of *Carousel* at the age of ten. I have a B.A. in theatre arts from Emerson College and studied acting in New

York with Pierreno Mascarino and Julie Bovasso. I am a member of Actors' Equity and have appeared with many theatre companies in New York, Massachusetts, Maine and New Hampshire. In 1980, I did a six-month tour of *Twelfth Night* with the Theatre of the Forgotten; in 1981, I appeared in *The Arabian Nights* with Chameleon Theatrix, and in 1982, I played the part of the narrator in the Balinese American Dance Theatre's *Night Shadow*. All of these productions were in New York City.

4. This prank actually took place early one morning during the later part of the season *in* the Pilgrim Village. I have seen a photograph of this enactment. An interpreter who witnessed the event told me that visitors were present, but they took it all very good-naturedly. I think that as the season comes to a close the Pilgrim impersonation becomes more and more vulnerable to this ironic, contradictory, comic spirit of inversion.

5. I don't want to overemphasize the extent of such bacchanalian behavior among the interpreters. In my own experience, there were at most two or three sleep overs in a season. However, I think the many ways in which these all-night blasts in the village contradict the illusory world of daytime performance is germane to this discussion of symbolic inversion.

CHAPTER 6: PILGRIMS AND TOURISTS: THE PERFORMER-AUDIENCE
INTERACTION

1. Here are the statistics of yearly visitation for the seven-year period from 1980 to 1986:

|        | *Mayflower II* | *Village* | *Total* |
|--------|----------------|-----------|---------|
| 1986 - | 369,124        | 349,292   | 718,416 |
| 1985 - | 357,000        | 347,000   | 704,000 |
| 1984 - | 362,000        | 332,000   | 694,000 |
| 1983 - | 333,000        | 304,000   | 637,000 |
| 1982 - | 351,000        | 290,000   | 641,000 |
| 1981 - | 336,000        | 300,000   | 636,000 |
| 1980 - | 354,000        | 276,000   | 630,000 |

These statistics are from the *Plimoth Plantation Annual Reports* 1983–86. During this time, attendance steadily increased, with the exceptions of the village in 1982 and the total in 1983. However, probably due to the recession, attendance began to drop a little in 1990. According to the 1991 *Plimoth Plantation Annual Report*, visitation in both 1990 and 1991 fell somewhat below the 700,000 mark.

2. All sixty-six interviews were taped on location at Plimoth Plantation. Each interview lasted approximately fifteen to twenty minutes. Forty-two

were done during Thanksgiving weekend, November 29, to December 1, 1985; fourteen were done on September 3, 1986. All of the visitors' quotations in this chapter are taken from this series of interviews.

3. Eric Marr, an interpreter in 1984 and 1985, once got himself in a little trouble with the Plantation administration for kicking some private school students out of the village. Their teacher wrote a letter of complaint to the plantation. Marr felt justified in his action because these students had been rowdy and disruptive. It seems that their teacher had told them that the interpreters were impervious to attempts to break them out of character, so the students made that the whole objective of their visit, aggressively barraging Marr with questions about twentieth-century sports. Finally, after observing their obnoxious behavior with other interpreters, Marr escorted them to the exit, breaking out of character to demand that they leave the premises (letter to the author, 27 January 1987). Marr received the support of his fellow interpreters, the visitor services staff, and the other tourists who were present for his action.

4. Of the sixty-six people I interviewed, forty-one said they thought the interpreters were actors and twenty-five said they did not. This 70 percent positive response is way below the 99 percent reported by visitor services. What the visitor services staff is basing their figure on, however, is people *asking* whether or not the interpreters are actors. They are curious as to whether or not this is so; they haven't totally made up their minds. Also, the statements of my respondents were qualified in so many ways that the information remains ambiguous. For instance, one interviewee said: "I guess they're better than just actors." Another responded: "No, they're not actors. They're too natural. It's like conversing with a neighbor."

5. During the 1984 season, interpreter David Hobbs was relentlessly pursued by a female visitor. While touring the village, she developed a crush on him and for weeks afterwards wrote him passionate love letters. Hobbs was a little embarrassed by the erotic content of her billets-doux: she described her sexual obsession with him, explicitly delineating her fantasies that included Hobbs's Pilgrim persona. For three months, she visited the Pilgrim Village three to four times a week. As Hobbs is a happily married man, he requested that she not be allowed in the village. Finally, she stopped pestering him. However, for Christmas 1984, she sent him a present—a book entitled *Social Customs in England* (letter to the author, 17 January 1987).

CHAPTER 7: THE EMERGENCE OF A NEW GENRE OF CULTURAL
PERFORMANCE

1. Barba's school focuses on the cross-cultural study of the "communi-

cation systems" of theatre. Barba brings together performers, many of whom are masters in their particular performance tradition, from all over the world. They direct workshops that are detailed investigations of the languages of dance, movement, gesture, mime. In the bulletin for the first session of the International School of Theatre Anthropology in 1980, he wrote: "Theatre anthropology is the study of the biological and cultural behaviour of man in a theatrical situation, that is to say, of man presenting and using his physical and mental presence in accordance with laws differing from those of daily life." This, of course, is very different from using improvisational role playing to re-create the daily behavior and symbolic action of various cultural groups to increase understanding of their cultures. For more on Barba's specialized approach, see his article "Theatre Anthropology" in *The Drama Review,* vol. 26, no. 2, Summer 1982 (T94).

2. Noel Arsenault, who considers herself an actress, has appeared in some 40 to 50 plays and worked in regional theatre. She has this to say about how working as an interpreter in the Pilgrim Village may have helped her grow as an actress: "One thing I always had trouble with was sustaining the mood of a character over a long period of time. I always did much better in plays where there were radical scene changes or the play was a one-act play. I found it very tiring to sustain a character for three acts. Now that I've had to sustain a character for eight hours, I think that I'll be better able to do long plays" (1985). Arsenault later decided to go into teaching. She told me that she thinks teaching is really a form of acting. Her comment clearly reflects the two sides of the actor/historian identity.

# References

BOOKS AND ARTICLES

Abrahams, Roger D. 1976. "The Complex Relations of Simple Forms." In *Folklore Genres*, edited by Dan Ben-Amos, 193–214. Austin: University of Texas Press.

Ainsworth, Henry. 1612. *The Book of Psalms, Englished Both in Prose and Metre*. Amsterdam: Imprinted by Giles Thorp.

Anderson, Jay. 1984. *Time Machines: The World of Living History*. Nashville, Tennessee: The American Association for State and Local History.

———. 1985. *The Living History Sourcebook*. Nashville, Tennessee: The American Association for State and Local History.

Anderson, Joan. 1984. *The First Thanksgiving Feast*. New York: Clarion Books.

Arber, Edward, ed. [1897] 1969. *The Story of the Pilgrim Fathers, 1606–1623 A.D.* Reprint. New York: Kraus Reprint Co.

Babcock, Barbara A. 1978. *The Reversible World: Symbolic Inversion in Art and Society*. Ithaca: Cornell University Press.

Baker, George Pierce. 1921. *The Pilgrim Spirit: A Pageant in Celebration of the Landing of the Pilgrims in Plymouth, Massachusetts, December 21, 1620*. Boston: Marshall Jones Company.

Banks, Edward Charles. [1929] 1965. *The English Ancestry and Homes of the Pilgrim Fathers*. Reprint. Baltimore: Genealogical Publishing Company.

Barish, Jonas. 1981. *The Anti-Theatrical Prejudice*. Los Angeles: University of California Press.

Bartlett, Robert M. 1971. *The Pilgrim Way*. Philadelphia: United Church Press.

Barton, Michael. 1978. "The Hearts and Minds of the Pilgrims." *Early American Life* 9, no. 5 (October): 44–78.

Ben-Amos, Dan, and Kenneth S. Goldstein, eds. 1975. *Folklore: Performance and Communication.* Paris: Mouton & Co. N.V., Publishers.

Benamou, Michel, and Charles Caramello, eds. 1977. *Performance in Postmodern Culture.* Madison: Coda Press, Inc.

Bittinger, Frederick W. 1923. *The Story of the Pilgrim Tercentenary Celebration at Plymouth in the Year 1921.* Plymouth, Massachusetts: The Memorial Press.

Bloomingdale, H., ed. 1921. *Plymouth Tercentary Illustrated.* New Bedford, Massachusetts: The Commercial Publishing Co.

Boorstin, Daniel J. [1961] 1987. *The Image: A Guide to Pseudo-Events in America.* 25th Anniversary Edition. New York: Atheneum.

———. 1962. *The Image or What Happened to the American Dream.* New York: Atheneum.

Bradford, William. 1981. *Of Plymouth Plantation 1620–1647.* Edited and introduced by Francis Murphy. New York: The Modern Library.

Bradford, William. 1981. *Of Plymouth Plantation 1620–1647.* New ed. Edited and introduced by Samuel Eliot Morrison. New York: Alfred A. Knopf.

Briggs, Rose T. 1971. "Pilgrim Progress, 1921–1971." Pilgrim Society, Plymouth, Massachusetts. Typescript.

———. 1982. *Plymouth Rock: History and Significance.* Boston: The Nimrod Press.

Brockett, Oscar. 1968. *History of the Theatre.* Boston: Allyn and Bacon, Inc.

Bruner, Edward M., and Barbara Kirshenblatt-Gimblett. 1985. "Tourist Productions: A Prospectus." Photocopy.

———. 1988. "Tourism: Performing Ethnographic Tropes." Photocopy.

———. 1989. "Tourism." In the *International Encyclopedia of Communications,* Vol. 4. 249–53. Oxford: Oxford University Press.

Campbell, Joseph, ed. 1970. *Myths, Dreams and Religion.* New York: E. P. Dutton & Co., Inc.

Carroll, James. 1984. "Pilgrim's Plymouth: Revisiting 1620." *New York Times,* 4 November, Travel section.

Carson, Cary. 1981. "Living Museums of Everyman's History." *Harvard Magazine* (Summer): 23–31.

Charlton, Warwick. 1957. *The Second Mayflower Adventure.* Boston: Little, Brown and Company.

Chekov, Michael. 1953. *To the Actor: On the Technique of Acting.* New York: Harper & Brothers, Publishers.

Claiborne, Craig. 1990. "Food of Our Fathers." *Phillip Morris Magazine* Nov./Dec.: 14–17.

Cohen, Erik. 1979. "A Phenomenology of Tourist Experiences." *Sociology* 13, no. 2 (May): 179–200.

Colby, Jean Poindexter. 1970. *Plimoth Plantation: Then and Now.* New York: Hastings House, Publishers.

Cole, David. 1975. *The Theatrical Event: A Mythos, A Vocabulary, a Perspective.* Middletown, Conn.: Wesleyan University Press.

Cole, Toby, ed. [1947] 1955. *Acting: A Handbook of the Stanislavski Method.* Introduction by Lee Strasberg. New York: Crown Publishers, Inc.

Cowing, Cedric B. and Glen Grant. 1985. "Missionaries in Hawaii." *Humanities News* 6, no. 1 (March): 1.

Deetz, James. 1969. "The Reality of the Pilgrim Fathers." *Natural History* (November): 32–45.

———. 1980. "A Sense of Another World: History Museums and Cultural Change." *Museum News* 58, no. 5 (May/June): 40–45.

———. 1981. "The Link from Object to Person to Concept." In *Museums, Adults and the Humanities,* edited by Zipporah W. Collins, 24–34. Washington, D.C.: American Association of Museums.

Deetz, James and Jay Anderson. 1986. *Partakers of Plenty: A Study of the First Thanksgiving.* Plymouth, Mass. Plimoth Plantation Educational Publication Series.

Demos, John. 1970. *A Little Commonwealth: Family Life in Plymouth Colony.* London: Oxford University Press.

Dittmar, Edwina. 1967. "Costumes—How Conceived—Construction of." Pilgrim Society, Plymouth, Massachusetts. Typescript.

Dix, Beulah Marie and Evelyn Greenleaf Sutherland. 1908. *A Rose O' Plymouth Town.* Chicago: The Dramatic Publishing Company.

Douglas, Mary. 1970. *Natural Symbols: Explorations in Cosmology.* New York: Pantheon Books.

Echeverria, Barbara. 1971. "Plymouth Colony Libraries 1627: A Report." Plimoth Plantation Research Department, Plymouth, Mass.

Eliade, Mircea. 1963. *Myth and Reality.* Translated by Willard R. Trask. New York: Harper & Row, Publishers.

———. 1965. *Rites and Symbols of Initiation: The Mysteries of Birth and Rebirth.* Translated by Willard R. Trask. New York: Harper & Row, Publishers.

———. 1973. *Australian Religions: An Introduction.* Ithaca: Cornell University Press.

Engstrom, John. 1985. "Buckle Up: Around Plimoth Plantation You've Got to Walk Like a Pilgrim, Talk Like a Pilgrim." *Boston Globe Magazine,* 24 November.

Fine, Elizabeth, and Jean Haskell Spear. 1984. "Tour Guide Performances as Sight-Sacralization." Department of Communication Studies, Virginia Tech. University, Blacksburg, Va. Photocopy.

Fiore, Jordan D., ed. 1985. *Mourt's Relation: A Journal of the Pilgrims at Plymouth.* Plymouth, Mass. Plymouth Rock Foundation.

Fitzgerald, Frances. 1979. *American Revised: History Schoolbooks in the Twentieth Century.* Boston: Little, Brown and Company.

Gebler, Ernest. 1950. *The Plymouth Adventure.* Garden City, New York: Doubleday & Company, Inc.

Geetz, Clifford. 1973. *The Interpretation of Cultures.* New York: Basic Books, Inc., Publishers.

———. 1980. "Blurred Genres: The Refiguration of Social Thought." *American Scholar* 49, no. 2 (Spring): 165–82.

Goffman, Erving. 1959. *The Presentation of the Self in Everyday Life.* Garden City, N.Y.: Doubleday & Company, Inc.

———. 1967. *Interaction Ritual.* New York: Pantheon Books.

———. 1974. *Frame Analysis.* New York: Harper & Row, Publishers.

Gomes, Peter. 1985. Lecture in conjunction with the Opening of "Aye, Call It Holy Ground: Victorian Images of the Pilgrims." Exhibit at Plimoth Plantation, Plymouth, Mass. 19 May.

Haley, Alex. 1976. *Roots: The Saga of an American Family.* New York: Dell Publishing Co., Inc.

Hassan, Ihab. 1981. "The Question of Postmodernism." *Performing Arts Journal* 16: 30–37.

Heath, Dwight B., ed. 1963. *Mourt's Relation: A Journal of the Pilgrims at Plymouth.* New York: Corinth Books.

Heinemann, Margot. 1980. *Puritanism and Theatre: Thomas Middleton and Opposition Drama Under the Early Stuarts.* Cambridge: Cambridge University Press.

Hobsbaum, Eric, and Terence Ranger, eds. 1983. *The Invention of Tradition.* Cambridge: Cambridge University Press.

Huizinga, Johan. 1955. *Homo Ludens: A Study of the Play-Element in Culture.* Boston: Beacon Press.

Jacobi, Jolande. [1942] 1973. *The Psychology of C. G. Jung.* Translated by Ralph Manheim. New Haven: Yale University Press.

James, Sydney V., Jr., ed. 1963. *Three Visitors to Early Plymouth.* Plymouth, Mass.: A Plimoth Plantation Publication.

Jennings, Francis. 1976. *The Invasion of America: Indians, Colonialism, and the Cant of Conquest.* New York: W. W. Norton & Company.

Jung, Carl G. [1953] 1966. *Two Essays on Analytical Psychology.* Translated by R. F. C. Hull. Rev. ed. Bollingen Series XX. Princeton: Princeton University Press.

Kaprow, Allan. 1966. *Assemblages, Environments, and Happenings.* New York: Harry Abrams.

Kirby, Michael, ed. 1974. *The New Theatre: Performance Documentation.* New York: New York University Press.

Kirk, G. S. 1970. *Myth: Its Meaning and Function in Ancient and Other Cultures.* Cambridge: Cambridge University Press.

Kirshenblatt-Gimblett, Barbara. 1984. "Place as a Cultural Concept: On the Construction of Sites and Their Interpretation." Paper presented at the Past Meets Present Conference, New York Council for the Humanities, 7 October.

————. 1988. "Authenticity and Authority in the Representation of Culture: The Poetics and Politics of Tourist Production." In *Kulturkontakt/kulturkonflikt*, edited by Ina-Marie Greverus, Konrad Köstlin and Heinz Schilling. Frankfurt: Institut für Kulturanthropologie und Europäische Ethnologie der Universität Frankfurt am Main.

————. 1991. "Confusing Pleasures." To appear in *Intercultural Performance*, edited by Richard Schechner (Routledge). Photocopy.

Lévi-Strauss, Claude. 1979. *Myth and Meaning.* New York: Schocken Books.

Lowenthal, David, and Marcus Binney, eds. 1981. *Our Past Before Us, Why Do We Save It?* London: Temple Smith.

MacAloon, John J., ed. 1984. *Rite, Drama, Festival, Spectacle: Rehearsals Toward a Theory of Cultural Performance.* Philadelphia: Institute for the Study of Human Issues.

MacCannell, Dean. 1976. *The Tourist: A New Theory of the Leisure Class.* New York: Schocken Books.

McCullough, Jack W. 1981. *Living Pictures on the New York Stage.* Ann Arbor: UMI Research Press.

McIntyre, Ruth A. 1963. *Debts Hopeful and Desperate: Financing Plymouth Colony.* Plymouth, Mass.: A Plimoth Plantation Publication.

MacKay, Patricia. 1977. "Theme Parks." *Theatre Crafts* (September): 27ff.

McNamara, Brooks. 1975. "The Pageant Era." *Theatre Crafts* (September): 11ff.

Miller, Perry. 1961. *The New England Mind.* Boston: Beacon Press.

Moore, Marianne. 1961. *Collected Poems.* New York: The MacMillan Company.

Moore, Sally Falk, and Barbara Myerhoff, eds. 1977. *Secular Ritual.* Amsterdam: Van Gorcum & Comp. B./V.

Moran, Maurice J., Jr. 1978. "Living Museums: Coney Islands of the Mind." Master's thesis, Department of Performance Studies, New York University.

Morgan, Edmund S. 1965. *Visible Saints: The History of a Puritan Idea.* Ithaca: Cornell University Press.

Murray, Henry A., ed. 1968. *Myth and Mythmaking.* Boston: Beacon Press.

Myerhoff, Barbara. 1974. *Peyote Hunt: The Sacred Journey of the Huichol Indians.* Ithaca: Cornell University Press.

Norbeck, Edward. 1971. "Man at Play." *Play, a Natural History Magazine Supplement* (December): 48–53.

Plimoth Plantation. n.d. *The Training Manual,* Vols. 1 and 2. Plimoth Plantation, Plymouth, Mass. Photocopy.

———. 1948. *The Pilgrim Memorial: The Program.* Cambridge, Mass.: University Press, Inc.

———. 1970. "A Letter to the Membership." December Plimoth Plantation, Plymouth, Mass. Photocopy.

———. 1983–86. *Plimoth Plantation Annual Reports.* Plymouth, Mass.: Plimoth Plantation.

———. 1986a. "Wanted: Time Travelers." Press Release, Plimoth Plantation, Plymouth, Mass.

———. 1986b. "History Lives at Plimoth Plantation." Press Release, Plimoth Plantation, Plymouth, Mass.

Rainolds, John. 1600. *Th' Overthrow of Stage-Playes.* Middleburg: Imprinted by Richard Schilders. (Harvard University Theatre Collection: STC 20617)

Rein, Lisa. 1986. "Portraying the Life of a Polish Pilgrim." *The Patriot Ledger,* 27 November.

Robinson, John. 1981. *The Works of John Robinson, Pastor of the Pilgrim Fathers.* Vol. 2, *A Justification of Separation.* Boston: Doctrinal Tract and Book Society.

Roth, Stacy. 1992. "Perspectives on Interpreter-Visitor Communications in First-Person Interpretation." Master's thesis, Department of American Studies, University of Pennsylvania.

Sauer, Carl O. 1980. *Seventeenth Century North America.* Berkeley: Turtle Island.

Schechner, Richard. 1973. *Environmental Theatre.* New York: Hawthorn Books.

———. 1977. *Essays on Performance Theory, 1970–1976.* New York: Drama Book Specialists.

———. 1979. "The End of Humanism." *Performing Arts Journal* 10/11 (Special Double Issue): 9–22.

———. 1981. "Restoration of Behavior." *Studies in Visual Communication* 7, no. 3 (Summer): 2–45.

————. 1985. *Between Theater and Anthropology*. Philadelphia: University of Pennsylvania Press.

Schechner, Richard, and Mady Schuman, eds. 1976. *Ritual, Play, and Performance: Readings in the Social Sciences/Theatre*. New York: The Seabury Press.

Shepard, Sam. 1977. *Rolling Thunder Logbook*. New York: The Viking Press.

"A Short Treatise Against Stage-Playes." 1625. London. (Harvard Theatre Collection: Thr 386.25).

Shurtleff, Nathaniel B. [1855] 1968. *Records of the Colony of New Plymouth*. Vol. I, 1633–1640; Vol. 2, 1641–1651. Reprint. New York: AMS Press.

Simpson, Alan. 1955. *Puritanism in Old and New England*. Chicago: University of Chicago Press.

Singer, Milton, 1972. *When a Great Tradition Modernizes: An Anthropological Approach to Indian Civilization*. New York: Praeger.

Smith, Valene L., ed. 1977. *Hosts and Guests: The Anthropology of Tourism*. Philadelphia: University of Pennsylvania Press.

Snow, Stephen. 1986. "Plimoth Plantation: Living History as Blurred Genre." *Kentucky Folklore Record* 32. nos. 1 & 2 (January–June): 34–41.

Spolin, Viola. [1963] 1985. *Improvisation for the Theater*. Rev. ed. Evanston: Northwestern University Press.

*Standard-Times*. 1984. "Seaside Issue." *Standard-Times* (New Bedford, Mass.), Summer.

Stanislavski, Constantin. [1936] 1963. *An Actor Prepares*. Translated by Elizabeth Reynold Hapgood. New York: Theatre Arts Books.

————. 1963. *An Actor's Handbook*. Edited and translated by Elizabeth Reynold Hapgood. New York: Theatre Arts Books.

Stoddard, Francis R. [1952] 1973. *The Truth About the Pilgrims*. Reprint. Baltimore: The Genealogical Publishing Co., Inc.

Stoeltje, Beverly. 1981. "Cowboys and Clowns: Rodeo Specialists and the Ideology of Work and Play." In *And Other Neighborly Names: Social Process and Cultural Image in Texas Folklore*, edited by Richard Bauman and Roger D. Abrahams. Austin: University of Texas Press.

Stowell, W. H., and D. Wilson. 1888. *A History of the Puritans and Pilgrim Fathers*. New York: Worthington Co.

Sumner, Mark. 1975. "Staging History Outdoors." *Theatre Crafts* (September: 15FF).

Thompson, Jay Earle. 1925. *The Land of the Pilgrims*. New York: D. C. Heath and Company.

Turnbull, Colin. 1979. *Anthropology, Drama, and the Human Experience: An Interdisciplinary Approach to the Study of Human Values*. Washington, D.C.: George Washington University.

Turner, Victor. 1969. *The Ritual Process*. New York Aldine Publishing Company.

———. 1973. "The Center Out There: Pilgrim's Goal." *History of Religions* 12, no. 3 (February): 191–230.

———. 1974. *Dramas, Fields, and Metaphors: Symbolic Action in Human Society*. Ithaca: Cornell University Press.

———. 1979. "Dramatic Ritual / Ritual Drama: Performative and Reflexive Anthropology." *Kenyon Review* 1, no. 3 (New Series): 80–93.

———. 1982. *From Ritual to Theatre: The Human Seriousness of Play*. New York: Performing Arts Journal Publications.

———. 1986. *The Anthropology of Performance*. New York City: Performing Arts Journal Publications.

Turner, Victor, and Edith Turner. 1982. "Performing Ethnography." *The Drama Review* 26, 2: 33–50.

Van Gennep, Arnold. 1960. *The Rites of Passage*. Translated by Monika B. Vizedom and Gabriella L. Caffee. Chicago: University of Chicago Press.

Villiers, Alan. 1958. *The New Mayflower*. New York: Charles Scribner's Sons.

Wagner, Roy. 1981. *The Invention of Culture*. Chicago: University of Chicago Press.

Wallace, Michael. 1981. "Visiting the Past: History Museums in the United States." *Radical History Review* 25: 63–96.

Webster, Daniel. 1825. *A Discourse Delivered at Plymouth, December 22, 1820. In Commemoration of the First Settlement of New-England*. 3rd ed. Boston: Wells and Lilly.

Willet, John, ed. and trans. 1964. *Brecht on Theatre: The Development of an Aesthetic*. New York: Hill and Wang.

Withington, Robert. 1920. *English Pageantry: An Historical Outline*. Vol. 2. Cambridge: Harvard University Press.

Young, Tom. 1972. "Indian Exhibits: A Proposal for Change." Plimoth Plantation, Plymouth, Mass. Photocopy.

Zook, Nicholas. 1971. *Museum Villages U.S.A.* Barre, Mass.: Barre Publishers.

UNPUBLISHED DUPLICATED MATERIALS FROM PLIMOTH PLANTATION, PLYMOUTH, MASSACHUSETTS

Curtin, Theodore J. 1985. "Scenario for a Meeting of the Governor's Council." Photocopy.

DeFabio, Donna. 1984a. "Some Notes on the Funeral of Mary Brewster." Photocopy.

———. 1984b. "Rational for a Festive Wedding." Photocopy.

———. 1985a. "Rational for a Festive Wedding." (Revised). Photocopy.

———. 1985b. "Some Notes on the Funeral of Mary Brewster." (Revised). Photocopy.

———. 1985c. "Wedding Scenario—April 27, 1985." Photocopy.

———. 1985d. "Mock-Up of a Pilgrim Wedding Contract." Transcribed in imitation of period script.

———. 1985e. "Scenario—The Wedding Day." Photocopy.

———. 1985f. "A Guide to Developing Characterizations." Photocopy.

Kemp, John. 1985. "Fur Trading." Photocopy.

Marten, Robert. 1977. "Plimoth Plantation Interpretation Defined." Photocopy.

"Personation Biograph: Richard Warren." 1984. Photocopy.

Travers, Leonard. 1984a. "Scenario for Quarter-Sessions." Photocopy.

———. 1984b. "Scenario Schedule—De Rasieres Days (October 6–8)." Photocopy.

———. 1984c. "Final Oration of De Rasieres (third day)." Photocopy.

# Interviews

I conducted all of these interviews. Since most were tape-recorded on the premises of Plimoth Plantation, I will designate method and geography only for the exceptions. The interviews are organized in three categories: (1) Plimoth Plantation Personnel (2) Visitors to Plimoth Plantation, and (3) Miscellaneous.

PLIMOTH PLANTATION PERSONNEL

Arsenault, Noel. 1985.
  1 December.
Baker, James. 1985a.
  9 October.
———. 1985b.
  15 October.
Beuchler, Hope. 1985.
  1 December.
Curtin, Theodore A. 1985.
  1 December.
Hale, Dorothy, Gerda Savery, and Henrietta Wolfenden. 1986.
  Home of Henrietta Wolfenden, Plymouth, Mass. 1 December.
Hall, Chris. 1986a.
  9 October.
———. 1985b.
  1 December.
Kelso, Tony. 1986.
  3 September.
Mindick, Nancy. 1985.
  Home of Nancy Mindick, Plymouth, Mass. 12 October.

Slevin, Peter. 1986.
    15 October.
Tompkins, Toby. 1985.
    14 October.
Travers, Carolyn. 1985.
    11 October.
Travers, Leonard. 1986.
    15 October.
Wall, Kathleen. 1986.
    3 September.

VISITORS TO PLIMOTH PLANTATION

Almagatta, Valerie. 1986.
    3 September.
Bordeaux, Debbie. 1986.
    3 September.
Cullingford, Joyce. 1986.
    3 September.
Dunn, Mr. and Mrs. Michael. 1985.
    1 December.
Haber, Jerry. 1985.
    29 November.
Haskell, Helen. 1985.
    30 November.
Holland, Leo P. 1985.
    30 November.
Jacobi, Mr. and Mrs. David. 1986.
    3 September.
Jendreas, Bruce. 1985.
    30 November.
Kawa, Mishi. 1985.
    30 November.
Kim, Oon June. 1986.
    3 September.
Laniere, Bill. 1985.
    1 December.
Lum, Al. 1985.
    1 December.
Meyerbachtal, Margo. 1985.
    30 November.

Sachs, Ed. 1985.
   1 December.
Schrock, Phillip. 1986.
   3 September.
Sewell, Marsha. 1985.
   30 November.
Wilkins, Jacklyn. 1986.
   3 September.

MISCELLANEOUS

Anderson, Jay. 1985.
   Interview with the author (conversation and notes). Annual Meeting of
   the American Folklore Society, Cincinnati, Ohio, 19 October.
Carroll, James. 1985.
   St. John the Divine Cathedral, New York City, 11 November.
Chapin, Caroline. 1985.
   Pilgrim Hall, Plymouth, 10 October.
Deetz, James. 1987.
   Telephone conversation with author. 24 March.
Ingram, Judith. 1987.
   Telephone conversation with author. 14 April.
Lonardo, Anthony. 1987.
   Telephone conversation with author. 31 March.
Spaulding, Joffrey. 1986.
   Manomet, Mass. 14 October.
Trask, Ruth. 1985.
   Home of Ruth Trask, Plymouth, Mass. 10 October.

# Sound Recordings

I made all of these sound recordings except for the first. They were made on the premises of Plimoth Plantation.

Kirshenblatt-Gimblett, Barbara. 1985.
Audiotapes of Interpreters Interacting with New York University Students. Plimoth Plantation, Plymouth, Mass. 12 April 1985.
Snow, Stephen. 1984a.
Audiotapes of Interpreters Performing in the Pilgrim Village. June.
_____. 1984b.
Audiotapes of Interpreters Performing in the Pilgrim Village. 14 November.
_____. 1984c.
Audiotapes of Interpreters Performing in the Pilgrim Village. 28 November.
_____. 1984d.
Audiotapes of "The Night of the Crappies." 1 December 1984.
_____. 1985a.
Audiotapes of Colloquium on "Living History." 12 April.
_____. 1985b.
Audiotapes of "Court Day" Performances. 21 September.
_____. 1985c.
Audiotapes of Interpreters Performing Aboard the *Mayflower II*. 1 December.
_____. 1986.
Audiotapes of "The 7th Annual Crappies." 30 November.

# Index

Lévi-Strauss, Claude, 187
Liminality, 123–24, 136–37. *See also* Turner, Victor
Liminoid Genre, 191, 198, 210–11
Living History Performance, 118, 159, 191, 202, 211; alienation effect in, 181; audience participation in, 189; authenticity of, 169, 209; as liminality, 184; as ritual, 185–87
Longfellow, Henry Wadsworth, author of "The Courtship of Miles Standish," 20
Ludic, 135, 137, 148, 182, 203, 210; function in postmodern culture, 148–52. *See also* Huizinga, Johan

MacCannell, Dean, 81–83, 118, 153–54, 161–62, 165–66, 169, 172, 207–08
Marshall, Cyril, 31–32
Marten, Robert, 39–45, 170
*Mayflower:* Compact, 14–15, 19; the original, 9–10; scenes aboard *Mayflower* II, 84–88, 176; Second Coming of, 27–29, 83
Mayflower Descendants, 156, 167–68
McLuhan, Marshall, 36, 192, 196
McNamara, Brooks, 17
Method Acting, 42–43. *See also* Stanislavski, Constantin
"Musket Day," 105–07. *See also* General Muster

Naruhito, His Imperial Highness, Prince, 87
Native American, 13n6, 158; Day of Mourning, 159; Program at Plimoth Plantation, 38–39; reenactment of Fur Trade, 97–101
Noh actor (Japanese), 41

Old Sturbridge Village, 7, 25–26. *See also* Restored Villages
Olsson, George C. P., 21

Pageant, 200; *The Pilgrim Spirit*, 17–20

Performance, derived from *parfournir*, 6, 183–84, 203
Performing Ethnography, 115–16, 197–98, 209. *See also* Turner, Edith and Victor
Pilgrims: *dramatis personae*, 10; history of, 8–12; images in the tourist trade, 82–84; "Pilgrim Century," 13; reenactment of Noon Meal, 71–73; Sabbath-day Services, 56n2
"Pilgrim-baiting," 71n6, 160, 165
Pilgrim Fathers, 26, 27, 82, 199, 202, 209
Pilgrims' Progress, 21–24, 201; modeled after the painting, *The Pilgrims Going to Church*, 22
Pilgrim Village: description of, 49–50, 53–60; scenes reenacted in, 88–114
Pitts, Edith, in role-play, 76–78, 79, 90–91, 137
Plimoth Plantation, 207; incorporation of, 26; site of, 29
Plymouth National Wax Museum, 33, 207
Plymouth Rock, 83, 186, 207
Pollard, Anthony (Nanepashemet), 99
Postmodernism, 191–98

*Ramlila*, 130
Restored Villages: Colonial Williamsburg, 7, 25, 36, 204; Fort Williams (Ontario), 204; Greenfield Village, 25; in Hawaii, 203–04; Old Sturbridge Village, 7, 25–26, 203
Robinson, John, 19, 55
Rothenberg, Jerome, 46, 192

Saints, 11, 155; "plain" style of, 71, 89
Schechner, Richard, 7, 82, 128, 132, 135, 147, 152, 176, 180, 182, 189–91, 194, 203, 204, 207; cool-down process, 80, 80n7, 112, 151; environmental theatre, 7–8, 48; liminality, 136; postmodernism, 192–93; processions, 178; restored behavior, 7, 115, 209; Theatre/Anthropology, 196; transformed performers, 124, 130–31